Microsoft® Official Academic Course:
Microsoft Office PowerPoint 2003

Microsoft Corporation

PUBLISHED BY
Microsoft Press
A Division of Microsoft Corporation
One Microsoft Way
Redmond, Washington 98052-6399

Library of Congress Cataloging-in-Publication Data pending.
      ISBN 0-7356-2091-1
      (Microsoft Press)
      ISBN 0-07-225574-9
      (McGraw-Hill)

Printed and bound in the United States of America.

2 3 4 5 6 7 8 9   QWE   8 7 6 5

Distributed in Canada by H.B. Fenn and Company Ltd.

A CIP catalogue record for this book is available from the British Library.

Microsoft Press books are available through booksellers and distributors worldwide. For further information about international editions, contact your local Microsoft Corporation office or contact Microsoft Press International directly at fax (425)
936-7329. Visit our Web site at www.microsoft.com/learning/. Send comments to *mspinput@microsoft.com*.

Acquisitions Editor: Linda Engelman
Project Editor: Dick Brown

Body Part No. X10-35369

PowerPoint

Contents

Course Overview

Welcome to the *Microsoft Official Academic Course* series for Microsoft Office System 2003 Edition. This series facilitates classroom learning, enabling you to develop competence and confidence in using Office applications. In completing courses taught with the *Microsoft Official Academic Course* series, you learn to use the software productively and discover how to make the software work for you. This series addresses core-level and expert-level skills in Microsoft Office Word 2003, Microsoft Office Excel 2003, Microsoft Office Access 2003, Microsoft Office PowerPoint 2003, Microsoft Office Outlook 2003, Microsoft FrontPage 2002/2003, and Microsoft Project 2002/2003.

The *Microsoft Official Academic Course* series provides:

- A time-tested, integrated approach to learning.
- Task-based, results-oriented learning strategies.
- Exercises based on realistic business scenarios.
- Complete preparation for Microsoft Office Specialist (MOS) certification.
- Attractive student guides with full-featured lessons.
- Lessons with accurate, logical, and sequential instructions.
- Comprehensive coverage of skills from the basic to the expert level.
- Review of core-level skills provided in expert-level guides.
- A CD-ROM with Microsoft's e-learning tool as well as practice files.

A Task-Based Approach Using Business Scenarios

The *Microsoft Official Academic Course* uses the time-tested approach of learning by doing. By studying with a task-based approach, you learn more than just the features of the software. You learn how to accomplish real-world tasks so that you can immediately increase your productivity using the software application.

The lessons are based on tasks that you might encounter in the everyday work world. This approach allows you to quickly see the relevance of the training beyond just the classroom. The business focus is woven throughout the series, from business examples within procedures, to scenarios chosen for practice files, to examples shown in the e-learning tool.

An Integrated Approach to Training

The *Microsoft Official Academic Course* series distinguishes itself from other series on the market with its consistent delivery and completely integrated approach to learning across print and online training media.

The textbook component of the *Microsoft Official Academic Course* series uses easily digested units of learning so that you can stop and restart lessons easily.

For those who prefer online training, this series includes an e-learning tool, the Microsoft e-Learning Library Version 2 (MELL 2). MELL 2 offers highly interactive online training in a simulated work environment, complete with graphics, sound, video, and animation. Icons in the margin of the textbook direct you to related topics within the e-learning tool so that you can choose to reinforce your learning more visually. MELL 2 also includes an assessment feature that students and teachers can use to gauge preliminary knowledge about the application.

Preparation for Microsoft Office Specialist (MOS) Certification

This series has been certified as approved courseware for the Microsoft Office Specialist certification program. Students who have completed this training are prepared to take the related MOS exam. By passing the exam for a particular Office application, students demonstrate proficiency in that application to their employers or prospective employers. Exams are offered at participating test centers. For more information, see *www.microsoft.com/traincert/mcp/officespecialist/requirements.asp*.

Designed for Optimal Learning

Lessons in the *Microsoft Official Academic Course* series are presented in a logical, easy-to-follow format, helping you find information quickly and learn as efficiently as possible. The colorful and highly visual series design makes it easy for you to see what to read and what to do when practicing new skills.

Lessons break training into easily assimilated sessions. Each lesson is self-contained, and lessons can be completed in sequences other than the one presented in the table of contents. Sample files for the lessons don't depend on completion of other lessons. Sample files within a lesson assume only that you are working sequentially through a complete lesson.

Each book within the *Microsoft Official Academic Course* series features:

- **Lesson objectives.** Objectives clearly state the instructional goals for the lesson so that you understand what skills you will master. Each lesson objective is covered in its own section, and each section or topic in the lesson is covered in a consistent way. Lesson objectives preview the lesson structure, helping you grasp key information and prepare for learning skills.

- **Key terms.** Terms with which you might not be familiar are listed at the beginning of the lesson. When these terms are used later in the lesson, they appear in boldface type and are defined. The Glossary contains all of the key terms and their definitions.

- **Informational text for each topic.** For each objective, the lesson provides easy-to-read, technique-focused information.

- **The Bottom Line.** Each main topic within the lesson has a summary of what makes the topic relevant to you.

- **Hands-on practice.** Numbered steps give detailed, step-by-step instructions to help you learn skills. The steps also show results and screen images to match what you should see on your computer screen. The accompanying CD contains the sample files needed for each lesson.

- **Full-color illustrations.** Illustrated screen images give visual feedback as you work through exercises. The images reinforce key concepts, provide visual clues about the steps, and give you something to check your progress against.

- **MOS icon.** Each section or sidebar that covers a MOS certification objective has a MOS icon in the margin at the beginning of the section. The complete list of MOS objectives and the location in the text where they are covered can be found in the MOS Objectives section of this book.

- **Reader aids.** Helpful hints and alternate ways to accomplish tasks are located throughout the lesson text. Reader aids provide additional related or background information that adds value to the lesson. These also include things to watch out for or things to avoid.

- **Check This Out.** These sidebars contain parenthetical topics or additional information that you might find interesting.

- **Button images in the margin.** When the text instructs you to click a particular button, an image of the button is shown in the margin.

- **Quick Reference.** Each main section contains a condensed version of the steps used in its procedures. This section is helpful if you want only a fast reminder of how to complete a certain task.

- **Quick Check.** These questions and answers provide a chance to review material covered in that section of the lesson.

- **Quick Quiz.** You can use the true/false, multiple choice, or short-answer Quick Quiz questions to test or reinforce your understanding of key topics within each lesson.

- **On Your Own exercises.** These exercises give you another opportunity to practice skills that you learned in the lesson. Completing these exercises helps you to verify whether you understand the lesson and to reinforce your learning.

- **One Step Further exercises.** These exercises give you an opportunity to build upon what you have learned by applying that knowledge in a different way. These might also require researching on the Internet.

- **Glossary.** Terms with which you might not be familiar are defined in the glossary. Terms in the glossary appear in boldface type within the lessons and are also defined within the lessons.

- **Index.** Student guides are completely indexed. All glossary terms and application features appear in the index.

- **MELL icons in the margin.** These icons direct you to related topics within the Micosoft e-Learning Library. For more information on MELL, please see the Microsoft e-Learning Library section later in this book.

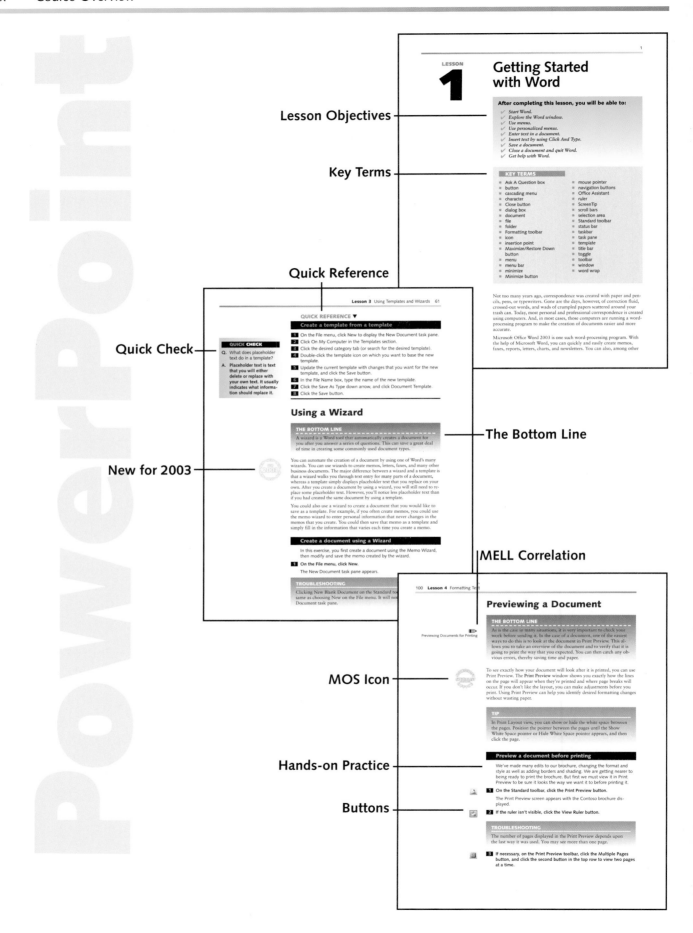

Lesson Objectives

Key Terms

Quick Reference

Quick Check

New for 2003

The Bottom Line

MELL Correlation

MOS Icon

Hands-on Practice

Buttons

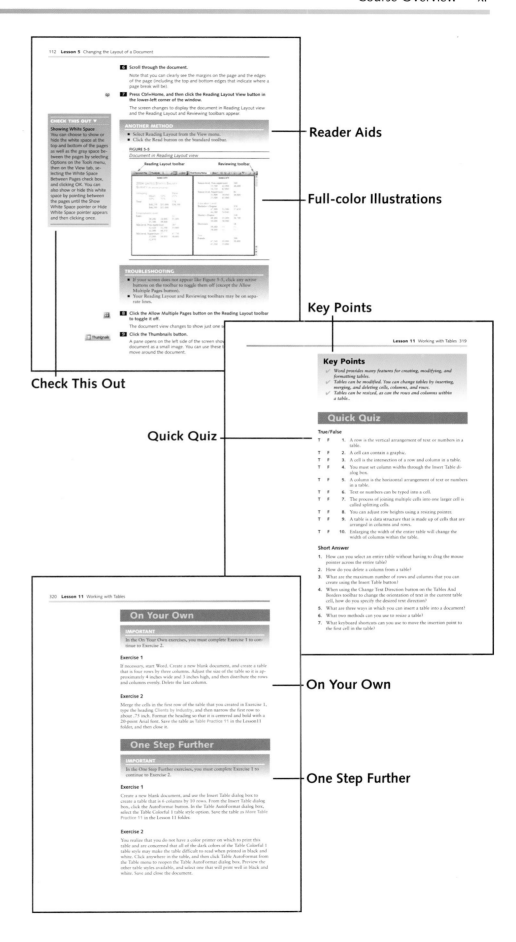

Reader Aids

Full-color Illustrations

Key Points

Check This Out

Quick Quiz

On Your Own

One Step Further

PowerPoint

PowerPoint

Conventions and Features Used in This Book

This book uses special fonts, symbols, and heading conventions to highlight important information or to call your attention to special steps. For more information about the features available in each lesson, refer to the "Course Overview" section.

Convention	Meaning
NEW FOR 2003 icon	This icon in the margin indicates a new or greatly improved feature in this version of the software.
MICROSOFT OFFICE SPECIALIST icon	This icon indicates that the section where it appears covers a Microsoft Office Specialist (MOS) exam objective. For a complete list of the MOS objectives, see the "MOS Objectives" section.
THE BOTTOM LINE	These paragraphs provide a brief summary of the material to be covered in the section that follows.
◆ Close the file.	Words preceded by a yellow diamond in a black box give instructions for opening, saving, or closing files or programs. They also point out items you should check or actions you should carry out.
QUICK REFERENCE ▼	These provide an "at-a-glance" summary of the steps involved to complete a given task. These differ from procedures because they're generic, not scenario-driven, and they're brief.
QUICK CHECK	This is a quick question and answer that serves to reinforce critical points and provides a chance to review the material covered.
TIP	Reader aids appear in green boxes. *Another Method* provides alternative procedures related to particular tasks, *Tip* provides helpful hints related to particular tasks or topics, and *Troubleshooting* covers common mistakes or areas in which you may have trouble. *Important* highlights warnings or cautions that are critical to performing exercises.

Convention	Meaning
CHECK THIS OUT ▼	These notes in the margin area provide pointers to information elsewhere in the book (or another book) or describe interesting features of the program that are not directly discussed in the current topic or used in the exercise.
🖫	When a toolbar button is referenced in the lesson, the button's picture is shown in the margin.
Alt+Tab	A plus sign (+) between two key names means that you must press those keys at the same time. For example, "Press Alt+Tab" means that you hold down the Alt key while you press Tab.
Boldface type	Indicates a key term entry that is defined in the Glossary at the end of the book.
Type Yes.	Anything you are supposed to type appears in red bold characters.
✏▶	This icon alongside a paragraph indicates reated coverage within the Microsoft e-Learning Library, (MELL)the e-learning tool. Find more information on MELL later in this book.

PowerPoint

Using the CD-ROMs

There are two CD-ROMs included with this student guide. One contains the practice files that you'll use as you perform the exercises in the book. You can use the other CD-ROM, described below, to install a 180-day trial edition of Microsoft Office Professional Edition 2003. By using the practice files, you won't waste time creating the samples used in the lessons, and you can concentrate on learning how to use Microsoft Office PowerPoint 2003. With the files and the step-by-step instructions in the lessons, you'll learn by doing, which is an easy and effective way to acquire and remember new skills.

System Requirements

Your computer system must meet the following minimum requirements for you to install the practice files from the CD-ROM and to run Microsoft PowerPoint 2003.

IMPORTANT

This course assumes that PowerPoint 2003 has already been installed on the PC you are using. Microsoft Office Professional Edition 2003—180-Day Trial, which includes PowerPoint, is on the second CD-ROM included with this book. Microsoft Product Support does not support these trial editions.

For information on how to install the trial edition, see "Installing or Uninstalling Microsoft Office Professional Edition 2003—180-Day Trial" later in this part of the book.

- A personal computer running PowerPoint 2003 on a Pentium 233-megahertz (MHz) or higher processor.
- Microsoft Windows® 2000 with Service Pack 3 (SP3), Windows XP, or later.
- 128 MB of RAM or greater.
- At least 2 MB of available disk space (after installing PowerPoint 2003 or Microsoft Office).
- A CD-ROM or DVD drive.
- A monitor with Super VGA (800 X 600) or higher resolution with 256 colors.
- A Microsoft mouse, a Microsoft IntelliMouse, or other compatible pointing device.

If You Need to Install or Uninstall the Practice Files

Your instructor might already have installed the practice files before you arrive in class. However, your instructor might ask you to install the practice files on your own at the start of class. Also, if you want to work through any of the exercises in this book on your own at home or at your place of business after class, you will need to first install the practice files.

Install the practice files

1 Insert the CD-ROM in the CD-ROM drive of your computer.

A menu screen appears.

IMPORTANT

If the menu screen does not appear, start Windows Explorer. In the left pane, locate the icon for your CD-ROM, and click this icon. In the right pane, double-click the file StartCD.

2 Click Install Practice Files, and follow the instructions on the screen.

The recommended options are preselected for you.

3 After the files have been installed, click Exit.

A folder called PowerPoint Practice has been created on your hard disk; the practice files have been placed in that folder.

4 Remove the CD-ROM from the CD-ROM drive.

Use the following steps when you want to delete the lesson practice files from your hard disk. Your instructor might ask you to perform these steps at the end of class. Also, you should perform these steps if you have worked through the exercises at home or at your place of business and want to work through the exercises again. Deleting the practice files and then reinstalling them ensures that all files and folders are in their original condition if you decide to work through the exercises again.

Unistall the practice files from the Windows XP or later operating system

1 On the Windows taskbar, click the Start button and then click Control Panel.

2 If you are in Classic View, double-click the Add Or Remove Programs icon. If you are in Category View, single-click the Add Or Remove Programs link.

3 In the Add Or Remove Programs dialog box, scroll down and select Word Core Practice in the list. Click the Change/Remove button.

4 Click Yes when the confirmation dialog box appears.

PowerPoint

Uninstall the practice files from the Windows 2000 operating system

1 On the Windows taskbar, click the Start button, point to Settings, and then click Control Panel.

2 Double-click the Add/Remove icon.

3 Click PowerPoint Practice in the list, and click the Remove or the Change/Remove button.

4 Click Yes when the confirmation dialog box appears.

Using the Practice Files

Each lesson in this book explains when and how to use any practice files for that lesson. The lessons are built around scenarios that simulate a real work environment, so you can easily apply the skills you learn to your own work. The scenarios in the lessons use the context of the fictitious Contoso, Ltd, a public relations firm, and its client, Adventure Works, a resort located in the mountains of California.

By default, PowerPoint 2003 places the Standard and Formatting toolbars on the same row below the menu bar to save space. To match the lessons and exercises in this book, the Standard and Formatting toolbars should be separated onto two rows before the start of this course. To separate the Standard and Formatting toolbars:

■ Position the mouse pointer over the move handle at the beginning of the Formatting toolbar until it turns into the move pointer (a four-headed arrow), and drag the toolbar down until it appears on its own row.

The following is a list of all files and folders used in the lessons.

File Name	Description
02 PPT Lesson	File used in Lesson 2
03 PPT Lesson	File used in Lesson 3
04 Marketing Outline	File used in Lesson 4
04 Holiday Outline	File used in One Step Further Exercise 1
05 PPT Lesson	File used in Lesson 5
06 PPT Lesson	File used in Lesson 6
06 PPT Template	File used in Lesson 6
06 PPT Marx	File used in One Step Further Exercise 2
06 PPT Marx Template	File used in One Step Further Exercise 2
07 PPT Lesson	File used in Lesson 7
08 PPT Lesson	File used in Lesson 8
09 PPT Lesson	File used in Lesson 9
09 Future Picture	File used in Lesson 9

File Name	Description
10 PPT Lesson	File used in Lesson 10
10 Company Performance	File used in Lesson 10
10 PR Budget	File used in Lesson 10
11 PPT Lesson	File used in Lesson11
12 PPT Lesson	File used in Lesson 12
Arrowhit	File used in One Step Further Exercise 2
Cogs	File used in Lesson 12
13 PPT Lesson	File used in Lesson 13
13 PR Budget	File used in Lesson 13
14 PPT Lesson	File used in Lesson 14
14 PPT Edit	File used in Lesson 14

Replying to Install Messages

When you work through some lessons, you might see a message indicating that the feature that you are trying to use is not installed. If you see this message, insert the Microsoft Office PowerPoint 2003 CD or Microsoft Office CD 1 in your CD-ROM drive, and click Yes to install the feature.

Locating and Opening Files

After you (or your instructor) have installed the practice files, all the files you need for this course will be stored in a folder named PowerPoint Practice located on your hard disk.

Navigate to the PowerPoint Practice folder from within PowerPoint and open a file

1 On the Standard toolbar, click the Open button.

2 In the Open dialog box, click the Look In down arrow, and click the icon for your hard disk.

3 Double-click the PowerPoint Practice folder.

4 Double-click the file that you want to open.

All the files for the lessons appear within the PowerPoint Practice folder.

If You Need Help with the Practice Files

If you have any problems regarding the use of this book's CD-ROM, you should first consult your instructor. If you are using the CD-ROM at home or at your place of business and need additional help with the practice files, contact McGraw-Hill for support:

E-mail: techsup@mcgraw-hill.com

Phone: (800) 331-5094

Post: McGraw-Hill Companies

         1333 Burr Ridge Parkway

         Burr Ridge, IL 60521

IMPORTANT

For help using PowerPoint 2003, rather than this book, you can visit support.microsoft.com or call Microsoft Product Support at (425) 635-7070 on weekdays between 5 A.M. and 9 P.M. Pacific Standard Time or on Saturdays and Sundays between 6 A.M. and 3 P.M. Pacific Standard Time. Microsoft Product Support does not provide support for this course. Also please note that Microsoft Product Support does not support trial editions of Office.

Installing or Uninstalling Microsoft Office Professional Edition 2003—180-Day Trial

An installation CD-ROM for Microsoft Office Professional Edition 2003—180-Day Trial is included with this book. Before you install your trial version, please read this entire section for important information on setting up and uninstalling your trial software.

CAUTION

For the best performance, the default selection during Setup is to uninstall previous versions of Office. There is also an option not to remove previous versions of Office. With all trial software, Microsoft recommends that you have your original CDs available to reinstall if necessary. If you want to return to your previous version of Office, you need to uninstall the trial software. This should be done through the Add or Remove Programs icon in Microsoft Windows Control Panel.

Installation of Microsoft Office Professional Edition 2003—180-Day Trial software will remove your existing version of Microsoft Outlook. However, your contacts, calendar, and other personal information will not be deleted. At the end of the trial, if you choose to upgrade or to reinstall your previous version of Outlook, your personal settings and information will be retained.

Setup Instructions

1 **Insert the trial software CD into the CD drive on your computer. The CD will be detected, and the Setup.exe file should automatically begin to run on your computer.**

2 **When prompted for the Office Product Key, enter the Product Key provided with the software, and then click Next.**

3 **Enter your name and organization user name, and then click Next.**

4 **Read the End-User License Agreement, select the I Accept The Terms In The License Agreement check box, and then click Next.**

NOTE

Copies of the product License Agreements are also available for review at http://www.microsoft.com/office/eula.

5 **Select the install option, verify the installation location or click Browse to change the installation location, and then click Next.**

The default setting is Upgrade. You will have the opportunity to specify not to remove previous versions of Office from your computer later in the installation wizard.

6 **Verify the program installation preferences, and then click Next.**

CAUTION

For best performance, the default selection during setup is to uninstall (remove) previous versions of Office. There is also the option not to remove previous versions of Office. With all trial software, Microsoft recommends that you have your original CDs available to reinstall if necessary.

7 To finish Setup, select the check boxes you want so that you can receive the online updates and downloads or to delete the installation files, then click Finish.

Upgrading Microsoft Office Professional Edition 2003—180-Day Trial Software to the Full Product

You can convert the software into full use without removing or reinstalling software on your computer. When you complete your trial, you can purchase a product license from any Microsoft reseller and enter a valid Product Key when prompted during Setup.

Uninstalling the Trial Software and Returning to Your Previous Office Version

If you want to return to your previous version of Office, you need to uninstall the trial software. This should be done through the Add or Remove Programs icon in Control Panel.

1 Quit any programs that are running, such as Microsoft Word or Outlook.

2 In control Panel, click Add or Remove Programs.

3 Click Microsoft Office Professional Edition 2003, and then click Remove.

NOTE

If you selected the option to remove a previous version of Office during installation of the trial software, you need to reinstall your previous version of Office. If you did not remove your previous version of Office, you can start each of your Office programs either through the Start menu or by opening files for each program, such as Word, Microsoft Excel, and Microsoft PowerPoint files. In some cases, you may have to recreate some of your shortcuts and default settings.

MOS Objectives

Standard	Skill	Page
PP03S-1	**Creating Content**	
PP03S-1-1	Create new presentations from templates	7, 30
PP03S-1-2	Insert and edit text-based content	12, 15, 32, 35, 78, 80, 106, 124, 128, 131
PP03S-1-3	Insert tables, charts, and diagrams	242, 245, 246, 249, 254, 258
PP03S-1-4	Insert picture, shapes, and graphics	188, 209, 224, 230, 235
PP03S-1-5	Import objects	245, 246, 294, 297
PP03S-2	**Formatting Content**	
PP03S-2-1	Format text-based content	93, 112, 115, 119
PP03S-2-2	Format pictures, shapes, and graphics	199, 206, 211, 213, 215, 226, 228, 232, 235
PP03S-2-3	Format slides	168, 170, 173, 175, 177, 222
PP03S-2-4	Apply animation schemes	275
PP03S-2-5	Apply slide transitions	272
PP03S-2-6	Customize slide templates	138, 151, 161
PP03S-2-7	Work with masters	57, 138, 146, 148, 151, 155
PP03S-3	**Collaborating**	
PP03S-3-1	Track, accept, and reject changes in a presentation	350
PP03S-3-2	Add, edit, and delete comments in a presentation	340
PP03S-3-3	Compare and merge presentations	349
PP03S-4	**Managing and Delivering Presentations**	
PP03S-4-1	Organize a presentation	46, 86, 89, 324, 326
PP03S-4-2	Set up slide shows for delivery	286, 309, 326, 329
PP03S-4-3	Rehearse timing	303, 305
PP03S-4-4	Deliver presentations	266, 269
PP03S-4-5	Prepare presentations for remote delivery	353, 358
PP03S-4-6	Save and publish presentations	22, 161, 326
PP03S-4-7	Print slides, outlines, handouts, and speaker notes	59, 66
PP03S-4-8	Export a presentation to another Microsoft Office program	96

PowerPoint

Taking a Microsoft Office Specialist Certification Test

The Microsoft Office Specialist (MOS) program is the only Microsoft-approved certification program designed to measure and validate your skills with the Microsoft Office suite of desktop productivity applications: Microsoft Word, Microsoft Excel, Microsoft PowerPoint, Microsoft Access, and Microsoft Outlook.

By becoming certified, you demonstrate to employers that you have achieved a predictable level of skill in the use of a particular Office application. Employers often require certification either as a condition of employment or as a condition of advancement within the company or other organization. The certification examinations are sponsored by Microsoft but administered through Nivo International.

The MOS program typically offers certification exams at the "core" and "expert" levels. For a core-level test, you demonstrate your ability to use an application knowledgeably and without assistance in a day-to-day work environment. For an expert-level test, you demonstrate that you have a thorough knowledge of the application and can effectively apply all or most of the features of the application to solve problems and complete tasks found in business.

Preparing to Take an Exam

Unless you're a very experienced user, you'll need to use a test preparation course to prepare to complete the test correctly and within the time allowed. The *Microsoft Official Academic Course* series is designed to prepare you for either core-level or expert-level knowledge of a particular Microsoft Office application. By the end of this course, you should have a strong knowledge of all exam topics, and with some additional review and practice on your own, you should feel confident in your ability to pass the appropriate exam.

After you decide which exam to take, review the list of objectives for the exam. This list can be found in the "MOS Objectives" section at the front of the appropriate *Microsoft Official Academic Course* student guide. You can also easily identify tasks that are included in the objective list by locating the MOS symbol in the margin of the lessons in this book.

For an expert-level test, you'll need to be able to demonstrate any of the skills from the core-level objective list, too. Expect some of these core-level tasks to appear on the expert-level test.

You can also familiarize yourself with a live MOS certification test by downloading and installing a practice MOS certification test from www.microsoft.com/traincert/mcp/officespecialist/requirements.asp.

To take the MOS test, first see www.microsoft.com/traincert/mcp/office-specialist/requirements.asp to locate your nearest testing center. Then call the testing center directly to schedule your test. The amount of advance notice you should provide will vary for different testing centers, and it typically depends on the number of computers available at the testing center, the number of other testers who have already been scheduled for the day on which you want to take the test, and the number of times per week that the testing center offers MOS testing. In general, you should call to schedule your test at least two weeks prior to the date on which you want to take the test.

When you arrive at the testing center, you might be asked for proof of identity. A driver's license or passport is an acceptable form of identification. If you do not have either of these items of documentation, call your testing center and ask what alternative forms of identification will be accepted. If you are retaking a test, bring your MOS identification number, which will have been given to you when you previously took the test. If you have not prepaid or if your organization has not already arranged to make payment for you, you will need to pay the test-taking fee when you arrive. The current test-taking fee is $75 (U.S.). Prices are subject to change and may vary depending on the testing center.

Test Format

All MOS certification tests are live, performance-based tests. There are no multiple-choice, true/false, or short-answer questions. Instructions are general: you are told the basic tasks to perform on the computer, but you aren't given any help in figuring out how to perform them. You are not permitted to use reference material other than the application's Help system.

As you complete the tasks stated in a particular test question, the testing software monitors your actions. An example question might be:

> Open the file named AW Guests and select the word Welcome in the first paragraph. Change the font to 12 point, and apply bold formatting. Select the words at your convenience in the second paragraph, move them to the end of the first paragraph using drag and drop, and then center the first paragraph.

The sample tests available from www.microsoft.com/traincert/mcp/office-specialist/requirements.asp give you a clear idea of the type of questions that you will be asked on the actual test.

When the test administrator seats you at a computer, you'll see an online form that you use to enter information about yourself (name, address, and other information required to process your exam results). While you complete the form, the software will generate the test from a master test bank and then prompt you to continue. The first test question will appear in a window. Read the question carefully, and then perform all the tasks stated in the test question. When you have finished completing all tasks for a question, click the Next Question button.

You have 45 to 60 minutes to complete all questions, depending on the test that you are taking. The testing software assesses your results as soon as you complete the test, and the test administrator can print the results of the test so that you will have a record of any tasks that you performed incorrectly. A passing grade is 75 percent or higher. If you pass, you will receive a certificate in the mail within two to four weeks. If you do not pass, you can study and practice the skills that you missed and then schedule to retake the test at a later date.

Tips for Successfully Completing the Test

The following tips and suggestions are the result of feedback received from many individuals who have taken one or more MOS tests:

- Make sure that you are thoroughly prepared. If you have extensively used the application for which you are being tested, you might feel confident that you are prepared for the test. However, the test might include questions that involve tasks that you rarely or never perform when you use the application at your place of business, at school, or at home. You must be knowledgeable in all the MOS objectives for the test that you will take.

- Read each exam question carefully. An exam question might include several tasks that you are to perform. A partially correct response to a test question is counted as an incorrect response. In the example question on the previous page, you might apply bold formatting and move the words at your convenience to the correct location, but forget to center the first paragraph. This would count as an incorrect response and would result in a lower test score.

- You are allowed to use the application's Help system, but relying on the Help system too much will slow you down and possibly prevent you from completing the test within the allotted time. Use the Help system only when necessary.

- Keep track of your time. The test does not display the amount of time that you have left, so you need to keep track of the time yourself by monitoring your start time and the required end time on your watch or a clock in the testing center (if there is one). The test program displays the number of items that you have completed along with the total number of test items (for example, "35 of 40 items have been completed"). Use this information to gauge your pace.

- If you skip a question, you cannot return to it later. You should skip a question only if you are certain that you cannot complete the tasks correctly.

- Don't worry if the testing software crashes while you are taking the exam. The test software is set up to handle this situation. Find your test administrator and tell him or her what happened. The administrator will work through the steps required to restart the test. When the test restarts, it will allow you to continue where you left off. You will have the same amount of time remaining to complete the test as you did when the software crashed.

- As soon as you are finished reading a question and you click in the application window, a condensed version of the instruction is displayed in a corner of the screen. If you are unsure whether you have completed all tasks stated in the test question, click the Instructions button on the test information bar at the bottom of the screen and then reread the question. Close the instruction window when you are finished. Do this as often as necessary to ensure you have read the question correctly and that you have completed all the tasks stated in the question.

If You Do Not Pass the Test

If you do not pass, you can use the assessment printout as a guide to practice the items that you missed. There is no limit to the number of times that you can retake a test; however, you must pay the fee each time that you take the test. When you retake the test, expect to see some of the same test items on the subsequent test; the test software randomly generates the test items from a master test bank before you begin the test. Also expect to see several questions that did not appear on the previous test.

Microsoft e-Learning Library

Microsoft Learning is pleased to offer, in combination with our new *Microsoft Official Academic Course* for *Microsoft Office System 2003 Edition*, in-depth access to our powerful e-Learning tool, the Microsoft® e-Learning Library Version 2 (MELL 2) Desktop Edition for Office System 2003. The MELL Version 2 Desktop Edition for Office System 2003 will help instructors and students alike increase their skill and comfort level with Microsoft software and technologies—as well as help students develop the skills they need to succeed in today's competitive job market.

MELL Features

The MELL Version 2 Desktop Edition for Office System 2003 product included with this *Microsoft Official Academic Course* features:

- Fully customizable learning environments that help instructors pre-assess student's skill levels and direct them to the tasks that are appropriate to their needs.
- High-quality, browser-based training and reinforcement that offers students a familiar environment in which to acquire new skills.
- A powerful search tool that quickly scans a full library of learning materials and provides snappy answers to specific questions.
- Interactive exercises and focused lessons on specific subjects to help instructors direct their students quickly to exactly the content they need to know.
- Reliable, in-depth content, engaging simulations, automated support tools, and memorable on-screen demonstrations.
- An after hours and after class reference and reinforcement tool that students can take with them and use in their working lives.

Additionally, MELL Version 2 Desktop Edition for Office System 2003 fits easily into an existing lab and includes:

- Training solutions that are compatible with all existing software and hardware infrastructures.
- An enhanced learning environment that works without a separate learning management system (LMS) and runs in any SCORM-compliant LMS.
- The ability to send and receive shortcut links via e-mail to relevant help topics, which facilitates the learning experience in a classroom setting and encourages peer-to-peer learning.

Instructors who are preparing students for the MCSE/MCSA or MCAD credential can also use MELL 2 IT Professional Edition and MELL 2 Developer Edition to help students develop the skills they need to succeed in today's competitive job market. Both editions provide outstanding training and reference materials designed to help users achieve professional certification while learning real-world skills. Check out www.microsoft.com/mspress/business for more information on these additional MELL products.

Focused Students, Mastering Tasks

The MELL Version 2 Desktop Edition for Office System 2003 helps focus students on the tasks they need to know and helps them master those tasks through a combination of the following:

- Assessments that help determine the lessons that will require focus in the classroom or lab.
- Realistic simulations that mirror the actual software without requiring that it already be installed—making it ideal for students who may not have access to the latest Microsoft products outside of the classroom and labs.
- Within the simulation, the ability for a student to follow each step on his or her own, have the computer perform the step, or any combination of the two.

The MELL Version 2 Desktop Edition for Office System 2003 provides deep premium content that allows and encourages students to go beyond basic tasks and achieve proficiency and effectiveness—in class and eventually in the workplace. This depth is reflected in the fact that our desktop training titles are certified by the Microsoft Office Specialist Program.

The MELL Assessment Feature

MELL Version 2 Desktop Edition for Office System 2003 includes a skill assessment designed to help instructors identify topics and features that might warrant coverage during lecture or lab meetings. The skill assessment gives instructors an opportunity to see how much students already know about the topics covered in this course, which in turn allows instructors to devote meeting time to topics with which students are unfamiliar.

To use the assessment feature, follow these steps (note that the illustrations are specific to the Excel Core course, but the steps apply to all of the courses):

1 Insert the Microsoft Official Academic Course companion CD that accompanies this textbook into your CD drive.

2 From the menu, select "View e-Learning Course."

3 Click on the training course you are interested in via the left navigation pane.

4 Click on "Pre-Assessment" within any core training topic on the accompanying MELL Version 2 Desktop Edition for Office System 2003 CD-ROM.

5 Click on "Take the Pre-Assessment."

6 Input some correct answers and, if you choose, some incorrect answers as you move through the Pre-Assessment.

7 Click on "Show My Score" at the bottom of the Skills Assessment.

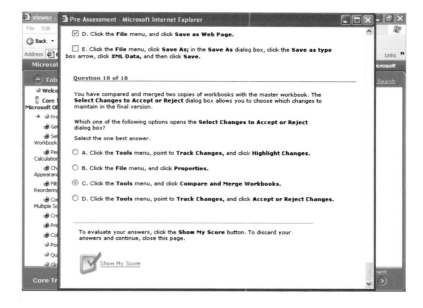

8 The "Show My Score" box details all the correct and incorrect answers and also provides correct answers for all the incorrect responses.

9 Additionally, the resultant table also provides a basic learning plan, directing you to areas you need to master while acknowledging the skills you already possess.

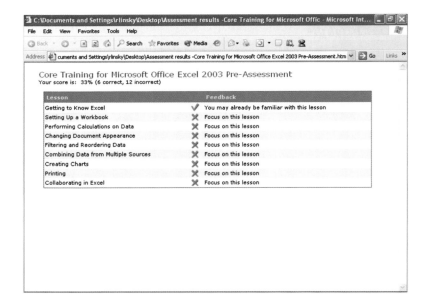

10 Click on either the "Print" or "Save" button to print or save to disk your Pre-Assessment results for future reference.

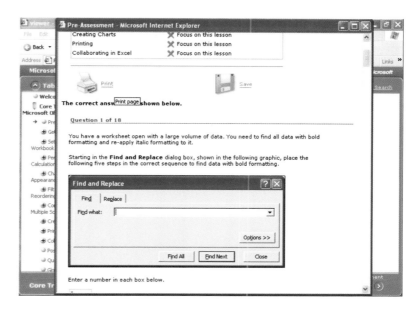

11 You are now ready to begin your interactive learning experience with MELL Version 2 Desktop Edition for Office System 2003!

Creating a Presentation

After completing this lesson, you will be able to:

✔ *Start Microsoft PowerPoint.*
✔ *Explore the PowerPoint window.*
✔ *Choose a method to start a presentation.*
✔ *Create a presentation using a wizard.*
✔ *Move around in a presentation.*
✔ *Change text in the Outline/Slides pane.*
✔ *Reverse one or more actions.*
✔ *Change and add text in the Slide pane.*
✔ *Change presentation views.*
✔ *Save a presentation.*

KEY TERMS

- bullet text
- menus
- Normal view
- Notes Page view
- Notes pane
- Outline/Slides pane
- paragraph
- presentation window
- ScreenTip
- selection box
- Slide pane
- Slide Show view
- Slide Sorter view
- status bar
- task pane
- text object
- title slide
- title text
- toolbars
- window

With Microsoft PowerPoint, you can create overhead slides, speaker notes, audience handouts, and outlines—all in a single presentation file. PowerPoint offers powerful tools to help you create and organize a presentation step by step.

As an example, suppose that you are the vice president of sales for the public relations firm Contoso, Ltd, and are responsible for developing a new employee training program. The president of Contoso has asked you to create a brief presentation to describe the project at the annual stockholders' meeting.

In this lesson, you will learn how to start PowerPoint, explore the PowerPoint window, create a presentation using the AutoContent Wizard, move around in a presentation, change and insert text, reverse changes that you make, look at content in different views, and save your work.

◆ Before you can use the practice files for this course, you must install them from the book's companion CD to their default location. See "Using the CD-ROM" at the beginning of this book for more information. You will not need any practice files for this lesson. Instead, you will create all of the files and folders that you need during the course of the lesson.

Starting Microsoft PowerPoint

THE BOTTOM LINE

Before you can create a new presentation or work on an existing one, you need to start PowerPoint on your computer. Starting PowerPoint opens the PowerPoint window, giving you access to PowerPoint's tools and features.

After you install PowerPoint, you are ready to start PowerPoint. As with other programs, there are several ways to start PowerPoint. One way is to use the Start button on the taskbar. Clicking the Start button displays the Start menu, where you can click All Programs to see a list of the programs available on your computer.

Depending how you installed PowerPoint, you may find an icon for it directly on the All Programs menu. If you installed PowerPoint as a part of the Microsoft Office system, you may find a Microsoft Office folder on the All Programs menu. Click the Microsoft Office folder to see a submenu of Office applications, including PowerPoint.

ANOTHER METHOD

You can also start PowerPoint by creating a shortcut icon on the Windows desktop. Shortcut icons allow you to launch the associated program by simply double-clicking. To create a shortcut, click the Start button, point to All Programs, right-click Microsoft Office PowerPoint 2003, point to Send To, and then click Desktop (create shortcut). A desktop shortcut is represented by an icon with a curved arrow in the left corner.

Use Start to open PowerPoint

1 On the taskbar, click Start.

The Start menu appears.

2 On the Start menu, point to All Programs or Programs.

The Programs menu appears, displaying all the programs on your hard disk drive, including Microsoft PowerPoint. A portion of the All Programs menu should look like the following illustration.

FIGURE 1-1

Portion of the All Programs menu

3 Click Microsoft Office PowerPoint 2003 on the All Programs menu, or point to Microsoft Office and then click the Microsoft Office PowerPoint 2003 icon to start PowerPoint.

◆ Keep PowerPoint open for the next exercise.

QUICK CHECK

Q: What do you call the Windows submenu that shows you all the applications available on your computer?

A: This menu is called All Programs.

QUICK REFERENCE ▼

Use Start to open PowerPoint

1 On the taskbar, click Start, and then point to All Programs.

2 Click Microsoft Office, if necessary, and then click Microsoft Office PowerPoint 2003.

Exploring the PowerPoint Window

Opening, Saving, and Closing a Presentation

THE BOTTOM LINE

The PowerPoint Window gives you access to important tasks and features you use to create and work with presentations. Becoming familiar with the presentation window elements allows you to work more quickly and efficiently with PowerPoint.

When Microsoft PowerPoint opens, it displays the program window. A **window** is an area of the screen that is used to display a PowerPoint program or presentation window. The **presentation window** is the electronic canvas on which you type text, draw shapes, create graphs, add color, and insert objects. As with any Microsoft Windows XP program, you can adjust the size of the PowerPoint and presentation windows with the Minimize and Restore Down/Maximize buttons, and you can close PowerPoint or the presentation window with the Close button.

FIGURE 1-2

Elements of the PowerPoint window

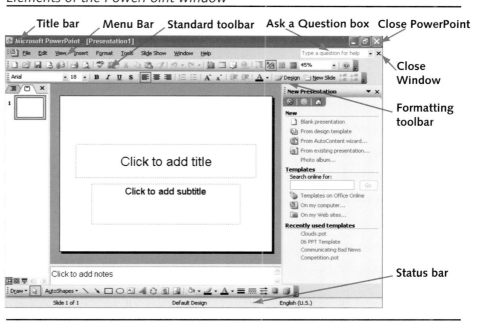

Along the top of the PowerPoint window are the menus and buttons you use to perform the most common presentation tasks. Another row of buttons appears along the bottom of the screen. The **menus** are lists of commands or options available in PowerPoint. The buttons you see are organized on **toolbars**. Toolbar buttons are shortcuts to commonly used menu commands and formatting tools. You simply click a button on the appropriate toolbar for one-step access to tasks such as formatting text and saving a presentation. At the top of the program window, you will also find the Ask a Question box, which you can use to type questions that the PowerPoint help system will answer for you.

TROUBLESHOOTING

What you see on your screen might not match the graphics in this book exactly. When you first open PowerPoint after installation, the Standard and Formatting toolbars share one row and show only the most frequently used buttons. The graphics in this book show the Standard and Formatting toolbars on two rows to make it easier for you to see the buttons you will be using. You can change your setup to match the graphics by clicking Customize on the Tools menu. On the Options tab, select the Show Standard And Formatting Toolbars On Two Rows check box, and then click Close.

The Standard and Formatting toolbars are located directly below the menu bar. Only the most commonly used commands appear on the toolbars by default. The toolbars on your computer might display buttons different from the ones shown in the figures in this lesson. To see the rest of the commands on either toolbar, click the Toolbar Options down arrow, shown in the margin. Once you use a button on the Toolbar Options list, it replaces a less frequently used button on the visible part of the toolbar. In this book, if you are instructed to click a button and you don't see it, click the Toolbar Options down arrow to display all of the buttons on a toolbar.

PowerPoint uses personalized menus and toolbars. When you click a menu name, a short menu appears, containing the most frequently used commands. These short menus save you time by displaying only the commands you use regularly. To make the complete long menu appear, you can leave the pointer over the menu name for several seconds, you can double-click the menu name, or you can click the menu name and then click the small double arrow at the bottom of the short menu.

IMPORTANT

You can turn off the personalized menus feature so that all commands appear all the time on the menus. On the Tools menu, click Customize, click the Options tab, click the Always Show Full Menus check box, and then click Close.

Messages appear at the bottom of the window in an area called the **status bar**. These messages describe what you are seeing and doing in the PowerPoint window as you work.

To find out about different items on the screen, you can display a **ScreenTip**. To display a ScreenTip for a toolbar button, you simply place the pointer over the button without clicking it, and a ScreenTip appears, telling you the name of the button, as shown in the margin.

TIP

You can turn toolbar ScreenTips on and off. On the Tools menu, click Customize, click the Options tab, clear the Show ScreenTips On Toolbars check box, and then click Close.

The default view, Normal, is made up of three panes: Outline/Slides, Slide, and Notes. The **Outline/Slides pane** has tabs that allow you to alternate between an outline of the slide text (the Outline tab) and a list of the presentation's slides displayed as thumbnails (Slides tab). The **Slide pane** shows the currently selected slide as it will appear in the presentation. The **Notes pane** is where you enter speaker notes. You can resize any of the panes by dragging the light-colored bar that separates them.

At the right side of the PowerPoint window is the **task pane**. The task pane displays commands and features you use often in working with presentations. Task panes let you work with commands without having to display menus or use toolbar buttons. Some task panes display automatically. For example, the Getting Started task pane opens along with PowerPoint each time the program starts. Other task panes display in response to a specific request. For instance, when you tell PowerPoint you want to insert a clip art picture, the Clip Art task pane opens to help you find a picture.

ANOTHER METHOD

To open the task pane manually, click Task Pane on the View menu. This command opens the task pane if it is hidden or closes it if it is open.

You can quickly switch from one task pane to another by clicking the Other Task Panes down arrow on any task pane to display the other task panes. When you're finished with a task pane, click its Close button to hide it.

FIGURE 1-3

Task pane in the PowerPoint window

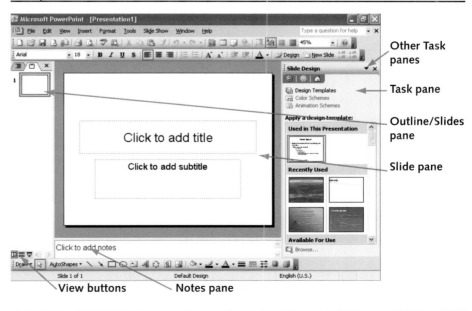

At the bottom of the Outline/Slides pane are view buttons that allow you to display the presentation's slides in different ways. When you open PowerPoint, the presentation is displayed in Normal view.

Work with PowerPoint window elements

In this exercise, you work with a PowerPoint menu, ScreenTips, and the task pane to become familiar with the PowerPoint window.

1 **On the menu bar, click Window.**

The Window menu appears.

2 **Click the arrows at the bottom of the Window menu to view the expanded menu.**

The expanded menu appears.

ANOTHER METHOD

You can also view the expanded menu by clicking the menu and waiting a few seconds for the expanded menu to appear or by double-clicking the menu name.

3 **Click Next Pane.**

4 **On the menu bar, click Window again.**

Notice that the Next Pane command is now displayed on the Window menu. PowerPoint has personalized the Window menu for you.

5 **Position the pointer on the slide icon in the Slides tab of the Outline/Slides pane.**

A ScreenTip appears when you position the pointer over the icon to identify the Slides tab.

6 **Click the Other Task Panes down arrow.**

The Other Task Panes menu opens, showing a list of all available task panes.

7 **Click New Presentation on the Other Task Panes menu.**

The Other Task Panes menu closes, leaving the New Presentation task pane open.

◆ **Keep PowerPoint open for the next exercise.**

Choosing a Method to Start a Presentation

THE BOTTOM LINE

Use the New Presentation task pane to start a new presentation when you open PowerPoint or at any time while you're working with another presentation. Choose the New Presentation task pane option that best fits the new presentation you want to create.

When you start PowerPoint, the Getting Started task pane displays along with a blank presentation. If you have created presentations recently, their names appear in the Open section of the Getting Started task pane. In this case, you can simply click the presentation name to open it and continue working with it.

If you want to create a new presentation, you can simply start adding text to the blank presentation in the Slide pane or display the New Presentation task pane to select from several options in the New section for creating a new presentation. Below are the default options available in the New Presentations task pane.

- Click Blank Presentation to start a new presentation from scratch.
- Click From Design Template to apply one of PowerPoint's design templates to a new, blank presentation.
- Click From AutoContent Wizard to let a wizard help you with both presentation content and a design.
- Click From Existing Presentation to base a new presentation on the content of a presentation you have already created.
- Click Photo Album to create an album of pictures or other images.

CHECK THIS OUT ▼

Create a Photo Album
The Photo Album feature allows you to create a presentation that contains nothing but photos or other images. This is a great way to display pictures from a trip to show your friends or organize images you intend to use in other projects.

Creating a Presentation Using a Wizard

Using a Wizard to Start a New Presentation

THE BOTTOM LINE

Use the AutoContent Wizard to help you create a sophisticated presentation with a design and suggested content. After you have answered the wizard's questions and the wizard has completed the presentation, you can replace the suggested content with your own text.

Creating a presentation with the AutoContent Wizard can save you time by helping you organize and write the presentation. The wizard takes you through a step-by-step process, prompting you for presentation information, beginning with the **title slide**, which is the first slide in the presentation. Although the AutoContent Wizard creates business-related presentations, you can adapt them to a wide variety of uses and save yourself a lot of planning and formatting time.

Create a presentation with the AutoContent Wizard

Now that you're more familiar with the PowerPoint window, you're ready to create your first presentation. You'll use the AutoContent Wizard for the new presentation.

1 **In the New Presentation task pane, click From AutoContent Wizard under New.**

The AutoContent Wizard dialog box opens, displaying the Start screen. On the left side of the dialog box is a list of the screens in the wizard.

2 **Read the introduction, and then click Next.**

The second screen in the AutoContent Wizard appears, and the square next to Presentation Type on the left of the dialog box turns green to indicate that this is the current screen. The AutoContent Wizard prompts you to select a presentation type. To help you identify presentation types quickly, the wizard organizes presentations by category.

3 **Click Projects.**

A list of project-related presentations displays.

4 **In the list on the right, click Project Overview if necessary.**

Your AutoContent Wizard dialog box should look like the following illustration.

FIGURE 1-4

Step 2 of the Wizard

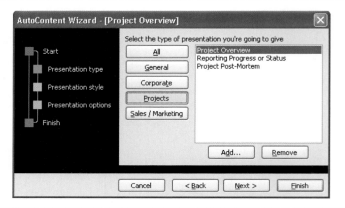

5 **Click Next.**

The AutoContent Wizard now prompts you to select a type of output, based on the media type you will be using for the presentation.

6 **Click the On-Screen Presentation option, if necessary, to select that presentation type.**

7 **Click Next.**

The AutoContent Wizard now prompts you to enter information for the title slide and for footer information to be included on each slide.

IMPORTANT

In the steps throughout this book, bold red type indicates text that you should type exactly as it appears. If you make a mistake as you type the information, press Backspace to delete the error, and then type the correct text.

8 **Click in the Presentation Title box, type New Employee Training Program and then press Tab.**

Pressing Tab takes you automatically to the next text box in the dialog box. You can also click inside the text box in which you would like to enter information.

9 **In the Footer box, type** Contoso, Ltd.

10 **Verify that the Date Last Updated and the Slide Number check boxes are selected.**

The Date Last Updated setting inserts the current date on each slide, and the Slide Number setting applies consecutive numbers to the slides.

FIGURE 1-5

Title and footer information for the new presentation

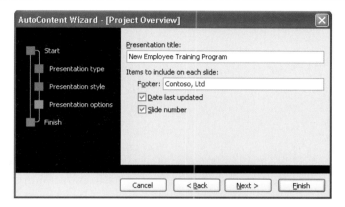

TROUBLESHOOTING

If you want to change any of the information you previously entered, click the Back button.

11 **Click Next, and then click Finish.**

The PowerPoint presentation window appears with content provided by the AutoContent Wizard in outline form in the Outline tab of the Outline/Slides pane and the title slide in the Slide pane. The name on the title slide is the name of the registered user. The task pane closes automatically.

◆ **Keep this file open for the next exercise.**

QUICK REFERENCE ▼

Use a wizard to create a new presentation

1 In the New Presentation task pane, click From AutoContent Wizard.

2 Read the introduction, click Next, and then click All.

3 In the list box on the right, click a presentation, and then click Next.

4 Click a presentation style, and then click Next.

5 Click the Presentation Title box, type a presentation title, and then press Tab.

6 In the Footer box, type footer text.

7 Select the Date Last Updated and the Slide Number check boxes.

8 Click Next, and then click Finish.

QUICK CHECK

Q: What is the name of the first slide in a presentation?

A: **The first slide in the presentation is the title slide.**

Moving Around in a Presentation

Viewing a Presentation

THE BOTTOM LINE

Because most presentations contain a number of slides, you need to master methods of moving from one slide to another so you can work efficiently with the slides. PowerPoint allows you to use both keys and mouse operations to move from slide to slide.

As you work with a presentation, you will find that you are constantly jumping from one slide to another to finalize content, add graphics, modify formats, and so on. Learning how to navigate a presentation quickly is an important skill.

You can move around in a presentation in several ways in PowerPoint. You can click the scroll arrows in the Slide pane to scroll slide by slide, click either side of the scroll box to scroll window by window, or drag the scroll box to move immediately to a specific slide. In the Slide pane, you can click the Next Slide and Previous Slide buttons, which are located at the bottom of the vertical scroll bar. You can also press the Page Up or Page Down key to scroll slide by slide.

FIGURE 1-6

Scroll bars and boxes in the PowerPoint window

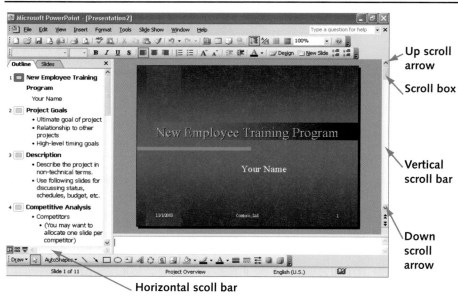

Move around in a PowerPoint presentation

In this exercise, you move around in the Outline tab and from slide to slide in the Slide pane.

1 **Click the down scroll arrow in the Outline tab a few times to see the text below the current pane.**

Each time you click a scroll arrow, PowerPoint changes the screen to show you one more line.

TIP

When you click below or above the scroll box, PowerPoint scrolls slide by slide.

2 Click below the scroll box in the scroll bar in the Outline tab.

The next window of information in the outline appears.

3 Drag the scroll box to the bottom of the scroll bar—you cannot drag it off the scroll bar.

The end of the outline appears. With this method, you can quickly jump to anywhere in the outline.

4 Click below the scroll box in the vertical scroll bar in the Slide pane.

Slide 2 appears in the Slide pane. Notice that the Outline tab jumps to slide 2 as well, and the slide icon next to slide 2 in the Outline tab is gray to indicate that this is the current slide.

5 Click the Previous Slide button.

Slide 1 appears in the Slide pane and is highlighted in the Outline tab

6 Click the Next Slide button until you reach the end of the presentation.

Each slide contains suggestions for developing and organizing the presentation.

7 Drag the scroll box up the vertical scroll bar to view the slide 3 slide indicator box, but don't release the mouse button.

Your presentation window should look like the following illustration.

FIGURE 1-7

Drag the scroll box to display the slide 3 indicator box

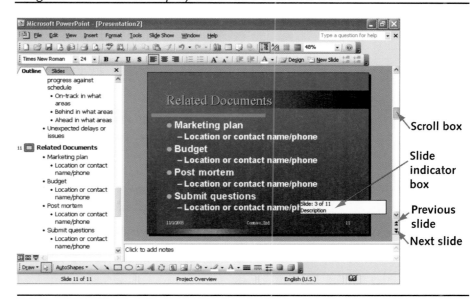

As you drag the scroll box, a slide indicator box appears, telling you the slide number and title of the slide to which the scroll box is pointing. The scroll box indicates the relative position of the slide in

the presentation on the scroll bar. To display the slide named in the indicator box, simply release the mouse button.

8 **Release the mouse button.**

The status bar changes from Slide 11 of 11 to Slide 3 of 11.

◆ **Keep this file open for the next exercise.**

ANOTHER METHOD

You can click the slide icon next to a slide in the Outline tab. The Slide pane jumps to the slide you clicked. Or, on the Slides tab, click on the thumbnail of the slide you want to display.

QUICK REFERENCE ▼

Move from slide to slide in the Slide pane

1 Click the Previous Slide button or the Next Slide button.

2 Click above or below the scroll box in the vertical scroll bar in the Slide pane.

3 Drag the scroll box up or down the vertical scroll bar.

Changing Text in the Outline/Slides Pane

Editing Text

THE BOTTOM LINE

Use the Outline tab when you want to concentrate on the text of a presentation rather than its design. You can see the text of a number of slides at a time in the Outline tab, making it easy for you to ensure consistency from slide to slide and to get information you might need from other slides.

You can edit presentation text in either the Outline tab of the Outline/Slides pane or in the Slide pane. When you are concentrating on the text of a presentation, the Outline tab is the most useful pane in which to work because you can easily see the text of the entire presentation.

Change text in the Outline tab

The AutoContent Wizard helps you get started with a suggested presentation outline. Now your job is to modify the suggested outline text to meet your specific needs.

1 **In the Outline tab, scroll up to slide 2, position the pointer (which changes to the I-beam) to the right of the text "Project Goals" in slide 2, and then double-click to select the title text.**

PowerPoint highlights the selected text so that once you select it, the subsequent text you type—regardless of its length—replaces the selection.

2 **Type** Program Overview.

If you make a typing mistake, press Backspace to erase it. Note that the text changes in the Slide pane also.

3 **Position the I-beam pointer (which changes to the four-headed arrow) over the bullet in the Outline tab next to the text "Ultimate goal of project" in slide 2, and then click to select the bullet text.**

4 **Type** Contoso's Goals.

5 **In slide 2, click the bullet next to the text "Relationship to other projects," and then type** Training Sessions.

6 **In slide 2, click the bullet next to the text "High-level timing goals," and then press Delete or Backspace.**

The text is deleted but the grayed-out bullet remains in view.

7 **Press Backspace twice.**

The first time you press Backspace, you remove the grayed-out bullet. The second Backspace removes the blank line and moves the insertion point back to the end of the second bullet item. Your presentation window should look like the following illustration.

FIGURE 1-8

New text added to slide

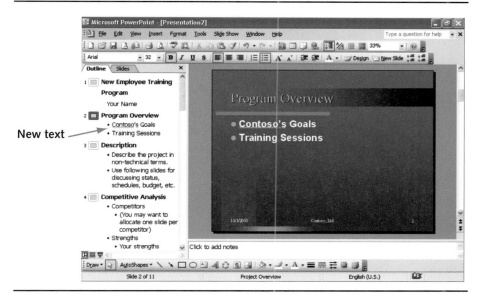

◆ **Leave this file open for the next exercise.**

QUICK CHECK

Q: Which pointer displays when you rest it on a bullet in the Outline tab?

A: **The four-headed arrow pointer displays when rested on a bullet.**

QUICK REFERENCE ▼

Change text in the Outline/Slides pane

1 In the Outline/Slides pane, click the Outline tab.

2 Position the pointer (which changes to the I-beam) to the right of the text, and then select the text.

3 Type the replacement text.

Reversing One or More Actions

Editing Text

THE BOTTOM LINE

As you work on a presentation, you may want to "take back" changes you have made to text, formatting, or other parts of the presentation. The Undo and Redo commands give you a very helpful "safety net" that allows you to feel comfortable making changes.

Whenever you perform an action that is not what you intended, you can reverse the action with a handy PowerPoint feature called the Undo command. Located on the Standard toolbar or the Edit menu, the Undo command can reverse up to the last 20 actions by default, one at a time. For example, choosing the Undo command now will restore the text you just deleted. If you decide that the undo action is not what you wanted, you can restore the undone action by clicking the Redo button or by clicking Redo on the Edit menu.

You must undo or redo actions in the order in which you performed them. That is, you cannot undo your fourth previous action without first reversing the three actions that followed it. To undo a number of actions at the same time, you can use the Undo button down arrow.

Use Undo and Redo

In the last exercise, you made some changes to the text on slide 2. In this exercise, you undo and redo these changes.

1 **On the Standard toolbar, click the Undo button to reverse your last action.**

The blank line reappears below the two bullet items on the slide.

ANOTHER METHOD

- Press Ctrl + Z.
- On the Edit menu, click Undo Typing. (The command name will change depending on what action has just been taken.)

2 **On the Standard toolbar, click the down arrow next to the Undo button.**

The Undo button menu appears.

3 **Click the third item in the list, Typing.**

The second bullet in slide 2 reverts to the AutoContent Wizard's text. Notice that the third bullet, which you deleted after changing the second bullet's text, also reappears.

4 **On the Standard toolbar, click the Redo button.**

The text you typed for the second bullet item reappears.

- Press Ctrl + Y.
- On the Edit menu, click Redo.

5 On the Standard toolbar, click the Redo button down arrow, and then click the item in the list, Typing, to restore the changes you just undid.

You should now see only the two bullet items you typed.

◆ Leave this file open for the next exercise.

TIP

You can change the number of actions the Undo command will undo by adjusting the number of Undo actions that appear on the Undo list. To do this, click Options on the Tools menu, click the Edit tab, change the maximum number of undos near the bottom of the dialog box, and then click OK.

QUICK CHECK

Q: How many actions can you undo at one time?

A: **You can undo up to 20 actions at one time.**

QUICK REFERENCE ▼

Use Undo and Redo

- On the Standard toolbar, click the Undo or Redo button.
- On the Standard toolbar, click the down arrow next to the Undo or Redo button, and then click an item in the list.

Changing and Adding Text in the Slide Pane

Editing Text

THE BOTTOM LINE

Besides editing text in the Outline pane, you can add and change text in the Slide pane, right on the slide. Working in the Slide pane lets you see your text at a larger size with the presentation's formatting applied, so you have a better idea how the slide will look when displayed during the presentation.

You can also work with presentation text in the Slide pane. In the Slide pane, you work with one slide at a time. An object containing slide text is called a **text object**. A typical slide contains a title, called **title text**, and the major points beneath the title, called a **paragraph** or **bullet text**. To add more bulleted text to the text object, you place the insertion point at the end of a line of text, press Enter, and then add another line of text.

Change and add text in the Slide pane

In this exercise, you work in the Slide pane to change and enter text.

1 Click the Next Slide button in the Slide pane to display slide 3.

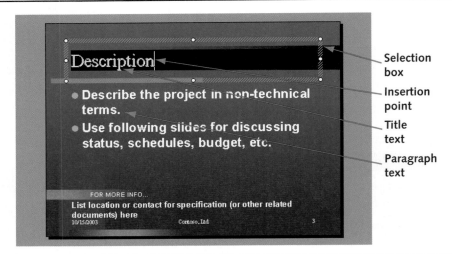

2 Position the pointer (which changes to the I-beam) over the title text in slide 3, and then click the title text.

The text is surrounded by a rectangle of gray slanted lines called a **selection box**, with the blinking insertion point placed in the high-lighted text. The selection box lets PowerPoint know what object you want to change on the slide.

FIGURE 1-9

Click in the title text to display the selection box

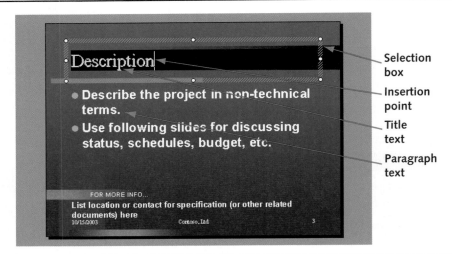

3 Double-click the title text "Description" to select it.

The text background becomes white to let you know the word is selected.

4 Type Training Session Development.

The new text replaces the selected text.

5 Position the pointer (which changes to the I-beam) over any of the bulleted text in slide 3, and then click the bulleted text.

6 Select all the text in the first bullet "Describe the project ...".

You can drag over the text to select it.

7 Type Content development stage.

8 Position the pointer (which changes to the four-headed arrow) over the bullet next to the text "Use following slides ..." in slide 3, and then click the bullet.

9 Type Lining up speakers for video and then press Enter.

A new bullet appears in the slide. The new bullet appears black until you add text.

10 Type Program will be ready in two weeks.

11 **Click outside of the selection box to deselect the text object.**

Your slide should look like the following illustration.

FIGURE 1-10

Text changed in Slide pane

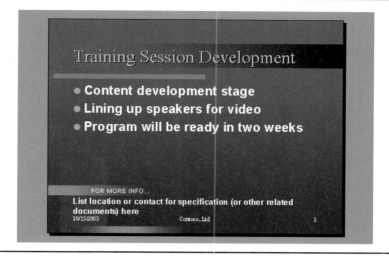

QUICK CHECK

Q: What are the major points beneath the title called?

A: The major points beneath the title are called paragraph or bullet text.

◆ **Keep this file open for the next exercise.**

QUICK REFERENCE ▼

Change or add text in the Slide pane

1 Position the pointer (which changes to the I-beam) over the text, and then select the text to change or click the text to which you want to add.

2 Type text.

Changing Presentation Views

THE BOTTOM LINE

PowerPoint's views let you perform different tasks to prepare a presentation for viewing. Switching frequently among these views helps you to identify problems and fine-tune the organization and content of a presentation.

Viewing a Presentation

PowerPoint has four views to help you create, organize, and display presentations: Normal, Slide Sorter, Notes Page, and Slide Show. You can click the view buttons at the bottom of the presentation window to switch among the different views. You can also access all of these view commands on the View menu. There is no view button for Notes Page view. Instead, to display this view you click Notes Page on the View menu.

You have been working in Normal view. In **Normal view,** you can work with your presentation in four different ways: Modify text in the Outline tab of the Outline/Slides pane; select slide miniatures in the Slides tab of the Outline/Slides pane; work with the slide and its design in the Slide pane; or add speaker notes to slides in the Notes pane.

In **Slide Sorter view,** you can preview an entire presentation as slide miniatures—as if you were looking at photographic slides on a light board—and easily reorganize the slides in a presentation.

Notes Page view differs slightly from the Notes pane. You can add speaker notes in the Notes pane, but if you want to add graphics as notes, you must be in Notes Page view.

Slide Show view allows you to preview slides as an electronic presentation. Slide Show view displays slides as you would see them in Normal view, but the slides fill the entire screen. Use this view at any time during the development of the presentation to check slides for accuracy and appearance.

Illustrations of Normal, Slide Sorter, Notes Page, and Slide Show view are shown below.

FIGURE 1-11

Four PowerPoint views

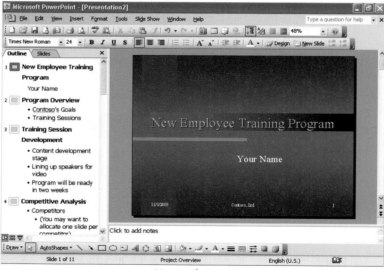

Normal view

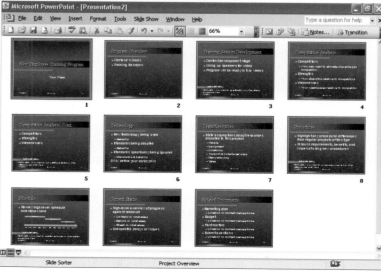

Slide Sorter view

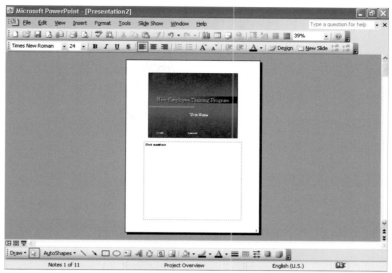

Notes Page view

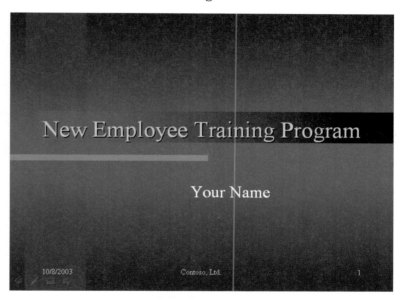

Slide Show view

Switch to different PowerPoint views

1 **In Normal view, click the Slides tab in the Outline/Slides pane.**

The Slides tab displays all slides in the presentation as slide miniatures. Click a slide in the Slides tab to display that slide in the Slide pane.

2 **Click slide 4 in the Slides tab.**

Your presentation should look like the following illustration:

FIGURE 1-12

Display slide 4

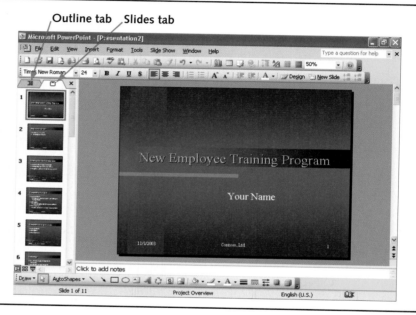

3 **Click the Slide Sorter View button.**

All the slides now appear in miniature on the screen, and the slide that you were viewing in Normal view is surrounded by a dark box, indicating that the slide is selected. You can scroll through the slides in Slide Sorter view to view all of the slides in a presentation.

ANOTHER METHOD

On the View menu, click Slide Sorter.

4 **Drag the scroll box on the vertical scroll bar to see the slides at the end of the presentation.**

TIP

If your screen is large enough to display all the slides in Slide Sorter view, you may not need to scroll.

5 Drag the scroll box to the top of the scroll bar.

The beginning slides of the presentation appear. Your presentation window should look like the following illustration.

FIGURE 1-13

Presentation in Slide Sorter view

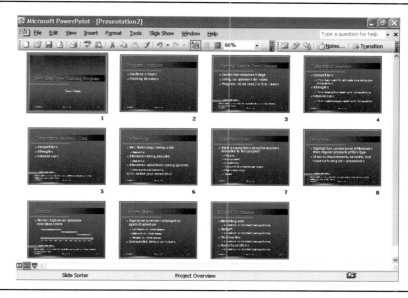

Note that your screen might display a different number of slides than shown in the illustration.

When PowerPoint displays slides that are formatted in Slide Sorter view, titles might be hard to read. You can suppress the slide formatting to read the slide titles.

6 Hold down Alt, and then click an individual slide.

The formatting for the slide disappears, and the title appears clearly. When you release the mouse button, the display format reappears.

7 Double-click slide 1 to switch to Normal view.

The presentation view changes back to Normal view, showing slide 1.

ANOTHER METHOD

- On the View menu, click Normal.
- Click the Normal View button.

◆ Keep this file open for the next exercise.

QUICK CHECK

Q: What view allows you to add graphics as notes?

A: **Notes Page view lets you add graphics as notes.**

QUICK REFERENCE ▼

Switch to different PowerPoint views

- Click the Normal View button.
- Click the Slide Sorter View button.
- Click the Slide Show button.
- On the View menu, click Notes Page.

Saving a Presentation

Opening, Saving, and
Closing a Presentation

THE BOTTOM LINE

Saving a presentation is an important skill to learn because saving stores the information on your system. Though you can recover presentations if the computer shuts down accidentally, it is better to save a presentation as soon as possible and to save changes frequently while you work.

The work you have completed so far is stored only in your computer's temporary memory. To save your work for further use, you must give the presentation a name and store it on your computer's hard disk drive.

The first time you save a new presentation, the Save As dialog box opens when you choose the Save command. In the Save As dialog box, you can name the presentation and choose where to save it. Once you name a presentation, you can save the changes you just made by clicking the Save button on the Standard toolbar or by selecting Save on the File menu. In other words, the newer version overwrites the original version. If you want to keep both the original file and the new version, you can choose the Save As command on the File menu to save the new version with a new name.

TIP

PowerPoint saves presentations for recovery in case the program stops responding or you lose power. Changes are saved in a recovery file based on the settings in the AutoRecover save features. On the Tools menu, click Options, click the Save tab, select the Save AutoRecover Info check box, specify the period of time in which to save, and then click OK.

Save a new presentation

You're finished working on this presentation, so you can save the presentation and close it.

1 **On the Standard toolbar, click the Save button.**

PowerPoint displays the Save As dialog box. The text in the box next to the label File Name shows the title of the presentation by default. This default name is selected so that you can type a different file name if you want.

FIGURE 1-14

Save As dialog box

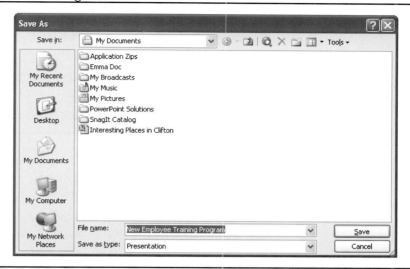

- Press Ctrl + S.
- On the File menu, click Save As.

2 **In the File Name box, type** Contoso Employee Training Report Pres 01.

The word *Pres* in the file name is an abbreviation for Presentation.

3 **Click the Save In down arrow, and then click the letter of your hard drive, which is usually C.**

If your hard disk uses a letter other than C, substitute the appropriate drive letter in place of C.

4 **In the list of file and folder names, double-click the PowerPoint Practice folder, and then double-click the Lesson01 folder.**

5 **Click Save or press Enter to save the presentation.**

The title bar name changes to Contoso Employee Training Report Pres 01.

◆ **If you are continuing to other lessons, close the Contoso Employee Training Report Pres 01 presentation and leave PowerPoint open. If you are not continuing to other lessons, click the Close button in the title bar of the PowerPoint window.**

To create a new presentation from existing slides, click File on the menu bar, click Save As, type a new name in the File Name box, and then click Save.

QUICK CHECK

Q: What command do you use to give a new name to an existing presentation?

A: Use the Save As command to give a new name to a presentation.

QUICK REFERENCE ▼

Save a new presentation

1 On the Standard toolbar, click the Save button.

2 In the File Name text box, type a file name.

3 In the Save In box, navigate to the location where you want to save the presentation.

4 Click Save or press Enter to save the presentation.

Key Points

✔ *Starting PowerPoint opens the PowerPoint window, giving you access to the features and tools you can use to create and work with presentations.*

✔ *The PowerPoint window contains typical features such as a menu bar, toolbars, and sizing and closing buttons. The default window displays Normal view, which consists of the Outline/Slides pane, the Slide pane, and the Notes pane.*

✔ *Choose one of four options in the New Presentation task pane to create a presentation: Blank Presentation, From Design Template, From AutoContent Wizard, or From Existing Presentation. You can also quickly create a Photo Album by clicking this link in the task pane.*

✔ *The AutoContent Wizard provides a slide design and suggested content on a number of business-related presentation topics. Use this option to quickly generate content you can change to suit your purpose.*

✔ *Text can be entered and modified in either the Outline tab or the Slide pane. Use the Outline tab when you want to concentrate on the text and the Slide pane when you want to concentrate on the presentation's appearance.*

✔ *To move from slide to slide in a presentation, use keys such as Page Up or use the mouse and the scroll bars.*

✔ *The Undo and Redo commands allow you to reverse or repeat actions. You can undo or redo one action at a time or a whole series of actions.*

✔ *PowerPoint's four views let you work with a presentation in specific ways. To switch from one view to another, use the view buttons or menu commands.*

✔ *It is important to save a presentation soon after you create it and at frequent intervals while working on it. Saving a presentation guards against loss from unexpected computer failure.*

Quick Quiz

True/False

T   F   **1.** There is only one way to start PowerPoint.

T   F   **2.** When you first open PowerPoint after installing the program, the Standard and Formatting toolbars appear on one row.

T   F   **3.** You can find the names of previously created presentations in the New Presentation task pane.

T   F   **4.** Using Redo is like undoing an Undo action.

T   F   **5.** After you have saved a presentation once, you can simply click the Save button to store your most recent changes.

Multiple Choice

1. To add toolbar buttons not on the Standard toolbar, click the _____.
   a. More Buttons arrow
   b. Toolbar Buttons arrow
   c. Toolbar Options arrow
   d. More Options button

2. The small message that tells you the name of a toolbar button is called a _____.
   a. What's This?
   b. ScreenTip
   c. ScreenName
   d. ToolHint

3. To create a presentation that suggests slide content as well as supplies a design, click _____.
   a. From Another Presentation
   b. From Design Template
   c. From Slide Wizard
   d. From AutoContent Wizard

4. To add more bulleted text to a slide in the Slide pane, place the insertion point at the end of a line of text and press _____.
   a. Enter
   b. Tab
   c. Down arrow
   d. Insert

5. The view that doesn't have a button at the bottom left of the screen is _____.
   a. Normal view
   b. Slide Sorter view
   c. Notes Page view
   d. Slide Show view

Short Answer

1. What are the options for starting a new presentation?
2. How do you create a presentation using a wizard?
3. How do you display a presentation as an outline?
4. What are the four PowerPoint views?
5. How do you clearly display a slide title in Slide Sorter view?
6. How do you save two versions of the same file?

On Your Own

Exercise 1

Your manager asks you to create a business plan. To help you get started, use the AutoContent Wizard to create the new presentation. Create an on-screen business plan presentation with the title Business Plan and the footer Contoso, Ltd. Save the presentation as Business Plan in the Lesson01 folder that is located in the PowerPoint Practice folder.

Exercise 2

A colleague needs a presentation slide on your current project for a larger presentation that he is working on for an upcoming business strategy meeting. Create a blank presentation. Change the new title slide to a Title and Text slide as follows: Display the Slide Layout task pane and select the second layout from the top at the left side of the task pane (use the ScreenTips to help you select the correct layout). Add the following title and bulleted list to the slide:

Brandson Ad Campaign
- Print media
- Commercial coverage
- Completion in Q4

Save the presentation as Brandson in the Lesson01 folder that is located in the PowerPoint Practice folder.

One Step Further

Exercise 1

You work for a computer services company named A. Datum Corporation that customizes systems for small businesses. Your company was counting on winning a contract to supply 25 new computers to a local school but was underbid by a new firm in your area. Use the AutoContent Wizard's Communicating Bad News template to break the news to your other employees. Modify the suggested content of the slides to fit your situation. Save the presentation as Badnews in the Lesson01 folder that is located in the PowerPoint Practice folder.

Exercise 2

A. Datum Corporation, your company, wants to avoid losing more contracts. Your boss has scheduled a sales meeting and wants you to put together a presentation that will help the sales force focus on A. Datum Corporation's services and strengths. Use the AutoContent Wizard's Selling a Product or Service template and then customize the slides to explain the needs of A. Datum Corporation's clients and how A. Datum Corporation can meet them with customer service and price strategies. Save the presentation as Selling in the Lesson01 folder that is located in the PowerPoint Practice folder and leave it open for the next exercise.

Exercise 3

View the Selling presentation in Slide Sorter view. Then change back to Normal view and display the Slides tab. Click the last slide in the tab to display the last slide in the Slide pane. Change the name on the first slide to that of your supervisor. Save and close the presentation.

LESSON

2

Working with a Presentation

After completing this lesson, you will be able to:

✔ *Create a new presentation using a design template.*
✔ *Enter text in the Slide pane.*
✔ *Create a new slide.*
✔ *Enter text in the Outline tab.*
✔ *Edit text in Normal view.*
✔ *Enter speaker notes in the Notes pane and Notes Page view.*
✔ *Insert slides from other presentations.*
✔ *Rearrange slides in Slide Sorter view.*
✔ *Show slides in Slide Show view.*

KEY TERMS

- design template
- text object
- text placeholder

To work efficiently with Microsoft PowerPoint, you need to become familiar with the important features of the product. In the previous lesson, you learned how to create a presentation using the AutoContent Wizard, change title and paragraph text, change views, move from slide to slide, and save a presentation.

After creating a progress report presentation for the employee training program at Contoso, Ltd, you decide to use PowerPoint to develop the program content. The next step is to start a new presentation and develop the content for the first training session, "Recruiting New Clients." Your sales manager has given you several slides to include in the presentation.

In this lesson, you will learn how to start a new presentation using a design template, enter and edit slide text, create new slides, enter speaker notes, insert slides from other presentations, rearrange slides, and show slides using the entire screen on your computer.

◆ Before you can use the practice files in this lesson, you must install them from the book's companion CD to their default location. See "Using the CD-ROM" at the beginning of this book for more information. To complete the procedures in this lesson, you will need to use a file named 02 PPT Lesson in the Lesson02 folder in the PowerPoint Practice folder located on your hard disk.

Creating a New Presentation Using a Design Template

Using a Template to Design a Presentation

THE BOTTOM LINE

Starting a new presentation with a design template displays a blank presentation with design formatting already applied. Design templates give you professional-looking formats and designs at the click of a button and save you considerable time in creating a good-looking presentation.

In addition to starting a presentation with sample text from the AutoContent Wizard as you did in Lesson 1, you can also start a new presentation without having PowerPoint insert any sample text. You can choose a design template or a blank presentation.

A **design template** is a presentation with a professionally designed format and color scheme to which you need only add text. Typically, design templates include background graphics that range from formal to playful. Each design template specifies where text placeholders appear on the slide and how the text in the placeholder is formatted. For example, some design templates specify round bullets for bullet text, whereas others use graphic pictures for bullets.

You can use one of the design templates that come with PowerPoint, or you can create your own. Design templates are displayed in the Slide Design task pane and can be applied to a presentation with a single click of the mouse. After you apply a design template, all slides you add to a presentation use the same template automatically.

◆ **If you quit PowerPoint at the end of the last lesson, restart PowerPoint now.**

Create a new presentation with a design template

In this exercise, you explore another option for creating a new presentation. You choose a design template and then save the presentation.

1 **On the View menu, click Task Pane, if necessary, to display the task pane.**

ANOTHER METHOD

Press Ctrl + F1.

2 **If necessary, click the Other Task Panes arrow, and then click New Presentation.**

3 **In the New Presentation task pane, click From Design Template.**

The Slide Design task pane appears with a variety of design templates shown as thumbnails.

4 **In the Slide Design task pane, point to any design template.**

The name of the design template appears as a ScreenTip, and a down arrow appears on the right side of the design.

5 **In the Slide Design task pane, click the down arrow on the right side of any design template.**

A menu appears with commands that let you apply the design template to the entire presentation or to selected slides, use the template as the default for all new presentations, or change the size of the preview design templates in the Slide Design task pane.

6 **In the Slide Design task pane, drag the scroll box down until the Maple slide design appears in the task pane, and then click the Maple slide design.**

The Maple slide design is applied to the blank slide in the Slide pane.

FIGURE 2-1

New slide design in place

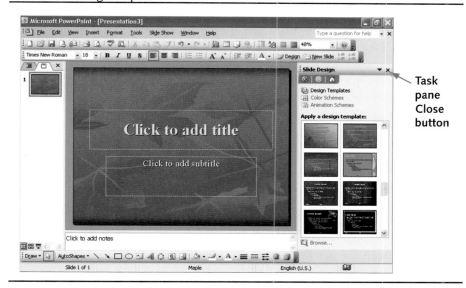

Task pane Close button

7 **In the Slide Design task pane, click the Close button to close the task pane.**

Closing the task pane gives you more room for the slide in the Slide pane.

ANOTHER METHOD

- Click Ctrl + F1.
- On the View menu, click Task Pane.

8 **On the File menu, click Save As.**

The Save As dialog box opens. Verify that the PowerPoint Practice folder appears in the Save In box.

9 **In the File Name box, type** Contoso Recruiting Pres 02, **and then click Save.**

PowerPoint saves the presentation, and the title bar changes to the new name.

◆ **Keep this file open for the next exercise.**

QUICK REFERENCE ▼

Create a new presentation with a design template

1 In the New Presentation task pane, click From Design Template.

2 Click a design template in the Slide Design task pane.

> **QUICK CHECK**
>
> **Q:** Why would you want to apply a design template to one or more selected slides?
>
> **A:** Applying a design template to selected slides emphasizes the slides in the presentation.

Creating Slides and Revising Their Layouts

Entering Text in the Slide Pane

THE BOTTOM LINE

Adding text in the Slide pane lets you see the text in its formatted form, so you know how it will look in the final presentation.

To add text to a presentation, including titles and subtitles, you can enter text into either the Slide pane or the Outline tab in Normal view. The Slide pane allows you to enter text on a slide using a visual method, whereas the Outline tab allows you to enter text using a content method.

The Slide pane displaying the Title Slide layout includes two text boxes called **text placeholders**. The upper box is a placeholder for the slide's title text. The lower box is a placeholder for the slide's subtitle text. Each placeholder on a PowerPoint slide includes text that tells you how to use it. For example, the title placeholder contains the text *Click To Add Title*. When you click this text, it disappears and an insertion point appears, ready for you to type your own title text. After you enter text into a placeholder, the placeholder becomes a **text object**, a box that contains text in a slide.

Most presentations begin with a title slide, which contains two placeholders: one for a title and one for a subtitle. You do not have to use all placeholders on a slide. If you choose not to use a placeholder, it won't display when you run the presentation.

Title a slide and add a subtitle

Now that you have applied a design template and saved the presentation, you're ready to begin entering text into the presentation.

1 **Click the Outline tab, if necessary, in the Outline/Slides pane.**

Though you will work in the Slide pane in this exercise, displaying the Outline tab lets you view the text not only on the slide but also as an outline.

You can resize the Outline tab by dragging its border to allow more room for the slide in the Slide pane.

2 **In the Slide pane, click the text placeholder Click To Add Title.**

A selection box surrounds the placeholder, indicating that the placeholder is ready for you to enter or edit text. The placeholder text disappears, and a blinking insertion point appears.

3 **Type Recruiting New Clients.**

Notice that the text appears in the Outline tab at the same time.

If you make a typing error, press Backspace to delete the mistake, and then type the correct text.

4 **Click the text placeholder Click To Add Subtitle.**

The title object is deselected, and the subtitle object is selected.

5 **Type Your Name, and then press Enter.**

Insert your own name in the placeholder rather than the words *Your Name* to customize the presentation.

6 **Type Contoso, Ltd.**

Your presentation window should look like the following illustration.

FIGURE 2-2

Completed title slide

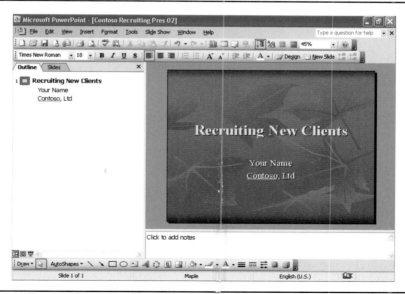

◆ **Keep this file open for the next exercise.**

QUICK CHECK

Q: What do you call a placeholder after text has been entered into it?

A: **A placeholder that contains text is called a text object.**

QUICK REFERENCE ▼

Enter text in the Slide pane

1 In the Slide pane, click the text placeholder Click To Add Title or click the text placeholder Click To Add Subtitle.

2 Type your text.

Creating a New Slide

Creating Slides and
Revising Their Layouts

THE BOTTOM LINE

New presentations have a single title slide, and in most cases you will have to add one or many more slides to cover your subject. PowerPoint offers 27 different slide layouts you can choose from to lay out specific types of slide content such as media objects, tables, graphs, and charts.

You can quickly and easily add more slides to a presentation in two ways: by clicking the New Slide button on the Formatting toolbar directly above the task pane or by clicking the New Slide command on the Insert menu. When you use either of these methods, PowerPoint inserts the new slide into the presentation immediately following the current slide, and the Slide Layout task pane appears with 27 predesigned slide layouts, any of which you can apply to your new slide. You select a layout by clicking it in the Slide Layout task pane. The layout title for the selected slide layout appears as you roll the mouse over each choice.

Slide layouts allow you to create slides with specific looks and functions. For example, you can choose a layout that displays only a title on a slide or a layout that provides placeholders for a title and a graph. The wide variety of different slide layouts means that you will most likely find one with exactly the layout you need, so you won't have to take the time to create it from scratch yourself.

Create a new slide

In this exercise, you add a slide to your presentation and then enter text on the new slide.

New Slide

1 **On the Formatting toolbar, click the New Slide button.**

The Slide Layout task pane appears. A new, empty slide is added after the current slide in the Slide pane and is created a new slide icon in the Outline tab. The default Title and Text slide layout (a title and bulleted list) is applied to the new slide. The status bar displays Slide 2 of 2.

ANOTHER METHOD

- Press Ctrl + M.
- On the Insert menu, click New Slide.

2 Type Develop a Plan.

TIP

If you start typing on an empty slide without first having selected a placeholder, PowerPoint enters the text into the title object.

3 In the Slide Layout task pane, click the Close button to close the task pane.

◆ Keep this file open for the next exercise.

QUICK REFERENCE ▼

Create a new slide

1 On the Formatting toolbar, click the New Slide button.
2 In the Slide Layout task pane, select a slide layout.

Entering Text in the Outline Tab

THE BOTTOM LINE

Working in the Outline tab lets you concentrate on the text of a presentation. The Outlining toolbar can help you work efficiently with an outline.

Creating Slides and
Revising Their Layouts

The Outline tab shows the presentation text in outline form just as if you had typed the text using Outline view in Microsoft Word. The Outline tab allows you to enter and organize slide title and paragraph text for each slide in a presentation. In the Outline tab, the slide title text appears to the right of each slide icon, and the paragraph text appears underneath each title, indented one level.

To enter text in the Outline tab, you click where you want the text to start, and then you begin typing. While working in the Outline tab, you can also create a new slide and add title and paragraph text by using the New Slide command or the Enter key.

PowerPoint offers an Outlining toolbar that supplies a number of tools useful for working efficiently with outlines. For example, the Promote and Demote buttons let you change the outline level of paragraph text. You can display the Outlining toolbar (or any toolbar) by clicking the View menu, clicking Toolbars, and selecting the toolbar name.

Enter text and create a new slide in the Outline tab

In this exercise, you enter text and create a new slide in the Outline tab.

1 **Position the pointer—which changes to the I-beam pointer—to the right of the title in slide 2 in the Outline tab, and then click the blank area.**

A blinking insertion point appears to the right of the slide title.

2 **Press Enter.**

PowerPoint adds a new slide in the Slide pane and a new slide icon in the Outline tab, with the blinking insertion point next to it. To add paragraph text to slide 2 instead of starting a new slide, you need to change the outline level from slide title to a bullet.

3 **Press Tab.**

Pressing Tab indents the text to the right one level and moves the text from slide 3 back to slide 2. The slide icon changes to a small gray bullet on slide 2 in the Outline tab.

4 **Type Develop a list of contacts, and then press Enter.**

PowerPoint adds a new bullet at the same indent level. Notice that once you press Enter after typing bulleted text, the preceding bullet becomes black. Also note that the text wraps to the next line in the Outline tab without your having to press Enter.

5 **Type Schedule periodic phone calls to prospective clients, and then press Enter.**

6 **Type Re-evaluate your strategy regularly, and then press Enter.**

Now you will display the Outlining toolbar and use one of its tools to work with the current outline.

7 **On the View menu, click Toolbars, and then click Outlining.**

The Outlining toolbar appears vertically to the left of the outline in the Outline tab.

ANOTHER METHOD

Right-click any displayed toolbar, and then click Outlining.

8 **On the Outlining toolbar, click the Promote button.**

PowerPoint creates a new slide with the insertion point to the right of the slide icon.

9 **Type Make the Client Number One, press Enter, and then press Tab.**

PowerPoint creates a new indent level for slide 3.

10 **Type Be creative, and then press Enter.**

A new bullet appears.

11 **Type Stay positive, press Enter, and then type Be tenacious.**

12 **Hold down Ctrl, and then press Enter.**

A new slide appears.

13 Type Summary, press Enter, and then press Tab.

PowerPoint creates a new indent level for slide 4.

14 Type Create a plan suitable to your temperament, and then press Enter.

15 Type Try to avoid cold calls, and then press Enter.

16 Type Keep current with the client's industry trends.

Your presentation window should look like the following illustration.

FIGURE 2-3

Summary slide with new text

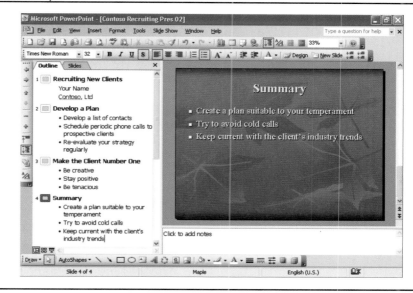

◆ **Keep this file open for the next exercise.**

QUICK REFERENCE ▼

Enter paragraph text in the Outline pane

1 Click in the blank area to the right of the slide title in the Outline tab.

2 Press Enter, and then press Tab.

3 Type your text.

Editing Text in Normal View

THE BOTTOM LINE

Most presentations require a certain amount of editing before they are finished. You can edit text in Normal view in either the Outline tab or the Slide pane. Editing can mean inserting text, changing text, or rearranging text on a slide.

Editing Text

QUICK CHECK

Q: What keystrokes can you use in the Outline tab to quickly create a new slide?

A: **Use Ctrl + Enter to quickly create a new slide in the Outline tab.**

After you have created a presentation, you frequently need to revise it. You may need to insert more text, for example, to "beef up" the content of a slide. Or, you may need to change existing content as you receive more recent information on the presentation's subject.

You can easily modify the text in a presentation using either the Outline tab or the Slide pane. Editing text in either location requires some basic skills that you should already be familiar with if you have worked with programs such as Microsoft Word. To insert text, for instance, you must click in the proper location to position the insertion point. To change text, you must first select it. You can select text by dragging the I-beam pointer over it or by double-clicking a word. In either the Outline tab or the Slide pane, you can select an entire bulleted item by simply clicking the bullet.

Besides modifying the text, you may want to rearrange it. For example, you may want to move the second bullet of paragraph text to be the first item, or even move one bullet item to another slide. You can easily rearrange text in this fashion by dragging it in the Outline tab.

Edit text in Normal view

In this exercise, you insert new text, select and replace text, and then select and rearrange text in the Outline tab.

1 **In the Outline tab, click the blank area to the right of the word "regularly" in slide 2.**

The blinking insertion point appears where you want to begin typing.

FIGURE 2-4

Place the insertion point

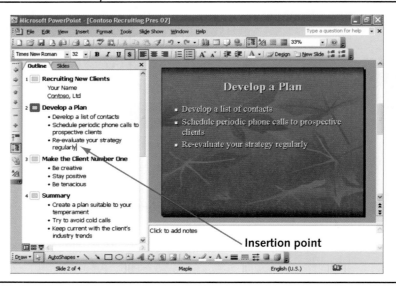

IMPORTANT

If you want to move the insertion point, reposition the I-beam pointer to the desired location, and then click the desired location.

2 **Press the Spacebar, and then type** and make adjustments as needed.

PowerPoint makes room in the outline for the new text.

3 **In the Outline tab, double-click the word "tenacious" in the third bullet point of slide 3.**

The text is now highlighted, indicating that it is selected.

ANOTHER METHOD

To select paragraph text or an individual slide in the Outline tab, click the associated bullet or slide icon to its left.

4 **Type** persistent.

The new word replaces the text in both the Outline tab and Slide pane.

5 **Move the pointer over the bullet next to "Be persistent" in slide 3.**

The pointer changes to the four-headed arrow.

6 **Click the bullet to select the entire line.**

7 **Drag the selected item up until a horizontal line appears above the bullet entitled "Stay positive," but do not release the mouse button yet.**

The horizontal line indicates where the selected text will go. The pointer changes to the two-headed arrow.

FIGURE 2-5

Moving selected text

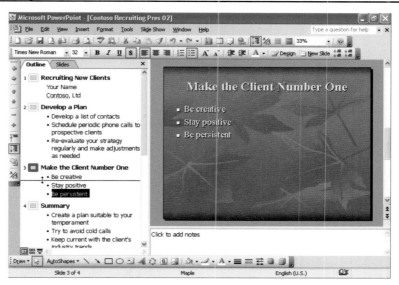

8 **Release the mouse button.**

The entire line moves up one line. You have now repositioned the text on this slide.

◆ **Keep this file open for the next exercise.**

QUICK CHECK

Q: What shape does the pointer take when you're dragging an entire bullet item in the Outline tab?

A: **The pointer takes the shape of a two-headed arrow.**

QUICK REFERENCE ▼

Select and replace text

1 Position the I-beam pointer over any part of the text that you want to replace.

2 Double-click or drag the text to select it.

3 Type the replacement text.

Select and rearrange bulleted text

1 Click the bullet to the left of the text.

2 Drag the selected item with the two-headed arrow until a horizontal line appears above the area where you want to place it.

3 Release the mouse button.

Entering Speaker Notes

THE BOTTOM LINE

Speaker notes supply additional information about a slide that a speaker can use when delivering the presentation. Using speaker notes helps you keep slide content relatively simple and uncluttered while also reminding you of important points to cover.

If you are going to deliver a presentation to a live audience, you may want to enter speaker notes on some or all of the slides in the presentation. Speaker notes relate to the content of the slide. For example, you may want to have available statistics associated with bullet items on a slide, or you may want to be able to give your audience more information about a person or place mentioned on a slide. Using speaker notes for this supplementary information can help you keep slide content simple for easy comprehension by your audience.

Speaker notes don't display along with the slides when you deliver the presentation. To have access to your speaker notes, you can print them, as you learn in the next lesson, or you can view them on one screen while you show the presentation on another, as you learn in Lesson 11.

You have two options for entering speaker notes: You can use the Notes pane or you can use Notes Page view. Which option you choose depends to some degree on how extensive the notes are as well as on your own working style.

Entering Notes in the Notes Pane

The Notes pane appears below the Slide pane in Normal view. If you have one or two sentences of notes to add, this is an appropriate place to insert the notes, because you don't have to change views.

To enter speaker notes in the Notes pane, click the Notes pane placeholder text, and then begin typing to insert text. You can modify the notes text the same way you would on a slide or in the Outline tab. If your notes run to more lines than the pane can display at one time, you can use the Notes pane's scroll bar to see them. You may also want to drag the top border of the Notes pane upward to increase the size of the pane.

Enter text in the Notes pane

You add a speaker note in the Notes pane in this exercise.

1 **Click the Notes pane in slide 3.**

The notes placeholder text disappears, and a blinking insertion point appears, as shown in the following illustration.

FIGURE 2-6

Insertion point in Notes pane

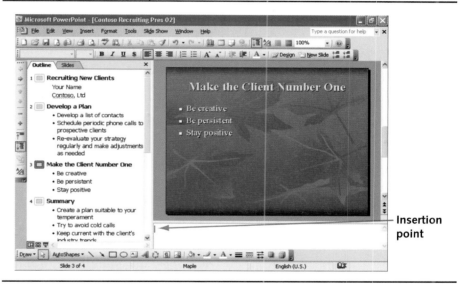

2 **Type the sentence below, but do not press Enter.**

Being persistent without being annoying is a skill you will need to perfect.

The Notes pane shows your new entry.

TIP

If you make a mistake, press Backspace to delete the mistake, and then type the correct text.

◆ **Keep this file open for the next exercise.**

QUICK CHECK

Q: What is the purpose of speaker notes?

A: These are notes on additional information relating to the slide's content that a speaker may want to share with an audience.

QUICK REFERENCE ▼

Enter text in the Notes pane

1 In Normal view, click the Notes pane.

2 Type your text.

Entering Notes in Notes Page View

PowerPoint's Notes Page view displays each slide in a presentation along with the notes that have been inserted for that slide. After you have inserted notes in the Normal view Notes pane, for example, you can see those notes under the slides in Notes Page view. To check all the speaker notes in a presentation, you can move from slide to slide using the Next Slide and Previous Slide buttons just as in Normal view.

Notes Page view is not just for displaying slides and their associated notes. You can also enter notes directly in Notes Page view. Because this view provides a much larger area for inserting notes, this is the option to choose if you want to enter a number of notes or a long note. You can also insert graphics such as a chart or picture into the notes area in this view.

By default, Notes Page view displays at a size that will fit the entire page in the window, such as 33% or 39%. At this size, you will have trouble inserting and reading speaker notes. You can use the Zoom box on the Standard toolbar to change the zoom percentage so you can read text more easily.

Enter notes in Notes Page view

In this exercise, you change the zoom percentage and add a note in Notes Page view to see how this compares to using the Notes pane.

1 **On the View menu, click Notes Page.**

Notes Page view appears at approximately 33% view on most screens to display the entire page. Your presentation window should look like the following illustration.

FIGURE 2-7

Notes Page view displays entire page

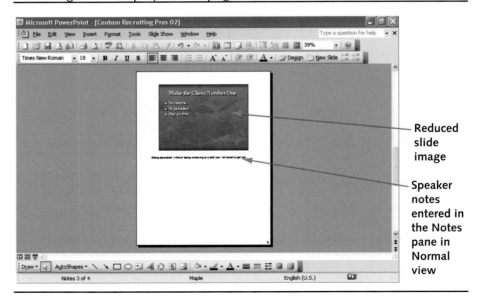

Reduced slide image

Speaker notes entered in the Notes pane in Normal view

Your view scale might be different, depending on the size of your monitor.

42%

2 **On the Standard toolbar, click the Zoom button down arrow, and then click 75%.**

The view scale increases to 75%.

3 **Click the Next Slide button.**

The status bar displays *Notes 4 of 4.*

4 **Select the Notes placeholder.**

The selection box surrounds the area that contains the notes text and the placeholder text disappears.

5 **Type** Experienced sales reps will lead a question-and-answer session immediately following this presentation.

6 **On the Standard toolbar, click the Zoom down arrow, and then click Fit.**

Choosing this option displays the page at the largest size that will fit in the window.

7 **Click the Normal View button.**

ANOTHER METHOD

- Double-click the reduced slide image in Notes Page view.
- On the View menu, click Normal.

◆ **Keep this file open for the next exercise.**

Q: How would you change the display size of a notes page to the actual page size?

A: **Click the Zoom button down arrow, and then click 100%.**

QUICK REFERENCE ▼

Enter speaker notes in Notes Page view

1 On the View menu, click Notes Page.

2 Select the Notes placeholder.

3 Type your text.

Inserting Slides from Other Presentations

THE BOTTOM LINE

To save time when creating a presentation, you can insert slides that have already been created in other presentations. This is also a good way to maintain consistency when creating a number of presentations on one subject or for one client.

Creating presentations can be a time-consuming process. You can save time while creating a presentation by using slides that you or someone else has already made. For example, you can pick up your company's title slide or a slide that contains contact information to avoid having to recreate these slides every time you do a company presentation.

PowerPoint's Slides From Files command allows you to pick up one or more—or all—slides from another presentation to insert into the current presentation. You don't have to worry if the other presentation has the same design template as your current presentation. When you insert slides from one presentation into another, the slides conform to the color and design of the current presentation, so you don't have to make many changes.

TIP

If you want to keep the original formatting for inserted slides, click the Keep Source Formatting check box in the Slide Finder dialog box.

Insert slides from one presentation into another

You're now ready to add slides from another presentation your sales manager has given you to beef up your presentation.

1 **On the Insert menu, click Slides From Files.**

The Slide Finder dialog box appears.

2 **Click the Find Presentation tab if necessary, and then click Browse.**

The Browse dialog box appears.

3 **In the Look In box, verify that your hard disk is selected.**

4 **In the list of file and folder names, double-click the PowerPoint Practice folder, and then double-click the Lesson02 folder.**

5 **Click the file titled 02 PPT Lesson, and then click Open.**

The Slide Finder dialog box reappears.

6 **Click Display, if necessary.**

All of the slides in the selected presentation are displayed as thumbnails.

TIP

If you use one or more slides in several presentations, you can click Add To Favorites to save the selected slides in the List Of Favorites tab in the Slide Finder dialog box.

7 **Click slide 2, click slide 3, click the right scroll arrow, and then click slide 4 to select the slides you want to insert.**

The Slide Finder dialog box should look like the following illustration.

FIGURE 2-8

Slide Finder dialog box

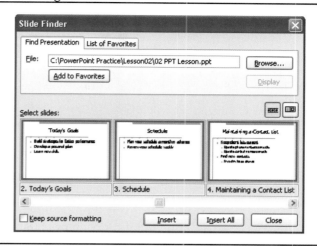

8 **Click Insert.**

PowerPoint inserts the slides into the new presentation after the current slide. The Slide Finder dialog box remains open so you can insert other slides from the same or a different presentation if desired.

9 **Click Close.**

The Slide Finder dialog box closes, and the last inserted slide appears in the Slide pane. The inserted slides adopt the design template of the current presentation.

◆ **Keep this file open for the next exercise.**

QUICK REFERENCE ▼

Insert slides from other presentations

1 On the Insert menu, click Slides From Files.

2 Click the Find Presentation tab, and then click Browse.

3 In the Look In box, navigate to the location of the presentation that you want to insert.

4 In the list of file names, click the presentation you want to open, and then click Open.

5 Click Display, if necessary.

6 Click the slides that you want to insert.

7 Click Insert.

8 Click Close.

Rearranging Slides in Slide Sorter View

THE BOTTOM LINE

Use Slide Sorter view to quickly reorganize a presentation so you can make sure the slides are arranged in the best order. The advantage of using this view is that you can usually see all slides of a presentation at one time, making it easy to move them around.

Creating a presentation often requires reorganizing slides. You want to make sure they appear in the best order to communicate your message effectively. For example, you may want to move a slide that reviews the presentation content from the end of the presentation to the beginning, to give the audience a preview of the presentation's topics.

Although you can rearrange slides in both the Outline and Slides tabs, you will find reorganizing slides to be easiest in Slide Sorter view. This view shows you all slides as thumbnails. To rearrange slides, you simply click a slide and drag it to its new position. As you drag, a vertical gray line appears to show where you can "drop" the slide. You can move a slide to the end or the beginning of the presentation or between existing slides. After you drop the slide, PowerPoint renumbers the slides to reflect their new order.

Rearrange slides in Slide Sorter view

After you added slides from the other presentation in the last exercise, your Summary slide is no longer the last slide in the presentation. You reorganize the presentation in this exercise.

1 **Click the Slide Sorter View button.**

Notice that the Slide Sorter toolbar appears above the presentation window.

ANOTHER METHOD

On the View menu, click Slide Sorter.

2 **Click slide 4 ("Summary"), and then drag it to the empty space after slide 7 ("Maintaining a Contact List").**

Slide 4 displays a heavy blue border to indicate it is selected. Notice that the pointer changes to the drag pointer when you begin to drag (see illustration below). When you release the mouse button, slide 4 moves to its new position, and the other slides in the presentation are repositioned and renumbered.

FIGURE 2-9

Repositioning a slide

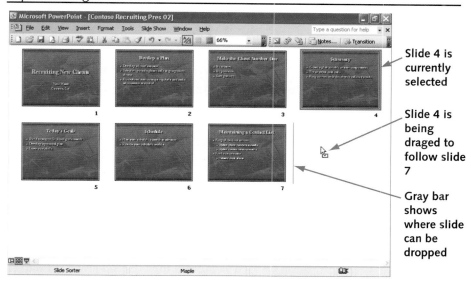

Slide 4 is currently selected

Slide 4 is being draged to follow slide 7

Gray bar shows where slide can be dropped

3 Click the current slide 4 ("Today's Goals").

4 Drag slide 4 between slides 1 and 2.

Drop the slide when you see the vertical gray bar appear between slides 1 and 2.

ANOTHER METHOD

In Slide Sorter view, you can also move slides between two or more open presentations. Open each presentation, switch to Slide Sorter view, and then click Arrange All on the Window menu. Drag the slides from one presentation window to another.

5 Double-click slide 1 to return to the previous view, Normal view.

ANOTHER METHOD

- Click the Normal View button.
- On the View menu, click Normal.

◆ Keep this file open for the next exercise.

QUICK CHECK

Q: What visual aid helps you to choose a place to drag a slide?

A: A vertical gray bar shows you where a slide will display when moved.

QUICK REFERENCE ▼

Rearrange slides in Slide Sorter view

1 Click the Slide Sorter View button.

2 Click a slide to select it.

3 Drag the slide to a new position.

4 Release the mouse button to "drop" the slide in its new position.

Showing Slides in Slide Show View

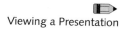

Viewing a Presentation

THE BOTTOM LINE

Slide Show view lets you see the slides in a presentation in order from first to last at full-screen size. Previewing a presentation in this view lets you review content and flow and identify errors or problems on the slides.

PowerPoint's Slide Show view gives you a full-screen view of the slides in a presentation. This allows you to see the presentation more nearly as it will appear when presented to an audience (or on-screen, if you are presenting the slides over the Internet or on an intranet). Slide Show view displays the slides in order by slide number.

It is a good idea to preview a presentation often as you create it. You can quickly and easily review the slides for accuracy and flow in Slide Show view. When you see slides at full-screen size, you can often catch errors that you missed in Normal view. You can also determine if slides are too crowded or need additional content, if the design template isn't exactly what you want, if you can easily read text, and so on.

To move from slide to slide in Slide Show view, click on the screen with the mouse button or use the Page Down or Enter key. If you want to end a slide show before you reach the last slide, click the Esc button.

Display slides in Slide Show view

1 In the Outline tab, click the slide 1 icon, if necessary.

The slide show begins with the currently selected slide, so displaying slide 1 ensures that you see the presentation from the beginning.

2 Click the Slide Show button.

PowerPoint displays the first slide in the presentation.

ANOTHER METHOD

- Press F5.
- On the View menu, click Slide Show.

3 Click the screen to advance to the next slide.

You can also press the Page Down or the Enter key to move to the next slide.

4 Click one slide at a time to advance through the presentation. After the last slide, click to exit Slide Show view.

PowerPoint returns to the current view.

◆ If you are continuing to other lessons, save the Contoso Recruiting Pres 02 presentation with the current name and then close it. If you are not continuing to other lessons, save and close the Contoso Recruiting Pres 02 presentation, and then click the Close button in the title bar of the PowerPoint window.

QUICK REFERENCE ▼

Show slides in Slide Show view

1 Verify that slide 1 appears in the Slide pane.

2 Click the Slide Show button.

3 Click the screen (or press Page Down or Enter) to advance to the next slide.

4 Click one slide at a time to advance through the presentation.

Key Points

✔ *You can create a new presentation using a design template that supplies professionally designed background color and graphics, text formatting, and layout.*

✔ *Use either the Outline tab or the Slide pane to enter and edit slide text. Working in the Outline tab allows you to concentrate on the presentation's text, whereas working in the Slide pane lets you see how text will look when presented.*

✔ *Most presentations need more than the single slide of a blank or design template presentation. You can select the layout of a new slide from the Slide Layout task pane.*

✔ *Speaker notes allow you to keep track of additional information you might want to share with your audience. Enter speaker notes in the Notes pane in Normal view or in Notes Page view.*

✔ *If another presentation contains slides you can use in your current presentation, you can use the Slides From Files command on the Insert menu to locate that presentation and select slides from it to insert. Inserted slides take on the design template of the current presentation by default.*

✔ *Use Slide Sorter view to rearrange slides so they appear in the best order to communicate your message. Because you can usually see all slides in the presentation at once, you can easily drag slides to new positions to reorganize them.*

✔ *To see how a presentation will look when delivered onscreen, use Slide Show view. Slide Show view displays slides using the entire screen on your computer, allowing you to easily check the presentation's flow and accuracy.*

Quick Quiz

True/False

T F **1.** You can create your own design template if you want.

T F **2.** One way to insert a new slide is to click New Slide on the Edit menu.

T F **3.** If you need to enter only a sentence or two of notes, the Notes pane in Normal view is your best bet.

T F **4.** To rearrange slides in Slide Sorter view, you can simply drag them from one location to another.

T F **5.** If a slide has speaker notes, they display at the bottom of a slide in Slide Show view.

Multiple Choice

1. If you are most concerned about how text is going to look on a slide, you should enter text in the _____.
   a. Outline tab
   b. Slides tab
   c. Slide pane
   d. Notes pane

2. If you want to select an entire bullet item at once, click _____.
   a. the bullet symbol
   b. the first word of the bullet item
   c. the last word of the bullet item
   d. anywhere in the bullet item

3. To insert a graphic speaker note, you should use _____.
   a. Normal view's Notes pane
   b. the Outline tab
   c. the Slide pane
   d. Notes Page view

4. If you don't see slides in the Slide Finder dialog box, click the _____.
   a. Show Slides button
   b. Display button
   c. Insert button
   d. Browse button

5. The easiest way to move from slide to slide in Slide Show view is to _____.
   a. use the Advance command on a shortcut menu
   b. press Esc
   c. click the screen
   d. press Ctrl + Enter

Short Answer

1. How do you start a new presentation using a design template with PowerPoint already running?

2. How do you add title text to a slide?

3. What are the ways you can create a new slide?

4. How do you change a paragraph text indent level in the Outline tab?

5. How do you move an entire line of text?

6. How do you enter text in the Notes pane?

7. How do you view the slides you want to insert from another presentation?

8. How do you move a slide in Slide Sorter view?

9. How do you advance to the next slide in Slide Show view?

On Your Own

Exercise 1

Your sales team has nominated you to choose the new design template for the monthly sales reports. You decide to use the following text to create a new presentation using a design template with a title slide, a new slide with a title and bullets, and speaker notes.

Southwest Sales Review Agenda	{title}
Today's Date	{subtitle}
Agenda	{title}
Introduction	{bullet}
Discussion	{bullet}
Summary	{bullet}
Elaborate only where projections significantly varied from actuals	{notes}

Save the presentation as SW Sales in the Lesson02 folder in the PowerPoint Practice folder.

Exercise 2

Your supervisor has asked you to help with a motivational presentation. You begin by creating a new presentation using a design template with the following slides:

Personal Strategic Planning	{title}
Sales Force	{subtitle}
Topics	{title}
Planning for Change	{bullet}
Identifying Barriers to Success	{bullet}
Getting the Right Skills and Knowledge	{bullet}

Switch the order of the second and third bullets on the slide. Insert slide 2 ("Today's Goals") at the end of the presentation from the file 02 PPT Lesson in the Lesson02 folder in the PowerPoint Practice folder. Move the slide so that it becomes the second slide.

Save the presentation as Motivate in the Lesson02 folder in the PowerPoint Practice folder.

One Step Further

Exercise 1

The personnel department at A. Datum Corporation wants to create several presentations to remind employees of company policies. Begin by creating a new presentation using a design template with the following slides:

A. Datum Corporation	{title}
Holidays and Personal Time	{subtitle}
Holidays	{title of Title Only slide}
Standard Holidays	{title of Title and Text slide}
New Year's Day	{bullet}
Memorial Day	{bullet}
Independence Day	{bullet}
Labor Day	{bullet}
Thanksgiving Day	{bullet}
Christmas Day	{bullet}

In the Outline tab, create a new slide with the title Expanded Holidays. Then type the following bullet items in the Outline tab:

Available to senior staff only
Six standard holidays
Day after Thanksgiving
Christmas Eve
New Year's Eve

Move the first bullet so that it becomes the last bullet on the slide. Save the presentation as Holidays 02 in the Lesson02 folder in the PowerPoint Practice folder.

Exercise 2

Create another new presentation for A. Datum Corporation's personnel department. Use the same design template as for the previous exercise and save the presentation as Vacation 02 in the Personnel folder. Create slide content as follows:

A. Datum Corporation	{title}
Vacation Policies	{subtitle}
Administration Staff	{title}
Less than 1 year, 0 days	{bullet}
From 1 to 5 years, 7 days	{bullet}
From 6 to 10 years, 14 days	{bullet}

Add the following note to the slide: Special arrangements may be made for employees with less than a full year's employment. Save and close the presentation.

Exercise 3

Create a new presentation using a design template for your company's cafeteria. The cafeteria staff want to inform the company's employees about new "lite" entrees and a coffee bar that offers coffee drinks such as those sold at chain coffee establishments. Develop the slide content and modify slide order as desired. Then view the slides in Slide Show view.

LESSON

Printing a Presentation

After completing this lesson, you will be able to:

✔ *Open an existing presentation.*
✔ *Add a header and a footer.*
✔ *Preview a presentation.*
✔ *Change the page setup.*
✔ *Choose a printer.*
✔ *Print slides, audience handouts, and speaker notes.*

KEY TERMS

- Grayscale
- Landscape
- Portrait

- Print Preview
- Pure Black and White

Microsoft PowerPoint gives you flexibility in printing the slides of a presentation and any supplements. For example, you can add headers and footers, preview your presentation in grayscale or black and white to see how color slides will look after printing, and print presentation slides, speaker notes, audience handouts, and outlines. You can easily customize the printing process by selecting the paper size, page orientation, print range, and printer type to meet your needs. When you are ready to print, you can preview your presentation on the screen to make sure it appears the way you want.

There are a number of reasons why you might want to print your presentation materials. Preparing a printed copy of the slides lets you review them easily or file the presentation hard copy for future reference. Printing the speaker notes gives you a hard copy of the notes to refer to during your presentation. You may also want to distribute printed handouts or the outline of the slides to your audience so they can refer to the material later or take notes during the presentation.

As the vice president of sales for Contoso, Ltd, you need to develop presentations for a new employee training program. In the previous lesson, you created a presentation for the first training session, "Recruiting New Clients," and now you want to open and print the presentation and accompanying speaker notes pages.

In this lesson, you will learn how to open an existing presentation; add a header and a footer; preview slides; change the page setup; choose a printer; and print slides, audience handouts, and speaker notes.

◆ Before you can use the practice files in this lesson, you must install them from the book's companion CD to their default location. See "Using the CD-ROM" at the beginning of this book for more information. To complete the procedures in this lesson, you will need to use a file named 03 PPT Lesson in the Lesson03 folder in the PowerPoint Practice folder located on your hard disk.

Opening an Existing Presentation

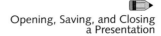
Opening, Saving, and Closing a Presentation

THE BOTTOM LINE

Before you can open an existing presentation, you have to find it. Use the Getting Started task pane or the Open dialog box to help you locate and open an existing presentation.

You can open an existing presentation—for example, one that you or a coworker has already created—and work on it in the same way that you would a new presentation. To open an existing presentation, you must first identify the presentation and its location.

One of the easiest ways to open an existing presentation that you have worked on recently is to look at the list of files in the Open section of the Getting Started task pane. This task pane displays automatically each time you start PowerPoint. To open one of the presentations listed near the bottom of this pane, simply click it. The task pane closes as the presentation opens.

If the presentation you want to work with doesn't appear in the Getting Started task pane, you can use the Open dialog box to locate the presentation. To display the Open dialog box, click the More link in the Open section of the Getting Started task pane or click the Open button on the Standard toolbar.

ANOTHER METHOD

If you can't remember the name of a presentation but you know part of the name or some of its contents, you can search for the presentation using the Basic or Advanced File Search task pane. Click File Search on the File menu or click the Search button on the Standard toolbar to open the Basic File Search task pane. You can specify a partial name and locations to search in the task pane. Use the Advanced File Search task pane if you want to be able to specify properties and conditions for the search.

◆ **If you quit PowerPoint at the end of the last lesson, restart PowerPoint now.**

Open an existing presentation

In this exercise, you open an existing presentation and then save the presentation with a new name.

1 **On the Standard toolbar, click the Open button.**

PowerPoint displays the Open dialog box, which is where you specify the name and location of the presentation you want to open.

FIGURE 3-1

Open dialog box

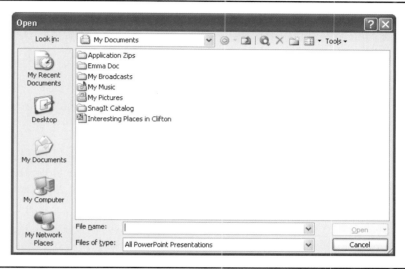

ANOTHER METHOD

- Press Ctrl + O.
- On the File menu, click Open
- On the Getting Started task pane, click More in the Open section of the task pane.

2 **In the Look In box, verify that your hard disk is selected.**

3 **In the list of file and folder names, double-click the PowerPoint Practice folder to open it.**

You can also click My Recent Documents in the Places bar in the dialog box to see a list of documents that you have worked on recently.

4 **In the list of file and folder names, double-click the Lesson03 folder, and then click 03 PPT Lesson, if it is not already selected.**

TIP

The Open button down arrow in the Open dialog box provides additional ways to open a file.

5 **Click Open.**

PowerPoint displays the presentation 03 PPT Lesson in Normal view. Your presentation window should look like the following illustration.

FIGURE 3-2

Presentation opens in Normal view

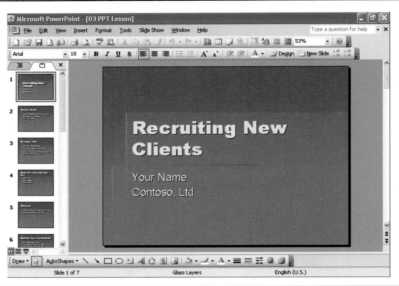

TROUBLESHOOTING

If the Outlining toolbar is open in Normal view, right-click the toolbar and select Outlining to close the toolbar.

6 **On the File menu, click Save As.**

The Save As dialog box opens. Verify that the PowerPoint Practice folder appears in the Save In box.

7 **In the File Name box, type** Contoso Recruiting Pres 03, **and then click Save.**

PowerPoint saves the presentation, and the title bar changes to the new name.

◆ **Keep this file open for the next exercise.**

QUICK REFERENCE ▼

Open an existing presentation

1 On the Standard toolbar, click the Open button.

2 In the Look In box, navigate to the location of the presentation that you want to open.

3 In the list of file names, click the presentation that you want to open.

4 Click Open.

Adding a Header and a Footer

Adjusting Headers and Footers

THE BOTTOM LINE

Headers and footers give additional information on a slide or page such as the date, the slide or page number, company name, author, and so on. This information helps you identify the slides and keep them organized.

Before you print your work, you can add a header or a footer, which will appear on every slide, handout, or notes page. Headers and footers contain useful information about the presentation, such as the author or company name, the date and time, and the page or slide number. This information helps you keep slides organized and can give a customized look to a presentation.

You can quickly and easily add a header and a footer to your slides, audience handouts, outlines, and speaker notes with the Header And Footer command on the View menu. This command opens the Header And Footer dialog box, which contains one tab for slides and one tab for notes and handouts. You can enter footers on each tab, so you can specify a footer on a notes page that differs from the footer on the presentation's slides. You can apply your header and/or footer information on the current slide or on all slides in the presentation. You can also choose to apply the slide footer information to all slides *except* the title slide, so the title slide has a clean look.

TROUBLESHOOTING

You can enter headers on notes pages and handouts only. Slides do not offer a placeholder for header information.

Header and footer information appears on the *slide master*, a slide that controls the display of items such as placeholders, background graphics, and text formatting. As you select items such as the date or slide numbers for a header or footer, these items appear in a specific location on the slide controlled by the slide master. You will learn more about working with masters in Lesson 6.

Add a header and a footer to a presentation

In this exercise, you apply footer information to the presentation's slides, and you also apply both header and footer information to the notes and handouts pages.

1 On the View menu, click Header And Footer.

The Header And Footer dialog box appears with the Slide tab on top.

2 **Select the Footer check box, and then type** Employee Training **to the right of the phrase Contoso, Ltd.**

In the Preview box, a black rectangle highlights the placement of the footer on the slides. Your dialog box should look like the following illustration.

FIGURE 3-3

Header And Footer dialog box

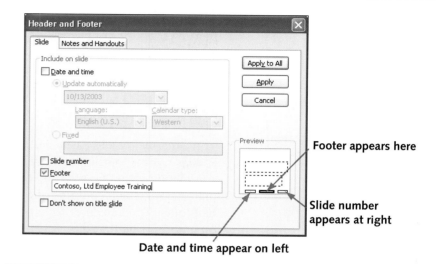

Footer appears here

Slide number appears at right

Date and time appear on left

3 **Click the Notes And Handouts tab.**

The header and footer settings for the notes and handout pages appear. All four check boxes are selected.

4 **Click the Header box, and then type** Recruiting New Clients.

5 **Click the Footer box, and then type** Contoso, Ltd.

6 **Clear the Date And Time check box.**

PowerPoint includes the header, footer, and page number on each note or handout page you print.

7 **Click Apply To All.**

The header and footer information is applied to the slides, notes pages, and handouts pages. Notice that the current slide appears with the slide footer in place.

◆ **Keep this file open for the next exercise.**

QUICK CHECK

Q: Where does a footer appear on a slide by default?

A: A footer appears at the bottom center of the slide by default.

QUICK REFERENCE ▼

Add a header and footer to slides

1 On the View menu, click Header And Footer.

2 Click the Slide or Notes And Handouts tab.

3 Select date and time, slide or page number, or header or footer options.

4 Click Apply To All.

Previewing a Presentation

Previewing and Printing
a Presentation

THE BOTTOM LINE

Print Preview allows you to check slides, handouts, notes pages, or an outline page before printing, which is a good way to identify errors or problems. You can change the color mode to pure black and white or grayscale in either Print Preview or Normal view to see how slides will look when printed to a black and white printer.

Print preview allows you to see how your presentation will look before you print it. While in print preview, you have the option of switching between various views, such as notes, slides, outlines, and handouts, and changing the print orientation. You can also view the current object close up by clicking the pointer on the slide or page. The pointer takes the shape of a magnifying glass in Print Preview. Click once to enlarge the view, and then click again to restore the previous size. Using the Print Preview tools can help you identify problems on slides or handouts before you commit them to paper or another medium.

If you are using a black and white printer to print a color presentation, you need to verify that the printed presentation will be legible. For example, dark red text against a shaded background shows up well in color, but when seen in black and white or shades of gray, the text tends to be indistinguishable from the background. To prevent this problem, you can preview your color slides in pure black and white or grayscale in Print Preview to see how they will look when you print them. **Pure Black and White** displays colors in black and white, whereas **Grayscale** displays colors in shades of gray.

You can also display your slides in black and white or grayscale in Normal view. Click the Color/Grayscale button on the Standard toolbar and select the desired option. Using this view allows you not only to see how your slides look in different color modes but also allows you to work with the text. When you change to black and white or grayscale in Normal view, the slide miniatures in the Slides tab retain the original design template colors.

Preview a presentation

You're ready to check your presentation before printing it. In this exercise, you preview your presentation, view your slides in Grayscale and Pure Black and White, and then change black and white settings.

1 **On the Standard toolbar, click the Print Preview button.**

The screen switches to Print Preview and shows your presentation in the currently selected settings.

FIGURE 3-4

Print Preview window

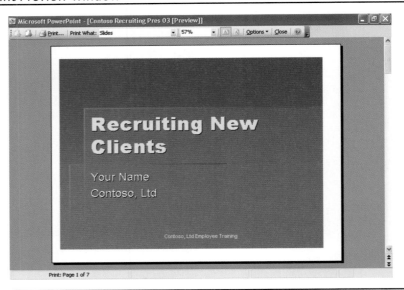

ANOTHER METHOD

On the File menu, click Print Preview.

IMPORTANT

If you are printing to a grayscale printer, your slides are shown in grayscale in Print Preview.

2 **On the Print Preview toolbar, click the Print What down arrow, and then click Handouts (2 Slides Per Page).**

The preview screen displays your presentation in handout format with two slides per page.

3 **On the Print Preview toolbar, click the Options down arrow, point to Color/Grayscale, and then click Grayscale.**

The preview screen displays your presentation in a shaded grayscale.

4 **On the Print Preview toolbar, click the Next Page button.**

The preview screen displays the next handout page.

5 Position the pointer (which changes to a magnifying glass with a plus sign) in the preview area, and then click anywhere in the top slide.

The preview screen magnifies to display a close-up view of the slide.

6 Position the pointer (which changes to a magnifying glass with a minus sign) in the preview area, and then click anywhere in the slide.

The preview screen zooms out to display the original preview of the two handout slides.

7 On the Print Preview toolbar, click the Previous Page button.

The preview screen displays the previous handout page.

8 On the Print Preview toolbar, click the Close Preview button.

The preview screen closes, and your slide appears in the previous view.

9 Click the Normal View button, if necessary, and then click the Slides tab if necessary to display slide miniatures in the Outline/Slides pane.

ANOTHER METHOD

On the View menu, click Normal.

10 On the Standard toolbar, click the Color/Grayscale button, and then click Grayscale.

The slide switches from color to grayscale and the Grayscale View toolbar opens. You can still view the slide miniatures in color on the Slides tab, making it easier to compare the color slides with the grayscale slides.

ANOTHER METHOD

On the View menu, point to Color/Grayscale, and then click Grayscale.

FIGURE 3-5

Slide in grayscale

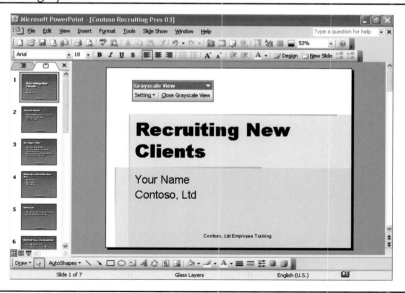

11 On the Standard toolbar, click the Color/Grayscale button and then click **Pure Black And White**.

The slide displays in pure black and white.

ANOTHER METHOD

On the View menu, point to Color/Grayscale, and then click Pure Black And White.

12 On the Grayscale View toolbar, click the Setting button, and then click **Black With Grayscale Fill**.

The slide background changes from white to gray.

13 On the Grayscale View toolbar, click the Setting button, and then click **White**.

The slide background is white again.

14 On the Grayscale View toolbar, click the **Close Black And White View** button.

The slide switches back to color.

◆ **Keep this file open for the next exercise.**

QUICK REFERENCE ▼

Preview a presentation

1 On the Standard toolbar, click the Print Preview button.

2 On the Print Preview toolbar, click the Print What down arrow, and then click an option on the list.

Preview slides in pure black and white or grayscale

1 On the Standard toolbar, click the Color/Grayscale button or if in Print Preview, click the Options down arrow, and point to Color/Grayscale.

2 On the menu, click Pure Black And White or Grayscale.

QUICK CHECK

Q: What shape does the pointer take after you have enlarged the view in Print Preview?

A: The pointer takes the shape of a magnifying glass with a minus sign in the middle.

Changing the Page Setup

THE BOTTOM LINE

Besides the default page size, you can specify 10 other page size options to allow you to print to various paper sizes, set up 35mm slides, or create a Web page banner. Use the Page Setup dialog box to make a page size selection.

Choosing the Correct Print Settings

Before you print a presentation, you can use the Page Setup dialog box to set the proportions and orientation of your slides, notes pages, handouts, and outlines on the printed page. For a new presentation, PowerPoint opens with default slide page setup: on-screen slide show, **Landscape** orientation (10 x 7.5 inches), and slide numbers starting at 1. Notes, handouts, and outlines are printed in **Portrait** orientation (7.5 x 10 inches). You can change these options at any time to customize your presentation for a particular type of output.

PowerPoint has 11 slide sizes from which to choose:

- **On-Screen Show** Use this setting when you are designing an on-screen slide show. The slide size for the screen is smaller than the Letter Paper size.
- **Letter Paper (8.5x11 in)** Use this setting when you are printing a presentation on U.S. letter paper.
- **Ledger Paper (11x17 in)** Use this setting when you are printing a presentation on legal-size paper.
- **A3 Paper (297x420 mm), A4 Paper (210x297 mm), B4 (ISO) Paper (250x353 mm), B5 (ISO) Paper (176x250 mm)** Use one of these settings when you are printing on international paper.
- **35mm Slides** Use this setting when you are designing a presentation for 35mm slides. The slide size is slightly reduced to produce the slides.
- **Overhead** Use this setting when you are printing overhead transparencies for an overhead projector (8.5 x 11 inch).
- **Banner** Use this setting when you are designing a banner (8 x 1 inch) for a Web page.
- **Custom** Use this setting to design slides with a special size.

TIP

You can print with the slides sized for any of the formats, but if you first choose the correct slide format, PowerPoint properly scales the slide for that medium.

Change the page setup

In this exercise, you change the slide size setting from On-Screen Show to Letter Paper.

1 On the File menu, click Page Setup.

The Page Setup dialog box appears.

2 Click the Slides Sized For down arrow, and then click Letter Paper (8.5x11 in).

3 Click OK.

The slide size changes to Letter Paper. You will not see a change in the slide size in Normal view.

◆ Keep this file open for the next exercise.

QUICK CHECK

Q: What page size do you use when printing to legal-sized paper?

A: **Use the Ledger size to print to legal-sized paper.**

QUICK REFERENCE ▼

Change the slide size

1 On the File menu, click Page Setup.

2 Click the Slides Sized For down arrow.

3 Click a format in the list.

4 Click OK.

Choosing a Printer

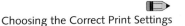
Choosing the Correct Print Settings

THE BOTTOM LINE

PowerPoint uses the Windows default printer unless you choose another printer to print a presentation. You may want to select a printer other than the default to print in color or if your default printer is busy.

PowerPoint prints presentations on your default Microsoft Windows printer unless you select a different printer. Your default printer is set up in the Windows print settings in the Control Panel.

TIP

To change the default printer in Windows XP, click Start on the taskbar, point to Control Panel, double-click Printers and Faxes in the Control Panel, right-click the printer you want to set as the default, and then click Set As Default Printer. For Windows 2000 users, point to Settings, click Control Panel, and then double-click Printers.

You can select another printer in PowerPoint's Print dialog box. After you have added a new printer to your system, it will appear on the list of available printers when you click the Name down arrow. Just click the printer to select it as the presentation's printer. You might select a different printer if it will do a better job of printing your presentation materials (for example, if it is a color printer and your default printer is black and white), if there is a problem with your default printer, or if your default printer is currently busy.

ANOTHER METHOD

If you are using Microsoft Windows 2000 or Windows XP and the Active Directory service, you can search for and use printers across your network, intranet, or the Web. Click the Find Printer button in the Print dialog box, and then click Find Now to locate all printers on the network, intranet, or Web site. You can then select the desired printer and it appears in the Name box in PowerPoint's Print dialog box.

Select a printer for a presentation

You've previewed the presentation and adjusted its page size. You're now ready to choose a printer to print the presentation materials.

1 **Verify that your printer is turned on, connected to your computer, and loaded with paper.**

Verifying these points can eliminate some common reasons why your presentation doesn't print when you tell it to.

2 **On the File menu, click Print.**

The Print dialog box appears.

FIGURE 3-6

Print dialog box

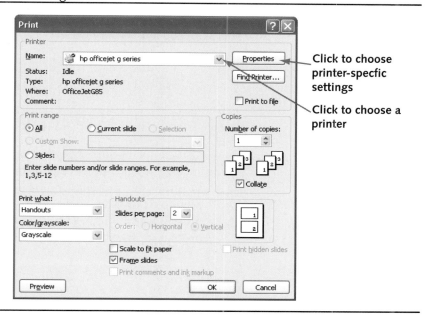

Click to choose printer-specfic settings

Click to choose a printer

3 **In the Printer area, click the Name down arrow.**

A drop-down list appears with the printers installed on your computer.

4 **Click one of the printers in the list.**

After choosing a printer, you can customize your printer settings.

5 **Click Properties.**

The Properties dialog box appears, showing the current printer settings. The Properties dialog settings differ depending on the specific printer you selected.

6 **Click OK in the Properties dialog box.**

The Properties dialog box closes to display the Print dialog box.

◆ **Keep this dialog box open for the next exercise.**

QUICK CHECK

Q: Give one reason why you might want to choose a printer other than your default printer.

A: **You might want to select another printer to print slides in color if your default printer is black and white, or if your default printer is busy or out of service.**

QUICK REFERENCE ▼
Choose a printer

1 On the File menu, click Print.

2 In the Printer area, click the Name down arrow.

3 Click a printer in the list.

4 Click Properties and make any necessary setting adjustments for the selected printer.

5 Click OK in the Properties dialog box.

Printing a Presentation

Previewing and Printing a Presentation

THE BOTTOM LINE

To make a hard copy of presentation materials, print them. You can print slides, notes pages, handouts, or the presentation outline. Choose other options in the Print dialog box to change output color, select slides or number of handouts to print, frame slides, and so on.

You can print your PowerPoint presentation in several ways: as slides, speaker notes, audience handouts, or an outline. PowerPoint makes it easy to print your presentation. It detects the type of printer that you chose—either color or black and white—and prints the appropriate version of the presentation. For example, if you select a black and white printer, your presentation will be set to print in shades of gray (grayscale).

TIP

If you are working with a professional printer to print your slides, you will need to print your slides to a file instead of a printer. To print your slides to a file, select the Print To File check box in the Printer section of the Print dialog box.

Slides and supplements are printed based on the settings in the Print dialog box. In the Print dialog box, you can select a printer or the option to print to a file. You set the print range, which defines which slides to print. You can choose to print multiple copies of a presentation, and if you do print more than one copy of each slide, you can choose to collate the presentation as you print. When you collate the presentation, a complete set of pages is printed before the next set starts printing. The Print dialog box also contains a Preview button that takes you to the Print Preview window, allowing you to preview any changes you might have made.

By clicking the Print What down arrow in the Print dialog box, you can choose to print a presentation as one of four output types:

- **Slides** Prints slides as they appear on the screen, one per page. You can print a slide as an overhead transparency in the same way that you print any other slide, except you put transparency film in the printer instead of paper.
- **Handouts** Prints one, two, three, four, six, or nine slides per page, with the option of ordering them horizontally or vertically.
- **Notes Pages** Prints each slide with the speaker notes under it.
- **Outline View** Prints an outline with formatting according to the current view setting. What you see in the Outline tab is what you get on the printout.

An example of each printing type is shown below.

FIGURE 3-7

PowerPoint printouts

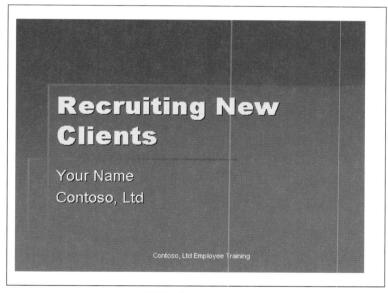

Slide (landscape)

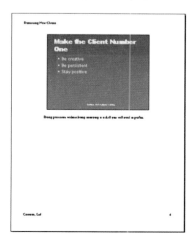

Notes page

Handout page

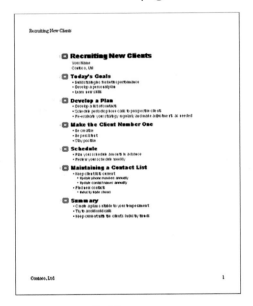

Outline page

By using the Color/Grayscale down arrow in the Print dialog box, you can choose to print a presentation as one of three color options:

- **Color** Use this option to print a presentation in color on a color printer. If you select a black and white printer with this option, the presentation prints in grayscale.
- **Grayscale** Use this option to print a presentation in grayscale on a color or black and white printer.
- **Pure Black And White** Use this option to print a presentation in black and white only with no gray on a color or black and white printer.

Finally, at the bottom of the Print dialog box, you can select from the following print options to enhance a printout:

- **Scale To Fit Paper** Use this option to scale slides to fit the paper size in the printer if the paper in the printer does not correspond to the slide size and orientation settings.
- **Frame Slides** Use this option to add a frame (a border) around the presentation slides when you print. This option is not available for the Outline print type.
- **Include Comments And Ink Markup** Use this option to print any comments and handwritten notes that you have inserted throughout the presentation. This option will be grayed out (unavailable) unless the presentation contains comments. You will learn about comments in a later lesson.
- **Print Hidden Slides** Use this option to print all hidden slides. This option will be grayed out (unavailable) unless the presentation contains hidden slides. You will learn about hidden slides in a later lesson.

 If you are satisfied with the current Print dialog box settings, you can click the Print button on the Standard toolbar to print directly without first viewing the settings. Otherwise, click the Print command on the File menu to adjust printer settings before printing.

Print presentation materials

Now that you have reviewed print output types and options, you're ready to print presentation slides, audience handouts, and speaker notes.

1 **On the File menu, click Print (if the Print dialog is not already displayed).**

The Print dialog box appears.

FIGURE 3-8

Options in the Print dialog box

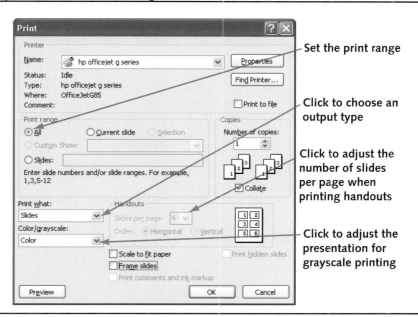

2 In the Print Range area, click the Current Slide option.

3 Click the Print What down arrow, and then click Slides.

4 Click the Color/Grayscale down arrow, click Grayscale, and then click OK.

PowerPoint prints the current slide in the presentation. A small print icon appears on the status bar, showing the printing status.

> **TIP**
>
> Every printer prints text and graphics slightly differently. PowerPoint presentation slides are sized to the printer you choose. Using scalable fonts, such as TrueType fonts, you can print a presentation on different printers with the same great results. When you print a presentation with scalable fonts, the size of the text is reduced or enlarged in the presentation for each printer to get consistent results.

5 On the File menu, click Print.

The Print dialog box appears.

6 Click the Print What down arrow, and then click Handouts.

> **TIP**
>
> You can print audience handouts in six formats: one, two, three, four, six, or nine slides per page.

7 Click the Slides Per Page down arrow, and then click 2.

Notice that PowerPoint selects the Frame Slides check box when you select handouts.

8 Click OK.

PowerPoint prints the presentation slides as handout pages.

9 On the File menu, click Print.

The Print dialog box appears.

10 Click the Print What down arrow, and then click Notes Pages.

11 In the Print Range area, click the Slides option.

The insertion point appears in the range box next to the Slides option.

> **TIP**
>
> You can print notes pages or slides in any order by entering slide numbers and ranges separated by commas.

12 Type 1-4,7.

You are telling PowerPoint you want to print pages 1 through 4 and 7.

13 Click OK.

PowerPoint prints notes pages 1, 2, 3, 4, and 7.

CHECK THIS OUT ▼

Save Slide as Picture
You can save a slide as a picture to use as an illustration in other programs. Because they usually display a colorful design and graphics, slides make good illustrations. Display or select the slide that you want to save, and then click Save As on the File menu. In the Save As Type box, click Windows Metafile, and then click the Save button. PowerPoint asks if you want to export every slide in the presentation or only the current slide. Now you can insert the slide as you would any picture.

◆ If you are continuing to other lessons, save the Contoso Recruiting Pres 03 presentation with the current name and then close it. If you are not continuing to other lessons, save and close the Contoso Recruiting Pres 03 presentation, and then click the Close button in the title bar of the PowerPoint window.

Q: If you want a border to appear around each printed slide or page, what option do you choose in the Print dialog box?

A: **Select the Frame Slides check box in the Print dialog box.**

QUICK REFERENCE ▼

Print a presentation

1 On the File menu, click Print.

2 Click the down arrow to the right of the Print What box, and then click the part of the presentation you want to print.

3 Select any other print options you want to apply.

4 Click OK.

Key Points

✔ *If you need to continue working on a presentation, you can open it from the Getting Started task pane or using the Open dialog box.*

✔ *Headers and footers provide additional information about notes pages, handouts, and slides. Use the Header And Footer dialog box to insert the date and time, a header, slide number, or a footer on slides, notes pages, outlines, and handouts.*

✔ *Preview slides to check their accuracy and impact. In the Print Preview window, you can move from slide to slide, change the view to see notes pages, handouts with various numbers of thumbnails, and the outline.*

✔ *You can change to a grayscale or black and white view in either Print Preview or Normal view to see how slides will look if printed with a black and white printer.*

✔ *Change the page setup if you need to print to a specific paper size or to a medium such as overhead transparency film or 35mm slides.*

✔ *You can choose the printer that will print a presentation in the Print dialog box. This dialog box also allows you to modify the printer's properties, choose what to print, specify what slides or pages to print, and select other options such as a frame for slides.*

Quick Quiz

True/False

T   F   1. The New Presentation task pane has a section that allows you to open existing presentations.

T   F   2. By default, the slide number appears at the bottom right side of all slides.

T   F   3. If you want to see an outline in Print Preview at a larger size, simply click the pointer on the outline.

T   F   4. You can create a custom page size for slides if desired.

T   F   5. When you collate a presentation as you print several copies, PowerPoint prints all page 1s, then all page 2s, and so on.

Multiple Choice

1. You can add a footer to one or more slides that includes _____.
    a. date
    b. slide number
    c. footer text
    d. all of the above

2. If you have a black and white printer, you may want to display slides in _____ to see how colors will look when printed.
    a. Grayscale
    b. Pure Color
    c. Pure Black And White
    d. either a or c

3. The default orientation for slides is _____.
    a. Portrait
    b. Landscape
    c. On-Screen
    d. Banner

4. To change the default printer in Windows XP, open the Control Panel and double-click _____.
    a. Network Printers
    b. All Printers
    c. Printers and Faxes
    d. Default Printers

5. If the paper in the printer doesn't correspond to the slide size and orientation, you can make slides fit the paper size by selecting _____ in the Print dialog box.
    a. Page Setup
    b. Scale To Fit Paper
    c. Print Comments
    d. Print Slides At Current Paper Size

Short Answer

1. Describe two methods for opening an existing presentation.
2. How do you change to Pure Black and White view?
3. What are four options you can specify in a header or a footer?
4. How do you select On-Screen Show as your slide size?
5. What are the print types from which you can print a presentation?
6. How do you print audience handouts with four slides per page?
7. How can you preview a presentation outline before printing?

On Your Own

Exercise 1

Open the presentation Contoso Recruiting Pres 03 in the Lesson03 folder that is located in the PowerPoint Practice folder, and then print two slides per page without a frame.

Exercise 2

Open the presentation Contoso Recruiting Pres 03 in the Lesson03 folder that is located in the PowerPoint Practice folder, and then print audience handouts with six grayscale slides per page in vertical order.

One Step Further

Exercise 1

Open the Holidays 02 presentation you created in Lesson 2. Add a footer to all slides that displays the date (choose the date option that updates automatically), the slide number, and the footer text A. Datum Corporation. For notes and handouts pages, add a header that includes the date (update automatically) and the text Holidays and Personal Time. Add a footer with the text A. Datum Corporation. Save the file as Holidays 03 in the Lesson03 folder and close the presentation.

Exercise 2

Open the Holidays 03 presentation and display the presentation in Print Preview. Change to Outline view. Magnify the view to see the header and footer text on the page. Print the presentation as an outline. Save and close the presentation.

Exercise 3

Open the Vacation 02 presentation you created in Lesson 2. Display the slides in Normal view in Pure Black and White. Change the view to Grayscale. Print Notes Pages in grayscale, with a frame around the pages. Save the file as Vacation 03 in the Lesson03 folder and close the presentation.

Outlining Your Ideas

After completing this lesson, you will be able to:

✔ *Create a blank presentation.*
✔ *View and enter text in an outline.*
✔ *Insert an outline from Microsoft Word.*
✔ *Change the view of an outline.*
✔ *Select text and delete slides in the outline.*
✔ *Rearrange slides, paragraphs, and text.*
✔ *Format text in an outline.*
✔ *Send an outline or slides to Word.*
✔ *Save a presentation as an outline.*

KEY TERMS

- export
- import
- Rich Text Format (RTF)

Outlining your thoughts and ideas makes it easier to organize a presentation. In Microsoft PowerPoint, you can enter and organize your thoughts and ideas in the Outline tab on the Outline/Slides pane to see the slide title text and paragraph text for each slide in the presentation. You can also edit and rearrange both title and paragraph text in the Outline tab, **import** outlines created in other programs into a PowerPoint outline, and **export** the results when you are done.

In previous lessons, you created a presentation for Contoso, Ltd's new employee training program. Now you need to develop a presentation that can be customized for prospective clients. You will present the slide show to the other department heads and to the CEO of Contoso at the next monthly meeting.

In this lesson, you will create a blank presentation, enter text into a PowerPoint outline, insert a Microsoft Word outline into a presentation, change the way you view an outline, select text, delete slides, rearrange and format text, export the outline into Word for later use, and then save a presentation as an outline.

◆ Before you can use the practice files in this lesson, you must install them from the book's companion CD to their default location. See "Using the CD-ROM" at the beginning of this book for more information. To complete the procedures in this lesson, you will need to create a new blank presentation and use a file named 04 Marketing Outline in the Lesson04 folder in the PowerPoint Practice folder located on your hard disk.

Creating a Blank Presentation

THE BOTTOM LINE

Start a new blank presentation when you want to concentrate on slide content. You can apply a design template at any time after you have begun entering slide text.

If you are not sure how you want your presentation to look, you can start a new presentation from scratch. You can create a blank presentation when you first start PowerPoint or after you have already started PowerPoint. Either way, a blank presentation appears, ready for you to use.

Working in a blank presentation allows you to concentrate on getting content on the slides, rather than spending time selecting just the right design. You can always apply and tweak a design at any time after you have begun to insert slide content. Keep in mind, however, that even the blank presentation has a template that controls the placeholder positions and text formatting.

◆ If you quit PowerPoint at the end of the last lesson, restart PowerPoint now.

Create a blank presentation

To start your task of creating a customizable presentation, you create a blank presentation and then save the presentation.

 1 Click the New button on the Standard toolbar.

PowerPoint displays a blank presentation with the default Title Slide layout, and the Slide Layout task pane appears, displaying various slide layouts.

ANOTHER METHOD

- Press Ctrl + N.
- On the File menu, click New.
- On the New Presentation task pane, click Blank Presentation.

FIGURE 4-1

PowerPoint displays a blank presentation with a title slide

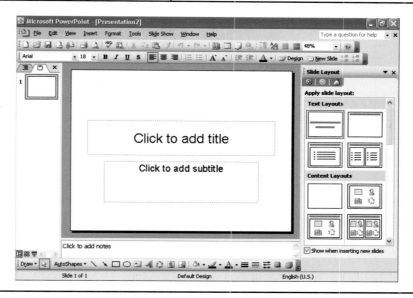

2 On the title bar of the Slide Layout task pane, click the Close button to close the task pane.

Because you want to start with the default title slide already displayed, you don't need to specify another layout. Closing the task pane gives you more room to work.

3 On the File menu, click Save As, and then type Contoso Company Pres 04 in the File Name box.

4 Navigate to the Lesson04 folder in the PowerPoint Practice folder, and then click Save.

◆ Keep this file open for the next exercise.

QUICK REFERENCE ▼

Create a blank presentation

On the Standard toolbar, click the New button or in the New Presentation task pane, click Blank Presentation under New.

Entering Text in an Outline

Creating Slides and Revising
Their Layouts

THE BOTTOM LINE

Enter slide text in the Outline tab when you want to be able to see the content of a number of slides at one time. Working in the Outline tab makes it easy to create a proper outline structure for your slides.

As you have already learned in Lesson 2, working in the Outline tab allows you to concentrate on the text of your presentation. The Outline tab displays the title and bullet points for each slide at a reduced size, making it possible for you to see most or all of the text in your presentation in one pane. This makes it simple for you to avoid repetition and stay on track with your main points. For example, after you create a slide that summarizes the topics that will be covered in the presentation, you can refer easily to that slide as you enlarge on each topic in subsequent slides.

If you are a skillful typist, working in the Outline tab has an additional benefit. You can do quite a lot of the labor of creating a presentation using keyboard keys. For example, you can insert a slide using keys so you don't have to take your hand away from the keyboard to use the mouse to click a command or button.

You need to know a few basic skills to work with an outline in the Outline tab. When you press Enter after inserting a title or paragraph, you automatically create another line at the same outline level. For instance, if you press Enter after typing a slide title, PowerPoint creates a new slide so you can enter the next title. Likewise, if you press Enter after typing a first-level bullet item, a new first-level bullet item is created.

To make sure your slide content is properly structured, you may need to *promote* or *demote* paragraphs. When you promote an item, you move it up to a higher level. For example, promoting a first-level bullet item turns it into a slide title. When you demote an item, you move it down to a lower level. Demoting a first-level bullet item turns it into a second-level bullet item. You can promote and demote using keyboard keys or buttons on the Outlining toolbar.

Enter text in the Outline tab

In this exercise, you use the Outline tab to complete the title slide.

Outline

1 **In the Outline/Slides pane, click the Outline tab, if necessary, and then click to the right side of slide 1 to place the insertion point.**

The slide icon for slide 1 is selected in the outline.

2 **On the View menu, point to Toolbars, and then click Outlining, if necessary, to display the Outlining toolbar.**

ANOTHER METHOD

Right-click any displayed toolbar, and then click Outlining.

FIGURE 4-2

Display the Outlining toolbar

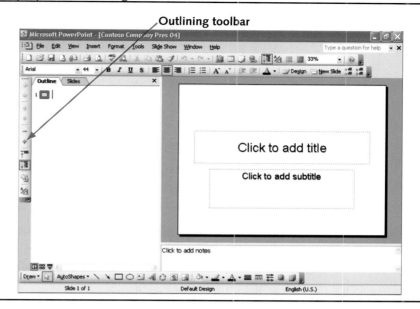

3 **Type** Give Your Image Impact**, and then press Enter.**

A new slide appears in the Outline tab.

 4 **On the Outlining toolbar, click the Demote button, or press Tab.**

The insertion point shifts to the right to start a new paragraph for the title text above it. Because this is a title slide, the new paragraph will be the subtitle.

TIP

Notice that there is no bullet next to the subtitle text on the title slide.

5 **Type** Contoso, Ltd **at the insertion point.**

Your screen should look similar to the following illustration.

FIGURE 4-3

New text displays in Outline tab

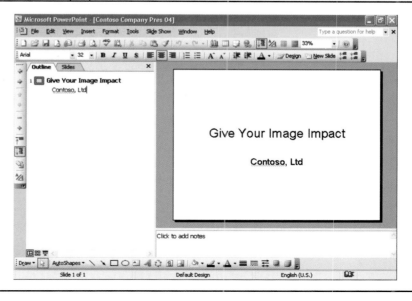

6 **On the Outlining toolbar, click the Promote button.**

The paragraph text shifts to the left to create title text for a new slide.
A slide icon appears next to the text.

7 **On the Outlining toolbar, click the Demote button.**

The title text shifts to the right to again create paragraph text for the
title text above it.

◆ **Keep this file open for the next exercise.**

QUICK REFERENCE ▼

View and enter text in an outline

1 In the Outline/Slides pane, click the Outline tab.

2 Click to place the insertion point, type your text, and then press Enter.

Inserting an Outline from Microsoft Word

THE BOTTOM LINE

To save time, create slides using an outline typed in another program.
You can insert text in Word (.doc) format, Rich Text Format (.rtf), or
plain text format (.txt).

Importing an Outline from Word

If you already have text in other programs, such as Microsoft Word, you
can insert the text into the Outline tab as titles and body text. Inserting an
outline in this way can save considerable time because you don't have to
retype the outline text in PowerPoint.

You can insert text in several formats, including Microsoft Word (.doc)
format, Rich Text Format (.rtf), or plain text format (.txt). When you insert a Word or Rich Text Format document, PowerPoint creates an outline
of slide titles and paragraphs based on the heading styles in the document.
When you insert text from a plain text document, paragraphs without tabs
at the beginning become slide titles, and paragraphs with tabs at the beginning become paragraph text. You can of course adjust the title and text
levels after you have imported the outline into PowerPoint.

TIP

Imported slides are inserted into the presentation following the currently selected slide.

Insert an outline developed in another program into a presentation

You have created the title slide for your new presentation, and you're now ready to add content. You will use an existing Word outline to create new slides.

1 **On the Insert menu, click Slides From Outline.**

The Insert Outline dialog box appears.

2 **In the Look In box, verify that the Lesson04 folder in the PowerPoint Practice folder is listed and that All Outlines appears in the Files Of Type box.**

3 **In the list of file and folder names, click 04 Marketing Outline.**

4 **Click Insert.**

PowerPoint inserts the Word outline into the PowerPoint outline following the current slide.

TROUBLESHOOTING

If you receive a message telling you that PowerPoint needs a converter, install the converter as directed.

5 **Click a blank area of the Outline tab to deselect the text.**

Your screen should look similar to the following illustration.

FIGURE 4-4

New text displays in Outline tab

Slides inserted from a Word outline

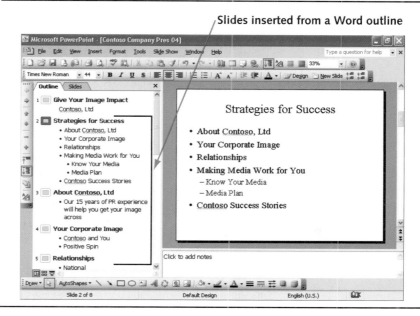

◆ **Leave this file open for the next exercise.**

TIP

You can start a new presentation from a Word outline using the Open command. On the Standard toolbar, click the Open button, click the Files Of Type down arrow, click All Files, and then click the outline file that you want to use.

QUICK REFERENCE ▼

Insert an outline from Microsoft Word

1 In the Outline tab, click a blank area to place the insertion point where you want to insert the outline.

2 On the Insert menu, click Slides From Outline.

3 In the Look In box, navigate to the location of the outline that you want to insert.

4 In the list of file and folder names, click an outline.

5 Click Insert.

QUICK CHECK

Q: You have an outline that a friend created in a simple text editor using tabs to indicate heading levels. Can you use this outline to create slides in PowerPoint?

A: Yes, you can use this outline as long as the file is saved with the .txt extension.

Importing an Outline from Word

Changing the View of an Outline

THE BOTTOM LINE

You can change the view of the outline in the Outline tab in a number of ways to make it easier to work with the outline. Zooming in or out lets you see more detail or more slides. Collapsing the outline lets you reorganize slides using only their titles. Showing formatting lets you see in the outline the same fonts and styles used on the slide.

The outline you are working on might contain more text than you can see on the screen at one time. To make it easier to view an outline, you can reduce the view scale of the presentation window. You can change the scale of your view by using the Zoom button on the Standard toolbar or the Zoom command on the View menu. When you change the view scale, the view of the presentation is increased or decreased in size, but the presentation itself does not change size.

The standard view scales available in the Outline tab are 25%, 33%, 50%, 66%, 75%, and 100%. Other panes use additional view scales: Fit, which means the view of the presentation is sized to fit your monitor; or 150%, 200%, 300%, and 400%, which are helpful for working on detailed items, such as graphics or objects. The Zoom command allows you to decrease the view size to see more of the presentation outline or increase the view size to see small text that is hard to read. You can also enter any view scale in the Zoom box on the Standard toolbar. The Zoom setting affects whatever pane is currently active.

To make it easier to work with the main points of an outline, PowerPoint lets you collapse and expand slide content to view entire slides or only slide titles. When you format text in the Outline tab, sometimes the text can be hard to read, so PowerPoint allows you to show or hide text formatting in the outline. The formatting information is not deleted or cleared. It is just turned off so that you can see the content more easily. When you print an outline, the outline will always appear with formatting on.

Change the view of the outline

Now that you have more content in the outline, you can become more familiar with some of the Outline tab's features. In this exercise, you change the view scale, and then you collapse and expand the outline.

1 **Click in the Outline tab, if necessary. On the Standard toolbar, click the Zoom button down arrow, and then click 25%.**

The view scale decreases from 33% to 25%. Your presentation window should look similar to the following illustration.

ANOTHER METHOD

On the View menu, click Zoom to open the Zoom dialog box.

TROUBLESHOOTING TIP

Your view scale might be different, depending on the size of your monitor.

FIGURE 4-5

Outline view scale decreased

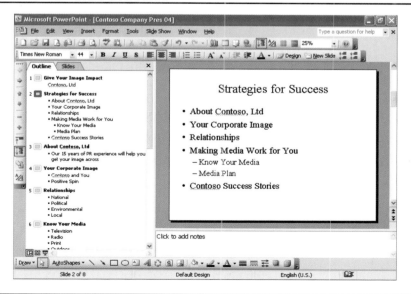

You can also enter a specific zoom percentage in the Zoom box.

2 **On the Standard toolbar, click in the Zoom box to type a percentage.**

3 **Type 38, and then press Enter.**

The view scale changes to 38%.

4 **Click the blank area to the right of the slide 2 title to place the insertion point in the line.**

5 **On the Outlining toolbar, click the Collapse button.**

Slide 2 collapses to show only the title. The rest of the outline remains fully expanded. Your presentation window should look like the following illustration.

FIGURE 4-6

Slide 2 is collapsed

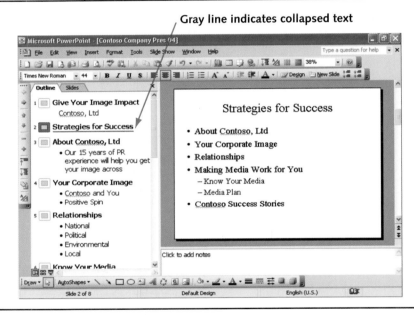

Gray line indicates collapsed text

To make it easier to work on the main points of the outline, you can view slide titles only for the presentation.

6 **On the Outlining toolbar, click the Collapse All button.**

The view switches from titles and paragraphs to titles only.

7 **Click the blank area to the right of the slide 6 title to place the insertion point in the line.**

8 **On the Outlining toolbar, click the Expand button.**

Slide 6 expands to include the paragraph text again.

9 **On the Outlining toolbar, click the Expand All button.**

The view switches to show all of the text in the outline. Now you will change the view to show in the outline the same text formatting applied in the Slide pane.

10 **On the Outlining toolbar, click the Show Formatting button.**

The text in the Outline tab changes from plain to formatted text, as shown in the following illustration. The formatting reflects the styles that were applied in the Word source file.

FIGURE 4-7

Outline text shows formatting

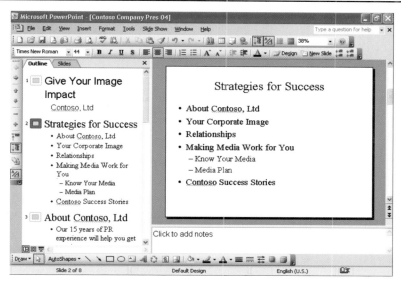

◆ **Keep this file open for the next exercise.**

QUICK REFERENCE ▼

Change the view of an outline

On the Standard toolbar, click the Zoom button down arrow, and then click a percentage.

Or

1 On the Standard toolbar, click in the Zoom box to select the current percentage size.

2 Type the percentage size, and then press Enter.

Collapse the outline

1 Click to the right of the slide title in the Outline tab to place the insertion point in the line.

2 On the Outlining toolbar, click the Collapse button or the Collapse All button.

Expand the outline

1 Click to place the insertion point in the line.

2 On the Outlining toolbar, click the Expand button or the Expand All button.

Show outline formatting

On the Outlining toolbar, click the Show Formatting button.

Selecting Text and Deleting Slides in an Outline

THE BOTTOM LINE

The Outline tab is the best location for making extensive text changes to a presentation because you can work in this tab just as in a word processing program to select, edit, and rearrange text.

The compact nature of the Outline tab makes it the best place to edit text because you can see a good part of the presentation's text in one place. Additionally, working in the Outline tab is similar to working in a word processor. In the Outline tab, you can select, edit, and rearrange slides, paragraphs, and text by using the Outlining toolbar buttons or by dragging the slides, paragraphs, or text.

As you will recall from Lesson 2, to edit or rearrange slides and paragraphs, you must first select the material you want to work with. To select a slide or paragraph, click the corresponding slide icon or paragraph bullet. To select a word, double-click the word. To select any portion of a title or paragraph, drag the I-beam pointer to highlight the text. In the Outline tab, you can also click the blank area at the end of a title or paragraph to select the entire line of text. This technique works especially well when selecting slide titles.

Select and delete slides and text in an outline

In this exercise, you select and delete a slide and a paragraph, and then you select text using different methods.

 1 **Position the I-beam pointer (which changes to the four-headed arrow) over the icon for slide 3, and then click the icon to select the slide.**

The entire slide, including all text, is selected. Your presentation window should look like the following illustration.

ANOTHER METHOD

You can also select a slide by clicking its slide number.

FIGURE 4-8

All text on the slide is selected

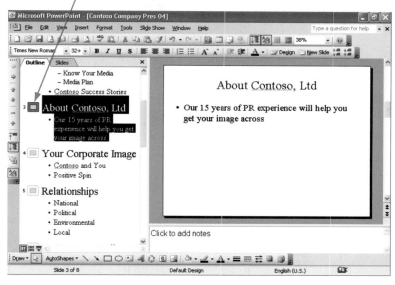
Click the slide icon to select all text for the slide

2 **Press Delete.**

PowerPoint deletes slide 3 and renumbers the other slides.

ANOTHER METHOD

On the Edit menu in any view, click Delete Slide.

3 **Scroll to the top of the outline and display slide 2.**

This slide's first paragraph refers to the slide you just deleted, so you will need to delete this paragraph. Selecting and deleting paragraphs works the same way as selecting and deleting slides.

 4 **Position the I-beam pointer (which changes to the four-headed arrow) over the bullet next to the paragraph titled "About Contoso, Ltd" in slide 2, and then click the bullet.**

PowerPoint selects the paragraph.

5 **Press Delete.**

PowerPoint deletes the paragraph.

6 **Click the bullet next to the paragraph titled "Your Corporate Image" in slide 2.**

TIP

You can also select multiple paragraphs.

7 Hold down Shift, and then click the bullet for the paragraph titled "Media Plan." Notice that the bulleted text in between is also selected.

Your presentation window should look like the following illustration.

FIGURE 4-9

Multiple paragraphs are selected

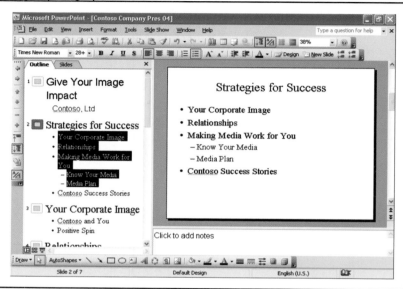

ANOTHER METHOD

You can also select multiple paragraphs by dragging the mouse. Click the I-beam pointer where you want the selection to begin, and then drag the I-beam pointer down to where you want the selection to end. PowerPoint selects everything between the first click and the ending point of the drag action.

8 Position the I-beam pointer in the middle of the word "Contoso" in the last paragraph in slide 2.

9 Drag the I-beam pointer to the right, through the text "Contoso Success Stories," to select all the text that follows in the line.

Although you started the selection in the middle of the word *Contoso*, because the Automatic Word Selection feature is turned on, PowerPoint selects the entire word.

◆ Keep this file open for the next exercise.

TIP

You can turn off the Automatic Word Selection command by clicking Options on the Tools menu, clicking the Edit tab, and then clearing the When Selecting, Automatically Select Entire Word check box.

QUICK REFERENCE ▼

Select text

1 Position the I-beam pointer.

2 Drag the I-beam pointer to select the desired text.

Select multiple paragraphs

1 Click the bullet next to a paragraph.

2 Hold down Shift, and the click the bullet next to another paragraph.

Select and delete a paragraph or slide

1 Position the I-beam pointer over a bullet or slide icon, and then click to select the bullet text or slide.

2 Press Delete.

QUICK CHECK

Q: Besides clicking the slide icon, what can you click in the Outline tab to select an entire slide?

A: **You can click the slide number to select the entire slide.**

Rearranging Slides, Paragraphs, and Text

Rearranging a Presentation

THE BOTTOM LINE

Take advantage of the Outline tab's Outlining toolbar to rearrange slides and slide text to improve your presentation's flow.

One of the most important tasks you can perform in the Outline tab is rearranging slide content. As you work with a presentation, you will often realize that a slide would fit better at some other location in the presentation, or that the paragraphs on a slide aren't in quite the right order. You may also feel that the phrasing of a particular paragraph could be improved by rearranging words.

You can rearrange slides and paragraphs in the Outline tab by using the Move Up button and the Move Down button on the Outlining toolbar or by dragging selected slides and paragraphs to the desired location. You can also drag a paragraph so that it becomes a part of another paragraph. To move selected words, you simply drag the selection to the new position.

Rearrange a slide, paragraphs, and words

You're ready to begin the process of fine-tuning the presentation outline. In this paragraph, you rearrange slides, paragraphs, and words.

1 Scroll down so that slide 4 is the top slide in the window.

2 Position the four-headed arrow over the slide icon for slide 4, Relationships, and click to select it.

3 Drag the slide icon down between slides 6 and 7.

As you drag, the pointer changes to the vertical two-headed arrow, and a horizontal line appears, showing you where you can place the slide. Your screen should look similar to the following illustration.

FIGURE 4-10

Moving a slide to a new location

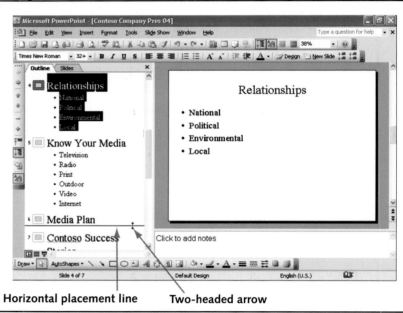

Horizontal placement line   Two-headed arrow

After you release the mouse button, the selected slide content is dropped into its new location, and PowerPoint reorders and renumbers the slides.

4 Click the bullet to the left of the word "Local" in slide 6.

The paragraph is selected.

5 On the Outlining toolbar, click the Move Up button three times.

Local becomes the first bulleted item.

6 Scroll to the top of the outline, and then in slide 2, position the four-headed arrow over the bullet of the text line titled "Know Your Media."

7 Drag the text line horizontally to the left one level, as shown in the following illustration.

FIGURE 4-11

Move a bullet item up one level by dragging

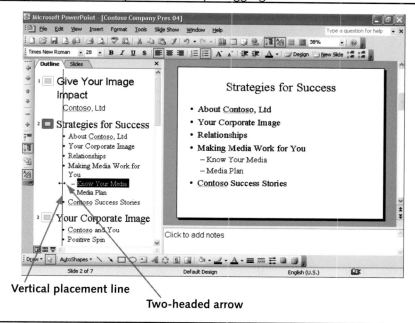

Vertical placement line

Two-headed arrow

 As you drag, the pointer changes to the horizontal two-headed arrow, and a vertical line indicates at what level the text will be placed. The text line moves one indent level to the left. This is the same action as promoting the paragraph.

8 **Drag the text line titled Media Plan horizontally to the left one level.**

You have promoted this bullet item to the first level.

TIP

You can also drag a paragraph horizontally to the right to demote it.

9 **Click the bullet next to the text "Making Media Work for You," and then press Delete.**

10 **Scroll down so that you can see all of slide 7 at the bottom of the outline, and then position the I-beam pointer over the word "Bits" in slide 7.**

11 **Select the entire word, the comma, and the space that follows it, and then drag the selection to the left of the word "Bytes" on the same line.**

 As you drag, a gray indicator line shows where the text will be placed. When you release the mouse button, the word *Bits* moves to its new position.

FIGURE 4-12

Indicator line shows where text will move

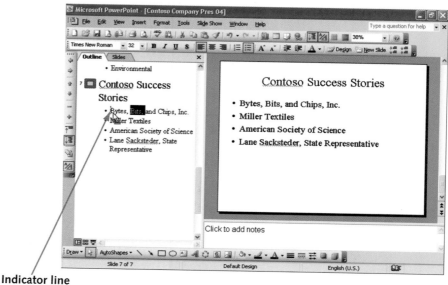

Indicator line

◆ **Keep this file open for the next exercise.**

QUICK REFERENCE ▼

Rearrange a slide

1 Position the four-headed arrow over the icon of the slide to rearrange.

2 Drag the slide icon between the slides where you want the selected slide to appear.

Rearrange paragraphs

1 Position the four-headed arrow over the bullet of your text line.

2 Drag the text line horizontally to the left or to the right to promote or demote one level.

Rearrange words

1 Position the I-beam pointer over a word in the slide, and then drag the I-beam pointer to select the words that you want to rearrange.

2 Drag the selection to a new position.

QUICK CHECK

Q: What happens when you select a bullet item and drag it to the left?

A: The item is promoted one level.

Formatting Text in an Outline

Formatting Text and Text Objects

THE BOTTOM LINE

Apply formatting right in the Outline tab to save time while you're working with outline text. You can change fonts, font sizes, and styles using Formatting toolbar buttons.

You can apply formatting in the Outline tab just as you would in the Slide pane. (You will learn more about formatting text in the Slide pane in the next lesson.) If you are working extensively in the Outline tab, it makes good sense to apply formatting to the outline text rather than switch to the Slide pane to do so.

TIP

If you prefer creating and formatting slide text as an outline, you can drag the Outline/Slides pane border to the right to provide plenty of room to work on the outline. This is especially useful if you're showing formatting in the Outline tab because you have room for the formatted text to display at a larger scale.

You can change fonts, sizes, and styles in the Outline tab. To format text, you first select it and then apply the specific formatting you want, using the commands on the Formatting toolbar. The Formatting toolbar includes commands to change the font type and size and to apply the bold, italic, and underline styles.

Format text in an outline

Now that you're satisfied with the reorganization of the presentation, you can turn your attention to formatting text. In this exercise, you change the style, font, and size of the text.

1 Scroll to the top of the outline.

2 Double-click the blank area to the right of the word "Impact" in the title of slide 1.

The title text is selected.

B

3 On the Formatting toolbar, click the Bold button.

ANOTHER METHOD

Press Ctrl + B.

4 Position the four-headed arrow pointer to the left of the word "Contoso" in the paragraph text of slide 1.

5 Click the blank area to select the entire line.

I

6 On the Formatting toolbar, click the Italic button.

The selected text is formatted. Your screen should look similar to the following illustration.

ANOTHER METHOD

Press Ctrl + I.

FIGURE 4-13

Text formatted with bold and italic styles

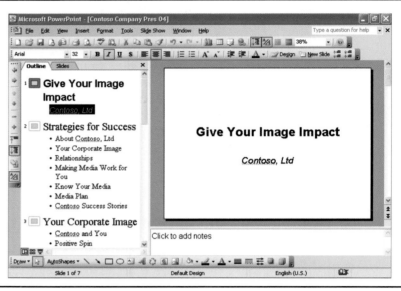

7 **With the subtitle text still selected, on the Formatting toolbar, click the Font Size button down arrow, and then click 28.**

The subtitle text is reduced in size.

8 **Double-click the blank area to the right of the slide title "Give Your Image Impact."**

The entire line is selected.

9 **On the Formatting toolbar, click the Increase Font Size button.**

The slide title font changes from 44 to 48 points. The Increase Font Size button increases the font size by a set increment and thus can be used when you just want to increase the size without worrying about a specific font size.

10 **On the Formatting toolbar, click the Font down arrow, and then scroll down and click Times New Roman.**

The selected text changes from Arial to Times New Roman.

11 **On the Formatting toolbar, click the Font down arrow again.**

Notice that the Times New Roman font is at the top of the list. PowerPoint places the fonts you recently used at the top of the list, separated by a double line, so you don't have to scroll down the list of fonts if you want to use the font again.

12 **Click a blank space in the Outline tab.**

The font list closes, and PowerPoint deselects the slide 1 title text, as shown in the following illustration.

FIGURE 4-14

Slide formatted with new styles

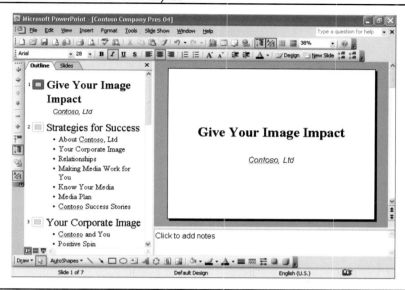

◆ **Keep this file open for the next exercise.**

QUICK REFERENCE ▼

Change text style

1 Select the text in which you want to change text style.

2 On the Formatting toolbar, click a formatting button such as Bold or Italic.

Change the font

1 Select the text in which you want to change the font.

2 On the Formatting toolbar, click the Font down arrow, and then click a font.

Change the font size

1 Select the text in which you want to change the font size.

2 On the Formatting toolbar, click the Font Size down arrow, and then click a size, or on the Formatting toolbar, click the Increase Font Size button or the Decrease Font Size button.

QUICK CHECK

Q: What is a quick way to make text larger without specifying an exact font size?

A: **Use the Increase Font Size button to increase font size by a set amount at each click.**

Sending an Outline or Slides to Word

Sending an Outline or Notes to Word

THE BOTTOM LINE

Send an outline or slides to Word when you want to take advantage of Word's formatting and text-handling features. Exported outlines and slides are editable documents that can provide good alternatives to printing presentation materials from PowerPoint.

You may find that you need output options other than simply printing a presentation's slides, pages, or outline. Suppose, for example, you want to study further and perhaps edit the outline you have created for Contoso in this lesson. You can use PowerPoint's Send To command to send the outline to Microsoft Word, where you can edit it just like any other Word document. (And you can then, if desired, insert the edited outline back into a PowerPoint presentation to eliminate the need for correcting each slide with your edits.)

As long as Word is installed on your computer, you can export a presentation outline or slides and their associated speaker notes directly from PowerPoint into a Word document. You can choose to arrange the presentation's slides in two different ways as well as choose whether to include the notes or instead create blank lines beside or beneath each slide. Because the slides and notes display in a Word table, you can use table-editing tools to adjust layout and format notes text. This is an excellent alternative to printing handouts or notes pages.

CHECK THIS OUT ▼

Link Presentation to Word Document

The Send To Microsoft Office dialog box, where you choose settings for exporting presentation materials to Word, allows you either to paste the presentation content or Paste Link it. When you use Paste Link, changes you make to the presentation will automatically be made to the Word document the next time you open it. Use this feature when you want to keep an archive copy of a presentation and don't want to have to keep exporting as the presentation is modified.

Send an outline to Word

You have finished tweaking the presentation outline. You're now ready to export the outline to Word, where you'll be able to edit it if you need to.

1 On the File menu, point to Send To, and then click Microsoft Office Word.

The Send To Microsoft Office Word dialog box appears with five page layout options and two pasting options. The page layout options determine the type of information you want to send to Word. The pasting options determine how you want to send the information.

2 Click the Outline Only option, and then click OK.

The pasting options gray out, indicating that you don't have the option to link the outline. PowerPoint launches Word and inserts the presentation slides with the title text and main text format into a blank Word document. Your Word document should look similar to the following illustration.

FIGURE 4-15

Exported outline in Word

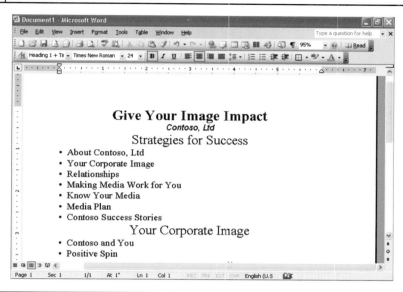

3 On the Word File menu, click Save As.

The Save As dialog box opens.

4 In the Save In box, verify that the Lesson04 folder in the PowerPoint Practice folder is open.

5 In the File Name box, type Contoso Company Doc 04 and click Save.

Word saves the presentation slide text in a document called Contoso Company Doc 04 in the Lesson04 folder.

6 On the Word File menu, click Exit.

Word closes, and PowerPoint is redisplayed.

> **TIP**
>
> If you don't have Word installed, you can save a presentation in a common file format called Rich Text Format (RTF). For more information on RTF, see "Saving a Presentation as an Outline" in the next section.

◆ Keep this file open for the next exercise.

QUICK REFERENCE ▼

Send an outline or notes to Word

1 On the File menu, point to Send To, and then click Microsoft Office Word.

2 Click a layout option and pasting option.

3 Click OK.

QUICK CHECK

Q: What is one reason why you might export a presentation to Word?

A: Exporting allows you to keep an archive copy, create an editable version of an outline, or prepare handouts that can be formatted.

Saving a Presentation as an Outline

Sending an Outline or Notes to Word

THE BOTTOM LINE

Save a presentation as an outline when you want to make the text available to other programs that can read only a limited number of file formats.

When you need the text portion of a presentation for use in another program, you can save the presentation text in a format called **Rich Text Format (RTF)**. Saving an outline in RTF allows you to save any formatting you made to the presentation text in a common file format that you can open in other programs. There are many programs, such as Word for Macintosh or older versions of PowerPoint, that can import outlines saved in RTF.

TIP

As with an outline created in Word, you can use the Slides From Outline command to create slides from an outline you have saved in RTF.

Save a presentation as an outline

For your last task, you'll save the current presentation, then save it as an outline in RTF format.

 1 **On the Standard toolbar, click the Save button.**

The next time you open this presentation, PowerPoint opens it with the Outline displayed in the same view scale in which you last saved it. Now that you have saved the changes to a presentation in Normal view, you can save it as an RTF file.

ANOTHER METHOD

- Press Ctrl + S.
- On the File menu, click Save.

2 **On the File menu, click Save As.**

3 **In the Save In box, verify that the Lesson04 folder in the PowerPoint Practice folder is open.**

4 **Type** Contoso Outline RTF **in the File Name box.**

5 **Click the Save As Type down arrow, and then click Outline/RTF.**

6 **Click Save.**

PowerPoint saves the presentation slide text in RTF format in a document called Contoso Outline RTF in the Lesson04 folder.

◆ If you are continuing to other lessons, save the Contoso Company Pres 04 presentation with the current name, and then close it. If you are not continuing to other lessons, save and close the Contoso Company Pres 04 presentation, and then click the Close button in the title bar of the PowerPoint window.

QUICK REFERENCE ▼

Save a presentation as an outline

1 On the File menu, click Save As.

2 In the Save In box, navigate to the location in which you want to save the outline file.

3 In the File Name box, type the file name.

4 Click the Save As Type down arrow, and then click Outline/RTF.

5 Click Save.

QUICK **CHECK**

Q: What does RTF stand for?

A: **RTF stands for Rich Text Format.**

Key Points

✔ *Create a blank presentation when you want to concentrate more on content, rather than slide design.*

✔ *The Outline tab lets you see much of your presentation at one time, making it easy to avoid repetition and emphasize your main points.*

✔ *If text useful for slides has already been typed in a word processing outline, use the Slides From Outline command to import the text into a PowerPoint presentation. The text is designated as titles or bullet items according to the outline formatting in the word processing document.*

✔ *Change an outline's zoom setting to see the text at a larger or smaller size. Collapsing and expanding slide content makes it easier to reorganize slides. You can display the same text formatting in the outline as is shown in the Slide pane.*

✔ *Use the Outline tab to easily select and delete slides, paragraphs, or words.*

✔ *The Outline tab can be used to reorganize slides, paragraph text, and words just by dragging.*

✔ *Apply formats such as fonts, sizes, and styles right in the Outline tab to save time.*

✔ *Send an outline or slides to Word to create an editable document that can be used for archive purposes or as an alternative to PowerPoint's printed materials.*

✔ *Save a presentation as an RTF outline when you want to make it available to other programs.*

Quick Quiz

True/False

T   F   **1.** You can create a new blank presentation by starting to enter text in the first window that opens when you start PowerPoint.

T   F   **2.** When the Outline tab is active, changing the zoom setting scales text in the outline.

T   F   **3.** You can delete a slide in any view by clicking Delete Slide on the Format menu.

T   F   **4.** If you drag a first-level bullet to the left in the Outline tab, you turn it into a slide title.

T   F   **5.** You can easily send presentation handouts to Word for further editing.

Multiple Choice

1. If you drag a bullet item to the right, you have _____ the item.
   a. promoted
   b. demoted
   c. deleted
   d. formatted

2. You can import an outline in which of these formats?
   a. .doc
   b. .rtf
   c. .txt
   d. all of the above

3. To select all of the content for a slide in the Outline tab, click the _____.
   a. paragraph bullet
   b. slide icon
   c. slide number
   d. either b or c

4. To apply underline formatting to text, you would click a button on the _____ toolbar.
   a. Formatting
   b. Outlining
   c. Standard
   d. Drawing

5. In the Send To Microsoft Office Word dialog box, you select a layout option and a _____ option.
   a. formatting
   b. saving
   c. pasting
   d. color/grayscale

Short Answer

1. What are the two ways you can change the view scale?
2. How do you insert an outline from another file?
3. How do you delete multiple paragraphs?
4. How do you display the same text fonts and styles in the Outline tab that are displayed in the Slide pane?
5. How do you send an outline to Word?
6. How do you save a presentation in RTF?

On Your Own

Exercise 1

Open the Contoso Company Pres 04 in the Lesson04 folder that is located in the PowerPoint Practice folder. Move slide 6 after slide 3, and then add the following bulleted list to the Media Plan slide:

Target audience
Budget
Time frame

Save and close the presentation.

Exercise 2

Create a blank presentation, display the Outline tab, and then insert the Contoso Outline RTF from the Lesson04 folder that is located in the PowerPoint Practice folder. In the Outline tab, change the view scale to 100%, and then save the presentation as Contoso Company Pres Outline in the Lesson04 folder that is located in the PowerPoint Practice folder. Close the presentation.

One Step Further

Exercise 1

Open Holidays 03 from the Lesson03 folder that is located in the PowerPoint Practice folder and position the insertion point at the end of the last slide in the Outline tab. Insert the 04 Holiday Outline from the Lesson04 folder that is located in the PowerPoint Practice folder so that its slides follow the original four slides. Delete the last slide in the outline. Move the *Vacation* slide to become slide 6. Change the view scale to 25% to see all the new slides at once. Save the presentation as Holidays 04 in the Lesson04 folder that is located in the PowerPoint Practice folder and leave the presentation open for the next exercise.

Exercise 2

Demote the *Maternity leave* slide title so it becomes paragraph text on slide 9. Demote the next two slide titles to become second-level bullets below *Maternity leave*. Demote the *Disability* slide one level. On slide 8, demote *Immediate family only* one level. Collapse all text to see only the headings. Select all slides and change the font to another appropriate font. Expand all text again. Apply bold formatting to all slide titles, if they aren't already bold. Change paragraph formatting on the inserted slides to match that on the original slides (remove italic formatting as necessary). Increase the font size of the title text on the first slide. Save and close the presentation.

Exercise 3

You have been asked to lead a discussion on your company's wellness and enrichment programs, which include a new exercise room, classes in yoga and Pilates, smoking and diet counseling, company-supported teams for local running and cycle races, and so on. Create a new, blank presentation. Working in the Outline tab of the Outline/Slides pane, create several slides that list the company's programs and reasons for investing in the health and well-being of their workers. Use tools on the Outlining toolbar to re-organize slides and slide text. Format slide text as desired. Save the presentation as Wellness 04 in the Lesson04 folder that is located in the PowerPoint Practice folder and close the presentation.

Adding and Modifying Text

After completing this lesson, you will be able to:

✓ *Select and deselect objects.*
✓ *Add text to slides.*
✓ *Adjust text objects.*
✓ *Format text.*
✓ *Change text alignment and spacing.*
✓ *Move a text object.*
✓ *Find and replace text and fonts.*
✓ *Correct text while typing.*
✓ *Check spelling.*
✓ *Check presentation styles.*
✓ *Use the Research task pane.*

KEY TERMS

- dotted selection box
- object
- resize handles
- slanted-line selection box
- text label
- word processing box
- word wrap

In Microsoft PowerPoint, you can add to and modify your presentation text to fine-tune your message. PowerPoint offers several alternatives for placing text on your slides: text placeholders for entering slide titles and subtitles, text labels for short notes and phrases, and word processing boxes for longer text. You can also place text inside objects, such as circles, rectangles, or stars.

As the vice president of sales at the public relations firm Contoso, Ltd, you have been working on a presentation that you want to customize for new clients. After working with your presentation outline in the previous lesson, you are ready to fine-tune your message.

In this lesson, you will learn how to create several kinds of text objects, edit text, change the appearance of text, find and replace text, replace fonts, let PowerPoint correct text while you type, check spelling and presentation styles, and use PowerPoint's new Research task pane.

◆ Before you can use the practice files in this lesson, you must install them from the book's companion CD to their default location. See "Using the CD-ROM" at the beginning of this book for more information. To complete the procedures in this lesson, you will need to use a file named 05 PPT Lesson in the Lesson05 folder in the PowerPoint Practice folder located on your hard disk.

Selecting and Deselecting Objects

Editing Text

THE BOTTOM LINE

Knowing the ways you can select objects can speed editing. Click in an object to work with its content individually. Click on an object to work with the object as a single unit.

An **object** is anything that you can manipulate. For example, the title object on a slide is all the text in the title, which is treated as a unit. To make formatting changes to all of the text in a text object, you need to first select the object. To select an object, you click a part of the object by using the pointer. To deselect an object, you move the pointer off the object into a blank area of the slide and then click the blank area.

In PowerPoint, you can select a text object in two ways. First, you can click inside a text object. This places the insertion point in the object and surrounds the text object with a **slanted-line selection box**, consisting of gray slanted lines. When the slanted-line selection box is displayed, you can edit any content within the box. For example, you can insert or delete a word. Second, you can click on the outside edge of a text object. This surrounds the object with a fuzzy outline, called a **dotted selection box**. When the dotted selection box is displayed, the entire object is selected and ready for you to edit as an object. That is, you can manipulate it as a whole. The white circles at each corner of either type of selection box are **resize handles**, which you use to adjust and resize the object. A sample of each selection box is shown in the following illustrations.

FIGURE 5-1

Slanted-line and dotted selection boxes

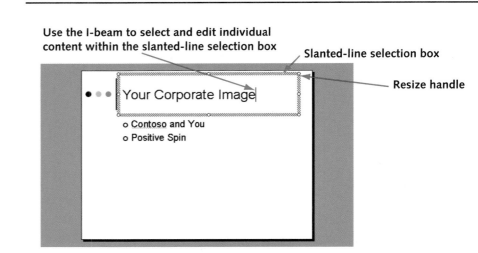

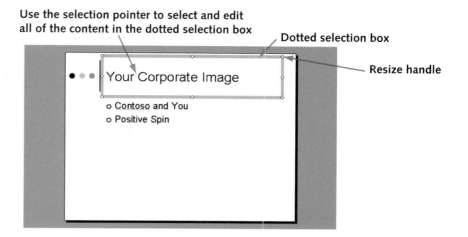

Use the selection pointer to select and edit
all of the content in the dotted selection box

Dotted selection box

Resize handle

Select and deselect objects

In this exercise, you review selection boxes and then select and deselect a text object.

◆ **Start PowerPoint, if necessary, click the Open button on the Standard
toolbar, navigate to the Lesson05 folder in the PowerPoint Practice
folder, and then open the 05 PPT Lesson file. Save the file as Contoso
Company Pres 05 in the same folder.**

1 **Display slide 3 and click directly on top of the title object.**

The text box is selected with the slanted-line selection box and an
insertion point displays where you clicked.

2 **Position the pointer directly on top of an edge of the slanted-line
selection box.**

The pointer changes to the selection pointer, shown in the margin.

3 **Click the edge of the slanted-line selection box.**

The selection box changes to a dotted selection box.

FIGURE 5-2

Placeholder shows dotted selection box

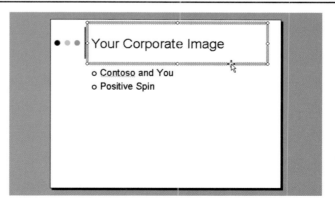

> **TIP**
>
> You can select an entire object with only one click without having to first select the individual text content inside the object. Position the pointer above or below the object until it changes to the selection pointer, and then click the slide. The dotted selection box appears.

4 **Click outside the selection box in a blank area of the slide.**

The text box is deselected.

◆ **Keep this file open for the next exercise.**

QUICK REFERENCE ▼

Select and deselect objects

- Click directly on top of the title object.
- Click directly on top of an edge of the slanted-line selection box.
- Click outside the selection box in a blank area of the slide to deselect it.

Adding Text to Slides

Editing Text

> **THE BOTTOM LINE**
>
> When you want to add text in a location that doesn't have a place-holder, add a text box. Use a text label for a single line of text and a word processing box for text that wraps.

Usually, slides contain text boxes for title and bulleted text into which you enter your main ideas. You can also place other text objects on a slide by using the Text Box button on the Drawing toolbar. You use text boxes when you need to include annotations or minor points that do not belong in a list.

You can create two types of text objects: a **text label**, which is text that does not **word wrap** within a defined box, and a **word processing box**, which is text that wraps inside the boundaries of an object. Use a text label to enter short notes or phrases and a word processing box for longer text or sentences.

You can create a text label on a slide by using the Text Box tool to select a place on the slide where you will begin typing your text. You can create a word processing box by using the Text Box tool to drag the pointer to create a text box of the appropriate width.

Once you have created a word processing box or a text label, you can change one object into the other by changing the word-wrap option and the fit text option in the Format Text Box dialog box. You can also change a text label to a word processing box by dragging one of the corner resize handles. The text rewraps to adjust to the new size.

Add text to slides

Your presentation would benefit from some additional information on several slides. In this exercise, you add text in an existing text object and then create a text label and a word processing box.

1 **Drag the scroll box in the Slide pane to slide 5.**

2 **Click immediately before the word "homework" in the first bulleted item.**

You will add a word in this text box to see how text wraps automatically in a placeholder.

3 **Type** your, **and then press the Spacebar.**

The paragraph wraps in the text object. Your slide should look like the following illustration.

FIGURE 5-3

Wrapping text in the text object

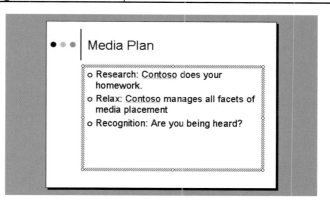

4 **Click anywhere outside the slanted-line selection box to deselect the text object.**

 5 **On the Drawing toolbar, click the Text Box button.**

The pointer changes to the upside-down T-pointer.

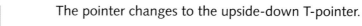
ANOTHER METHOD

On the Insert menu, click Text Box.

6 **Position the pointer at the bottom center of the slide.**

7 **Click to create a text label.**

A small, empty selection box composed of gray slanted lines appears with the blinking insertion point in it.

8 **Type** Media types are listed on slide 4.

Text in a new text box uses the current default font and font size, such as 18 point Arial. Your slide should look like the following illustration.

FIGURE 5-4

Text box added to slide

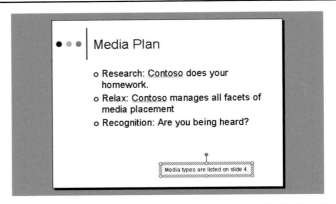

TIP

The text you create on a slide using the Text Box tool does not appear in the Outline tab. Only text entered in a title placeholder or a main text placeholder appears in the Outline tab.

9 Click a blank area of the slide to deselect the label.

10 Click the Next Slide button to advance to slide 6.

11 On the Drawing toolbar, click the Text Box button.

12 Position the pointer below the last bullet, about halfway between the bulleted item and the bottom of the slide, and then drag the pointer to create a box that extends a bit farther than the last bullet entry.

When you release the mouse button, a slanted-line selection box appears with the blinking insertion point in it. You can now enter your text.

13 Type It is worth it to create community relationships on several levels.

The width of the box does not change, but the words wrap, and the box height increases to accommodate the complete entry. Your slide should look like the following illustration.

FIGURE 5-5

Text box adjusts text automatically

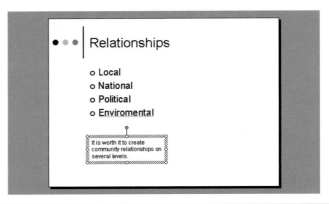

14 Click a blank area of the slide to deselect the text object.

◆ Keep this file open for the next exercise.

QUICK REFERENCE ▼

Create a text label

1 On the Drawing toolbar, click the Text Box button.

2 Click where you want the text label to appear.

3 Type the text.

Create a word processing box

1 On the Drawing toolbar, click the Text Box button.

2 Position the pointer on the slide, and then drag the pointer to create a box of the length you want.

3 Type the text.

Adjusting Text Objects

Formatting Text and
Text Objects

THE BOTTOM LINE

To ensure that text objects appear neatly on a slide, you can control word wrap and object size for both placeholders and text boxes you have added.

On occasion, you may need to adjust text objects to change object size or wrap options. For example, default bullet text placeholders usually take up a good portion of the slide, and if you want to insert a graphic or another text object near the bottom of the slide, you may want the unused portion of the placeholder out of the way. You may also want to change the wrap option for a text object to control the size of the object on the slide.

You can adjust text object settings for any text object on a slide—not only for text objects you have added, but also for the default text placeholders. Settings are adjusted in the Format Text Box or Format Placeholder dialog box. The Text Box tab in either of these dialog boxes offers check boxes that let you turn word wrap on or off and resize a placeholder to fit its text.

Adjust text objects

In this exercise, you experiment with changing word wrap options and adjust the size of a text placeholder.

1 Click the bottom text box on slide 6, and then click the edge of the text box to select it with the dotted selection box.

Remember that the dotted selection box means you can modify the object as a whole.

2 **On the Format menu, click Text Box.**

The Format Text Box dialog box opens. Note that the command on the menu is *Text Box* because this is a text box you added yourself.

3 **Click the Text Box tab.**

FIGURE 5-6

Format Text Box dialog box

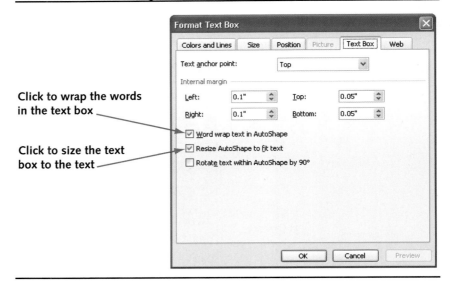

Click to wrap the words in the text box

Click to size the text box to the text

4 **Clear the Word Wrap Text In AutoShape check box.**

5 **Click OK.**

The word processing box changes to a text label and stretches across the slide.

6 **On the Standard toolbar, click the Undo button.**

7 Position the pointer near the bulleted text on slide 6 until it changes to the selection pointer, and then click to select the paragraph text object.

Notice that the dotted selection box is larger than it needs to be. (There is additional white space at the bottom that overlaps the word processing box you added.)

8 On the Format menu, click Placeholder.

The Format AutoShape dialog box appears. The menu command is *Placeholder* in this case because you have selected a default text placeholder.

ANOTHER METHOD

Right-click a placeholder, and click Format Placeholder on the shortcut menu.

---

9 Click the Text Box tab.

10 Select the Resize AutoShape To Fit Text check box, and then click OK.

The object adjusts to fit the depth of the text. You now have clear space at the bottom of this slide if you want to add another text box or a graphic.

11 Click a blank area of the slide to deselect the text box.

◆ Keep this file open for the next exercise.

QUICK REFERENCE ▼

To adjust word wrap in a text object

1 Select the text object.
2 On the Format menu, click Text Box.
3 Click the Text Box tab.
4 Clear or select the Word Wrap Text In AutoShape check box.
5 Click OK.

To adjust a text placeholder to fit text

1 Select the text object.
2 On the Format menu, click Placeholder.
3 Click the Text Box tab.
4 Select the Resize AutoShape To Fit Text check box.
5 Click OK.

QUICK CHECK

Q: Which menu option should you select to format the text of a placeholder object?

A: **You use the Format Placeholder option on the Format menu.**

Formatting Text

Formatting Text and
Text Objects

> **THE BOTTOM LINE**
>
> Though a design template specifies text formatting, you can adjust formats to suit your content or improve slide appearance. You can turn bullets or numbering on and off and change font styles, color, and size to add emphasis.

At any time while you work on a presentation, you can change text formatting. Although design templates specify fonts, font sizes, styles, colors, and bullets, you can modify these settings to add special emphasis to text or just to adjust the design's formats. With all text formatting changes, you need to select the text object before you can apply new changes.

Apply or Remove Bullets and Numbers

By default, paragraphs on text slides use bullets to indicate each item. You may sometimes want to remove bullets from paragraphs to achieve a different look on a slide or when you have only one paragraph on the slide. To remove bullets, select the placeholder and click the Bullets button on the Formatting toolbar. To reapply bullets, simply click the button again.

PowerPoint also has a Numbering button on the Formatting toolbar. You can number paragraphs rather than use bullets if you want to show order in the paragraphs. For example, you would use numbers rather than bullets when your paragraphs describe the process of applying for a credit card or the steps necessary to prepare a floor for tile installation.

> **TIP**
>
> You can use AutoNumbering to start a numbered list by typing. Remove any bullets at the beginning of the line, type a number 1, letter A or a, or Roman numeral I or i followed by a period or closing parenthesis, type text, and then press Enter. The numbering continues automatically.

Work with bullets and numbers

In this exercise, you work with bullets and numbers to decide which approach works best for the material on a slide.

1 Click the edge of the bulleted text box on slide 6 to select it with the dotted selection box.

2 On the Formatting toolbar, click the Bullets button.

You have turned off bullets, so the bullets for the four lines of text disappear.

3 On the Formatting toolbar, click the Numbering button to apply numbers to the paragraphs.

The text changes to a numbered list. This list doesn't need to be in a particular order, however, so it will be best to return it to a bulleted list.

 4 **On the Formatting toolbar, click the Bullets button again.**

The text changes back to a bulleted list.

◆ **Keep this file open for the next exercise.**

QUICK REFERENCE ▼

Add bullets or numbering to a text object

1 Click the edge of a text box on a slide to select it with the dotted selection box.

2 On the Formatting toolbar, click the Bullets button or click the Numbering button.

Remove bullets or numbering from a text object

1 Select the text object.

2 On the Formatting toolbar, click the Bullets button or click the Numbering button to deselect the button.

QUICK CHECK

Q: If your slide displays a list of materials required for a woodworking project, would you use bullets or numbers for the list?

A: A list of materials doesn't usually require a specific order, so bullets would be adequate.

Change Font Styles, Size, and Color

In all PowerPoint presentations, you can choose among three styles to emphasize text: **bold**, *italic*, and underline. Some design templates also make the shadow style available for use. Changing font style is as easy as clicking a button on the Formatting toolbar.

> **TIP**
>
> Additional font styles, bold italic and emboss, are available in the Font dialog box. This dialog box lets you make a number of font, size, and style selections at one time. To open this dialog box, click Font on the Format menu.

You already know that design templates provide the colors for text and background in a presentation. (You will learn more about design template color schemes in Lesson 7.) You can change text color at any time, however, to make text stand out by clicking the Font Color button, either on the Formatting toolbar or the Drawing toolbar. You can select another of the design template's colors, or you can choose a different color from PowerPoint's color palette.

Font size is also controlled by the design template, but you may want to adjust size to fill a placeholder better or to fit more text in placeholder. You can change the font size either by specifying an exact size in the Font Size box or by using the Increase Font Size or Decrease Font Size button, which increases or reduces font size by set intervals.

Change font styles

You will change text formatting in several ways in this exercise to emphasize portions of the presentation.

 1 Click the Next Slide button to go to slide 7.

 2 Position the pointer near the edge of the quote in the text box until the pointer changes to the selection pointer, and then click to select it.

A dotted selection box appears around the text object, indicating that it is selected.

 3 On the Formatting toolbar, click the Italic button.

The text in the object changes to italics.

ANOTHER METHOD

Press Ctrl + I.

 4 On the Formatting toolbar, click the Decrease Font Size button to reduce the font size to 20 points.

 5 On the Drawing toolbar, click the Font Color button down arrow.

A text color palette of the current color scheme appears.

6 Click the blue color as indicated in the following illustration.

FIGURE 5-7

Use the blue color on the color palette

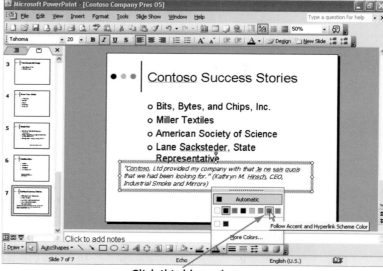

Click this blue color

The font color in the word processing box changes to blue.

TIP

The line on the Font Color button also changes, indicating the currently selected font color.

7 Select the words "Je ne sais quois."

The slanted-line selection box appears, and you can format individual text.

8 On the Formatting toolbar, click the Italic button.

You have turned off italic formatting. This is the usual way to emphasize text that is already italicized.

9 Click a blank area of the slide to deselect the text object.

◆ Keep this file open for the next exercise.

QUICK REFERENCE ▼

Format text in a text object

1 Select the text object.

2 On the Formatting toolbar, click a formatting button (such as Bold, Italic, Underline, Shadow, or Font Color).

3 Click a blank area of the slide to deselect the text object.

Changing Text Alignment and Spacing

THE BOTTOM LINE

To add emphasis to text, you can change how it lines up in a placeholder. Adjust the line spacing to fit more text in a placeholder or to fill space in a placeholder.

Formatting Text and Text Objects

PowerPoint enables you to control the way text lines up on the slide. You can align text to the left or to the right or to the center in a text object. You can adjust the alignment of text in an object by selecting the object and clicking an alignment button on the Formatting toolbar. The Align Left button aligns text evenly along the left edge of the text box and is useful for paragraph text. The Align Right button aligns text evenly along the right edge of the text box and is useful for text labels. The Center button aligns text in the middle of the text box and is useful for titles and headings. You can also justify text in a paragraph so it lines up evenly along both edges of the text box.

You can adjust the vertical space between selected lines and the space before and after paragraphs by selecting the object and clicking a line spacing button (Increase Paragraph Spacing or Decrease Paragraph Spacing) on the Formatting toolbar or by using the Line Spacing command on the Format menu.

Change text alignment and spacing

In this exercise, you change the alignment of text in a text object, decrease paragraph spacing, and adjust line spacing.

1 Select the text box at the bottom of slide 7.

 2 On the Formatting toolbar, click the Center button.

The text in the text object aligns to the center.

ANOTHER METHOD

- Press Ctrl + E.
- On the Format menu, click Alignment, and then click Center.

3 Click a blank area of the slide to deselect the text box.

 4 Click the edge of the bulleted paragraph text box on slide 7 with the selection pointer.

The dotted selection box appears. You are now ready to change the paragraph spacing, but to do so, you may need to add a button to your Formatting toolbar.

5 On the Formatting toolbar, click the Toolbar Options down arrow, point to Add or Remove Buttons, and then point to Formatting.

A list of all the buttons currently available for the Formatting toolbar appears.

6 In the list of additional buttons, click the Decrease Paragraph Spacing button to place it on the toolbar.

A check mark appears next to the entry.

TROUBLESHOOTING

If a check mark appears by the button when you open the list of additional buttons, the button is already active. Don't click the button or you will deactivate it.

7 Click the Toolbar Options down arrow to close the list.

 8 On the Formatting toolbar, click the Decrease Paragraph Spacing button.

The paragraph spacing in the text box decreases by 0.1 lines, from 1.0 to 0.9.

9 Click a blank area of the slide to deselect the text box.

10 Click the edge of the bulleted paragraph text object on slide 7 to select it.

11 On the Format menu, click Line Spacing.

The Line Spacing dialog box appears.

12 Click the Before Paragraph down arrow until 0.1 appears, and then click OK.

FIGURE 5-8

Line Spacing dialog box

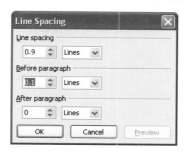

The paragraph spacing before each paragraph decreases by 0.1 lines.

13 **Click a blank area of the slide to deselect the text box.**

> **TIP**
>
> Everything you can do to manipulate a text label or word processing box you can also do to any text object, including title and paragraph text objects, and vice versa.

◆ **Keep this file open for the next exercise.**

QUICK REFERENCE ▼

Change text alignment

1 Select the text box.

2 On the Formatting toolbar, click an alignment button (such as Align Left, Center, or Align Right).

3 Click a blank area of the slide to deselect the text box.

Decrease or increase paragraph spacing

1 Select the text object.

2 On the Formatting toolbar, click the Decrease Paragraph Spacing button or the Increase Paragraph Spacing button.

Adjust line spacing

1 Select the text object.

2 On the Format menu, click Line Spacing.

3 Adjust the Line Spacing measurement to increase or decrease space between lines, or click the Before Paragraph or After Paragraph arrow to increase or decrease space above or below a paragraph.

4 Click OK.

QUICK CHECK

Q: What alignment button would you choose to make text line up at the right side of the text box?

A: **Use the Align Right button to line text up at the right side of the text box.**

Moving a Text Object

Editing Text

THE BOTTOM LINE

Move a text object to place it more attractively or usefully on a slide.

You can move a text object to any place on a slide to improve the appearance of a presentation. You can use the mouse to drag a text object from one location to another on a slide. Any text object on a slide can be moved, including both the default placeholders and text labels and word processing boxes you add yourself. The most efficient way to move a text object is to drag it from one location to another.

Move a text object

In this exercise, you move a text object by dragging the edge of the text object's selection box.

1 Click the edge of the text box at the bottom of slide 7 with the selection pointer.

The dotted selection box appears.

2 Drag the edge of the selection box to center the text object between the bottom of the slide and the bulleted text box.

ANOTHER METHOD

You can use the arrow keys on the keyboard to "nudge" an object by small increments in any direction.

TIP

To copy a text object, hold down Ctrl, and then drag the selection box of a text object to a new location on the slide.

3 Click a blank area of the slide to deselect the text box.

Your slide should look like the following illustration.

FIGURE 5-9

Text box has been repositioned

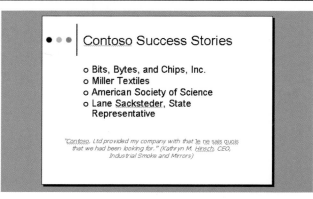

◆ Keep this file open for the next exercise.

QUICK REFERENCE ▼

To move a text object

1 Select the text object.

2 Drag the edge of the selection box to place the text object where you want it.

Finding and Replacing Text and Fonts

The Find and Replace commands on the Edit menu allow you to locate and change specific text in a presentation. Find helps you locate each occurrence of a specific word or set of characters, whereas Replace locates every occurrence of a specific word or set of characters and replaces it with a different one. You can change every occurrence of specific text all at once, or you can accept or reject each change individually.

The Find and Replace commands also give you options for more detailed searches. If you want to search for whole words so the search doesn't stop on a word that might contain only part of your search word, you select the check box for Find Whole Words Only. If you want to find a word or phrase that matches a certain capitalization exactly, you select the Match Case check box.

In addition to finding text, you can also find and replace a specific font in a presentation. The Replace Fonts command allows you to replace every instance of a font style you have been using with another. You cannot choose to replace a font only in certain locations.

Find and replace text and fonts

In this exercise, you use the Replace command to find and replace a word and then use Replace Fonts to replace a font.

1 On the Edit menu, click Replace.

The Replace dialog box appears.

ANOTHER METHOD

Press Ctrl + H.

2 Click in the Find What box, and then type facets.

3 Press Tab or click in the Replace With box.

4 Type aspects.

FIGURE 5-10

Replace dialog box

5 Click **Find Next.**

PowerPoint finds and selects the word facets on slide 5.

TROUBLESHOOTING

If the dialog box covers up the selected text, drag the Replace dialog box title bar out of the way so that you can see the text.

6 Click **Replace.**

An alert box appears, telling you that PowerPoint has finished searching the presentation. If you do not want to replace an instance, you could click Ignore, and if you want to replace all instances, you could click Replace All.

7 Click **OK, and then click Close in the Replace dialog box.**

The Replace dialog box closes.

8 Click **a blank area of the slide to deselect any text boxes.**

9 On the Format menu, click **Replace Fonts.**

The Replace Font dialog box appears.

10 Click the Replace down arrow, and then click **Tahoma.**

11 Click the With down arrow, scroll down, and then click **Arial.**

12 Click **Replace.**

Throughout the presentation, the text formatted with the Tahoma font changes to the Arial font.

13 Click **Close in the Replace Font dialog box.**

◆ Keep this file open for the next exercise.

QUICK REFERENCE ▼

Replace text

1 On the Edit menu, click Replace.

2 Click the Find What box, and then type the text you want to replace.

3 Press Tab or click in the Replace With box.

4 Type the replacement text.

5 Click Find Next, and then click Replace, Replace All, or Ignore.

6 Click OK, and then click Close in the Replace dialog box.

Replace fonts

1 On the Format menu, click Replace Fonts.

2 Click the Replace down arrow.

3 Click a font.

4 Click the With down arrow, and then click a font.

5 Click Replace.

6 Click Close in the Replace Font dialog box.

Correcting Text While Typing

Checking Spelling and
Word Choice

THE BOTTOM LINE

Automatic correction and text-fitting features can save time by fixing errors and adjusting layouts for you. AutoCorrect replaces common typing errors with correct words, and AutoFit reduces text size as necessary to fit in a placeholder.

As you type text in a presentation, you might be aware of making typographical errors, but when you look at the text, the mistakes have been corrected. PowerPoint's AutoCorrect feature corrects common capitalization and spelling errors as you type. For example, if you frequently type *tehm* instead of *them*, you can create an AutoCorrect entry named *tehm*. Then, whenever you type *tehm* followed by a space or a punctuation mark, PowerPoint replaces the misspelling with *them*. You can customize AutoCorrect to recognize or ignore misspellings that you routinely make or ignore specific text that you do not want AutoCorrect to change. You can also use AutoCorrect to recognize abbreviations or codes that you create to automate typing certain text. For example, you could customize AutoCorrect to type your full name when you type in only your initials.

When you point to a word that AutoCorrect has changed, a small blue box appears under the first letter. When you point to the small blue box, the AutoCorrect Options button appears. The AutoCorrect Options button gives you control over whether you want the text to be corrected. You can change text back to its original spelling, or you can stop AutoCorrect from automatically correcting text. You can also display the AutoCorrect dialog box and change AutoCorrect settings.

As you type text in a placeholder, PowerPoint's AutoFit feature resizes the text, if necessary, to fit into the placeholder. The AutoFit Options button, which appears near your text the first time that it is resized, gives you control over whether you want the text to be resized. The AutoFit Options button displays a menu with options for controlling how the option works. For example, you can stop resizing text for the current placeholder while still maintaining your global AutoFit settings. You can also display the AutoCorrect dialog box and change the AutoFit settings so that text doesn't resize automatically.

Correct text while typing

In this exercise, you add an AutoCorrect entry, use AutoCorrect to fix a misspelled word, and then use AutoFit to resize text in a placeholder.

1 **On the Tools menu, click AutoCorrect Options, and then click the AutoCorrect tab, if necessary.**

The AutoCorrect dialog box appears. Note that PowerPoint has already added a number of commonly mistyped words and their correct equivalents.

2 **Click in the Replace box, and then type vidoe.**

Video is commonly mistyped as *vidoe*.

3 **Press Tab, type video, and then click Add.**

FIGURE 5-11
_____
AutoCorrect dialog box
_____

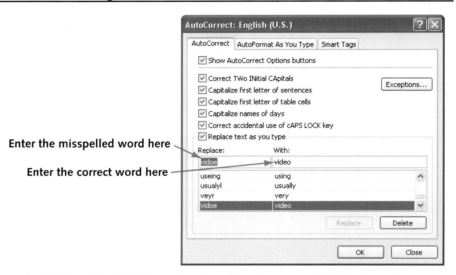

Enter the misspelled word here

Enter the correct word here

Now, whenever you type *vidoe* in any presentation, PowerPoint replaces it with *video*.

4 **Click OK.**

5 **Drag the scroll box to slide 4.**

6 **Click the blank space immediately after the word Outdoor.**

7 **Press Enter, and then type Vidoe.**

Press the Spacebar. The word corrects to *Video*.

8 **Point to the small blue box under the "V" of "Video" to display the AutoCorrect Options button, and then click the AutoCorrect Options down arrow.**

A short menu displays, as shown below, giving AutoCorrect options for the corrected word.

FIGURE 5-12

AutoCorrect options display

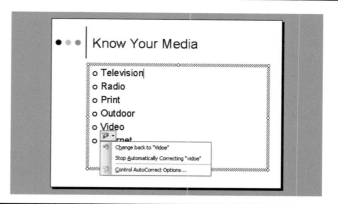

9 Click a blank area of the slide to deselect the AutoCorrect Options menu.

10 Click just to the right of the word "Television" at the top of the bulleted list.

11 Press Enter, and then press Tab.

12 Type Local.

13 Press Enter and then type National.

The text box automatically resizes to fit in the box. The AutoFit Options button appears at the bottom left of the text box.

14 Point to the AutoFit Options button, and then click the AutoFit Options down arrow.

The AutoFit Options menu gives you a number of options for fitting the text into the placeholder or creating a new slide to hold the runover content, as shown in the following illustration.

FIGURE 5-13

AutoFit options display

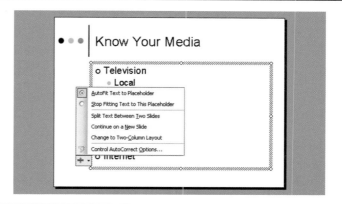

15 Click AutoFit Text To Placeholder if necessary and then click a blank area of the slide to deselect the text box.

PowerPoint reduces the font size to fit the text in the placeholder.

◆ Keep this file open for the next exercise.

QUICK REFERENCE ▼

Add an AutoCorrect entry

1 On the Tools menu, click AutoCorrect Options, and then click the AutoCorrect tab, if necessary.

2 Click the Replace box, and then type a misspelled word.

3 Press Tab, and then type the correctly spelled word.

4 Click Add.

5 Click OK.

Use AutoCorrect to fix a misspelled word

1 Click to position the insertion point where you want to type text.

2 Type the misspelled word.

3 Press the Spacebar or Enter.

Use AutoFit to fit text in a placeholder

1 Click the AutoFit button down arrow when the AutoFit button displays next to a text placeholder.

2 Select an option for fitting text in the current placeholder, changing slide layout, or creating a new slide to hold runover text.

QUICK CHECK

Q: What appears below a word that PowerPoint has AutoCorrected?

A: A blue line that, when clicked, opens the AutoCorrect Options menu appears.

Checking Spelling

THE BOTTOM LINE

Even if you're a good typist, you should always check spelling in a presentation to identify possible errors. Nothing is more amateurish than a presentation with glaring spelling mistakes for all to see.

Checking Spelling and Word Choice

PowerPoint's spelling checker checks the spelling of the entire presentation, including all slides, outlines, notes pages, and handout pages. To help you identify misspelled words or words that PowerPoint's built-in dictionary does not recognize, PowerPoint underlines them with a wavy red line. You have probably noticed this wavy underline under words such as *Contoso* in the current presentation. To turn off this feature, you can clear the Check Spelling As You Type check box on the Spelling and Style tab of the Options dialog box (available on the Tools menu).

PowerPoint includes several built-in dictionaries so you can check presentations that use languages other than English. You can also create custom dictionaries in PowerPoint to check the spelling of unique words, or you can use custom dictionaries from other Microsoft programs. If a word is a foreign language word, you can mark it as such, and PowerPoint won't flag it as a misspelling anymore.

You can correct misspelled words in documents in two ways. You can use the Spelling button on the Standard toolbar (or select Spelling from the Tools menu) to check the entire presentation, or, when you encounter a wavy red line under a word, you can right-click the word and choose the correct spelling from the list on the shortcut menu.

Correct spelling

You have finished entering and formatting text in the presentation. Now you need to check if the text is accurately spelled.

1 **Drag the scroll box to slide 7.**

The words *Je ne sais quois* appear with a wavy red underline, indicating that they are misspelled or not recognized by the dictionary. They aren't recognized because this is a common French phrase.

2 **Select the French phrase "Je ne sais quois" in the word processing box.**

3 **On the Tools menu, click Language.**

The Language dialog box appears.

4 **Scroll down, and then click French (France).**

You are telling PowerPoint that this is a French phrase (French as it is spoken in France, to be precise) that is correct as it stands.

FIGURE 5-14

Language dialog box

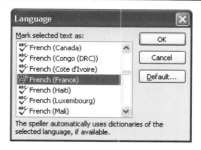

5 **Click OK, and then click to deselect the selected text.**

The dictionary now recognizes the words, though a wavy red line may still appear below *quois*.

6 **Drag the scroll bar to slide 6.**

7 **Right-click the word "Enviromental," and then click Environmental on the shortcut menu.**

PowerPoint corrects the misspelled word.

TIP

The custom dictionary allows you to add words that your dictionary doesn't recognize. Contoso is a proper name that you can add to your custom dictionary.

8 **On the Standard toolbar, click the Spelling button.**

PowerPoint begins checking the spelling in the presentation. The spelling checker stops and selects the proper name *Contoso*.

TROUBLESHOOTING

If you have just installed PowerPoint, the spelling feature may not be installed. PowerPoint may prompt you to install this feature before you can continue.

FIGURE 5-15

Spelling dialog box

Contoso does not appear in your dictionary, but you know it is a proper name that is spelled correctly.

9 **Click Add.**

The custom dictionary adds the word *Contoso* and continues to check the presentation. This word will no longer appear as an error in any presentation, because it has been added to the dictionary. The spelling checker stops on and selects the proper name *Sacksteder*.

TROUBLESHOOTING

Your spelling checker may not stop on the name *Sacksteder* if it has already been added to the custom dictionary.

10 **Click Ignore All if the spelling checker highlights "Sacksteder."**

The spelling checker may stop on *quois*, the French word that is part of the quote in the word processing box.

11 **Click Ignore if the spelling checker highlights "quois."**

The spelling checker ignores the proper name. The spelling checker stops when it fails to recognize the name *Hinsch*.

12 **Click Ignore All.**

The spelling checker now ignores all appearances of the word *Hinsch*. The spelling checker stops and selects the misspelled word *Realtionships*. The correct word spelling, *Relationships*, appears in the Suggestions list.

TIP

Click AutoCorrect in the Spelling dialog box to add the misspelling and the correct spelling of a word to the AutoCorrect table of entries.

13 Click Change to correct the spelling.

The spelling checker continues to check the presentation for misspelled words or words not found in the dictionary. A dialog box appears when PowerPoint completes checking the entire presentation.

14 Click OK, and then drag the scroll box up to slide 1.

◆ Keep this file open for the next exercise.

Mark a word as a foreign language word

1 Select the foreign phrase that you want to mark.

2 On the Tools menu, click Language.

3 Click the foreign language.

4 Click OK.

Correct the spelling of a word

1 Right-click a misspelled word.

2 Click the correct spelling on the shortcut menu.

Check the spelling in a presentation

1 On the Standard toolbar, click the Spelling button. The spelling checker stops when it fails to recognize a word.

2 Click Add to add the word to the dictionary.

Or

Click Ignore All to skip all instances of the word.

Or

Click the suggested spelling, and then click Change to correct the spelling.

3 Click OK.

Using Smart Tags

You have just seen that you can add frequently used proper names to a spelling dictionary to make future presentations easier to check. PowerPoint 2003 offers another feature called *smart tags* that can help you keep track of information such as names, dates and times, addresses, and telephone numbers.

You control smart tags from the AutoCorrect dialog box's Smart Tags tab. Select the Label Text With Smart Tags check box, and then select the kinds of information you want to tag. Click Check Presentation to search for information that can be tagged. Applicable items are underlined on the slides with a purple dotted line. If you point to the smart tag, the Smart Tag Actions button displays, as shown in the illustration below.

FIGURE 5-16

Smart Tag Actions menu

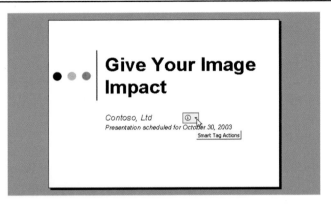

Click the Smart Tag Actions down arrow to display a menu of actions you can perform with the tagged information. For the date smart tag shown in the illustration above, for example, you can select Schedule A Meeting or Show My Calendar to schedule the presentation date in Microsoft Outlook.

Checking Presentation Styles

THE BOTTOM LINE

The presentation style checker helps you identify style and consistency errors in your presentation. This can save you a lot of time in the editing process.

PowerPoint's style checker works with the Office Assistant to help you correct common presentation style design mistakes so that your audience focuses on content and not on visual mistakes. When the Office Assistant is visible, the style checker reviews the presentation for typical mistakes, such as incorrect font size, too many fonts, too many words, inconsistent punctuation, and other readability problems. The style checker then suggests ways to improve the presentation. You can specify the style errors, such as text case or punctuation, that the style checker looks for.

TIP

As part of the style checking process, PowerPoint checks the text case, such as capitalization, of sentences and titles in the presentation, but you can independently change text case for selected text with a command on the Format menu. The Change Case command allows you to change text to sentence case, title case, uppercase, lowercase, or toggle case, which is a mixture of cases.

Check presentation styles

You have completed the spelling check. Now you need to check presentation styles to ensure that your slides are consistent.

1 **On the Tools menu, click Options.**

2 **Click the Spelling And Style tab.**

3 **Select the Check Style check box.**

If PowerPoint prompts you to enable the Office Assistant, click Enable Assistant.

4 **Click Style Options.**

The Style Options dialog box appears.

5 **Select the Body Punctuation check box if necessary to check for consistent body punctuation in the presentation.**

6 **Click the down arrow in the box next to Body Punctuation, and then click Paragraphs Have Consistent Punctuation in the list, if necessary.**

This style option will prompt the Office Assistant to point out paragraphs whose end punctuation differs from that of other paragraphs.

FIGURE 5-17

Style Options dialog box

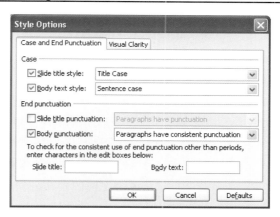

7 **Click OK, and then click OK again.**

The Options dialog box closes.

 8 **Drag the scroll box to slide 5.**

A light bulb appears on slide 5.

TROUBLESHOOTING

If you don't see a light bulb, click Show the Office Assistant on the Help menu.

9 Click the light bulb.

A dialog balloon appears over the Office Assistant, as shown below. The Office Assistant noticed that the second bulleted item does not have a period at the end of the sentence. The default style for main text is to have a period at the end of each bulleted item.

FIGURE 5-18

Office Assistant suggests changes

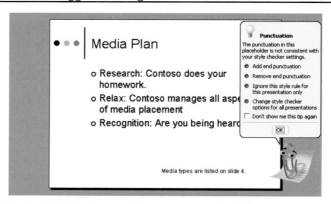

TIP

If you make a decision on a tip and then change your mind, you may need to display the tip again. To do this, you need to reset your tips so that the Office Assistant will display all of them again. To reset your tips, right-click the Office Assistant, click Options, click Reset My Tips, and then click OK.

10 Click the Add End Punctuation option.

PowerPoint adds a period at the end of the second bullet. The dialog balloon disappears.

11 Click the Next Slide button twice to scroll to slide 7.

12 Click the light bulb on slide 7.

The Office Assistant displays the same dialog balloon as before. The bulleted text items in this slide are not sentences, so they do not need end punctuation.

13 Click OK in the Office Assistant dialog balloon.

The Office Assistant closes.

14 To hide the Office Assistant, if necessary, right-click the Office Assistant, and then click Hide on the shortcut menu.

◆ Keep this file open for the next exercise.

QUICK REFERENCE ▼

Set style options

1 On the Tools menu, click Options.

2 Click the Spelling And Style tab.

3 Select the Check Style check box.

4 Click Style Options.

5 Select the style options that you want to set.

6 Click OK, and then click OK again.

QUICK CHECK

Q: What does a light bulb signify on a slide?

A: **The light bulb signifies that the Office Assistant has identified a style error.**

Check the style of a presentation

1 On the Help menu, click Show The Office Assistant if necessary.

2 Click the light bulb.

3 Click the option that you want from the list.

4 Click OK in the Office Assistant's dialog balloon.

5 On the Help menu, click Hide The Office Assistant.

Using the Research Task Pane

Checking Spelling and Word Choice

THE BOTTOM LINE

The Research task pane gives you access to a number of reference tools that you would otherwise have to have on hand to check facts, spelling, and word choice as you work.

As part of the process of entering and working with text, you need to make sure you're using correct information and words that exactly convey the meaning you intend. In the past, you might have turned to reference books on your bookshelf to locate the information you need. In PowerPoint 2003, you can use the Research task pane to open a reference and find information without leaving the program.

The Research task pane gives you access to a number of research sites such as encyclopedias, a thesaurus, a translation feature, and specialized search sites. Enter a word or phrase you want to research and choose the desired reference tool from the drop-down list. After the search is complete, information displays in the task pane.

PowerPoint's online Thesaurus works much the same way as a hard-bound thesaurus. It displays a list of synonyms for your selected word. If you don't find exactly the word you want, you can click one of the synonyms to display synonyms for that word.

CHECK THIS OUT ▼

Translate a Word
You can use the Research task pane's translation feature to translate a word from one language to another. This is a good way to check foreign language words or phrases you want to add to your presentation or add "local color" to a presentation. You need to have the desired languages installed before the translation feature will work.

Use the Thesaurus to replace a word

For your final action in fine-tuning the presentation, you will find a better word for one currently in the presentation.

1 **Go to slide 5 and select the word "homework" in the first bullet item.**

2 **On the Standard toolbar, click the Research button.**

The Research task pane opens and displays the word *homework* in the Search For box.

ANOTHER METHOD

On the Tools menu, click Research.

3 **Click the All Reference Books down arrow, and then click Thesaurus: English (U.S.).**

The task pane displays a list of synonyms for *homework*, as shown in the illustration below.

FIGURE 5-19

Synonyms display in the Research task pane

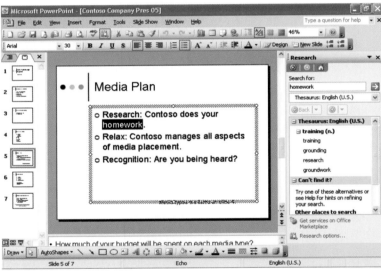

4 **Point to the last synonym in the upper part of the task pane, groundwork.**

A down arrow appears at the right of the word.

5 **Click the down arrow and click Insert.**

The word *homework* is replaced by the word *groundwork*.

6 **Click the Close button to close the Research task pane.**

QUICK REFERENCE ▼

Use the Thesaurus

1 Select the word you want to find a replacement for.

2 On the Standard toolbar, click the Research button.

3 Click the All Reference Books down arrow and select Thesaurus: English (U.S.).

4 Point to a word you want to use as a replacement to display the down arrow.

5 Click the down arrow and click Insert.

◆ If you are continuing to other lessons, save the Contoso Company Pres 05 presentation with the current name and then close it. If you are not continuing to other lessons, save and close the Contoso Company Pres 05 presentation, and then click the Close button in the title bar of the PowerPoint window.

Key Points

- ✓ Click in an object to display the slanted-line selection box that allows you to edit content within the box. Click the outside border to display the dotted selection box that allows you to manipulate the object as a whole.
- ✓ You can add text objects to slides either as text labels (a single line of text) or as word processing boxes (word-wrapped text).
- ✓ Any text object can be modified to change word wrap options or adjust the size of the placeholder to fit the text.
- ✓ Change text formatting by removing bullets, applying numbers, using text styles such as bold and italic, and changing text color, font style, or font size.
- ✓ Modify the position of text in a placeholder by changing alignment or adjusting paragraph spacing and spacing before and after lines.
- ✓ You can move a text object anywhere on a slide by simply dragging and dropping it at its new location to improve the slide appearance or usefulness.
- ✓ Use the Find and Replace commands to locate and change text quickly throughout a presentation. The Replace Fonts command lets you replace one font with another on all slides.
- ✓ AutoCorrect makes many corrections as you type. You can add words to the AutoCorrect list that you commonly mistype. AutoFit helps you adjust text in placeholders when you have too many lines to fit on the slide.
- ✓ You can correct the spelling of any word underlined with a wavy red underline by right-clicking and choosing the correct word. Use the spelling checker to move from slide to slide to identify and correct errors.
- ✓ The style checker lets you specify a number of style options to check for throughout the presentation. The Office Assistant appears to suggest style changes.
- ✓ Use the Research task pane to look up words or find information without having to leave the PowerPoint window.

Quick Quiz

True/False

T F **1.** To deselect an object, click in the middle of the object.

T F **2.** You should format a series of paragraphs explaining how to get from point A to point B with numbers rather than bullets.

T F **3.** If you used the Find Whole Words Only option in the Replace dialog box when searching for the word *cat*, PowerPoint would find both *cat* and *catastrophe*.

T F **4.** You could use AutoCorrect to insert your company name when you type its initials.

T F **5.** A wavy red line doesn't necessarily mean a word is misspelled.

Multiple Choice

1. To adjust the size of the default title text object, you would click _____ on the Format menu.
   a. Text Box
   b. Placeholder
   c. AutoShape
   d. Title

2. What is one text alignment option that you would probably not use for a slide title?
   a. Align Left
   b. Center
   c. Align Right
   d. Justify

3. To copy a text object, drag the object while holding down _____.
   a. Ctrl
   b. Alt
   c. Shift
   d. Ctrl + Alt

4. The style checker uses the _____ to offer suggested changes.
   a.. Presentation Assistant
   b. Office Checker
   c. Style Editor
   d. Office Assistant

5. The Research task pane gives you access to _____.
   a. an encyclopedia
   b. a thesaurus
   c. specialized search sites
   d. all of the above

Short Answer

1. How do you create a 2-inch word processing box that will word wrap?
2. How do you remove numbering from a list and insert bullets instead?
3. How do you change font color?
4. How do you adjust the line spacing of several paragraphs to 1.3 lines?
5. How do you find and replace a particular word?
6. How do you specify another language for a word or phrase to prevent the spelling checker from showing it as an error?

On Your Own

Exercise 1

Open the Contoso Company Pres 05 in the Lesson05 folder that is located in the PowerPoint Practice folder. Display slide 3 in Normal view, and then make the following changes:

- Add a text box with the text Create an image with impact!
- Change the formatting of the text to Impact font, 36-point size, italic style, and red color.
- Move the text box to the bottom center of the slide.

Save and close the presentation.

Exercise 2

Open the Contoso Company Pres 05 in the Lesson05 folder that is located in the PowerPoint Practice folder. Display slide 4, and then make the following changes:

- Add a text box with the text Create impact with the rigth media.
- Correct the spelling of the word *right* by using the wavy red underline.
- Add a trademark symbol to the end of the text *Create impact with the right media* using the AutoCorrect replacement (tm).

Save and close the presentation.

One Step Further

Exercise 1

Open the Holidays 04 presentation from the Lesson04 folder that is located in the PowerPoint Practice folder. Save it as Holidays 05 in the Lesson05 folder. Check the spelling of the entire presentation. On slide 3, add two new holidays after New Year's Day: Martin Luther King Day and Presidents Day. Solve the AutoFit problem by changing to a two-column format. Move half the holidays into the second text placeholder. Increase paragraph spacing to 1.2 lines for both placeholders. Save and close the presentation.

Exercise 2

Open the Holidays 05 presentation. Change the alignment of the subtitle on slide 1. (If the alignment is currently centered, right-align the subtitle, for example.) Replace one of the fonts in the presentation with another you like better. Change the color of the slide titles (except on slide 1) to another in the same group of colors offered by the design template. Save and close the presentation.

Exercise 3

Open Holidays 05. Add a new slide following slide 1 with the title Contents. (Format the title to match the other titles in the presentation.) Type the following paragraph text:

Holidays
Personal Time

Change the bulleted list to a numbered list. Replace the word *salary* with the word *wages* in all instances except the reference to *jury salary*. Use PowerPoint's thesaurus to find another word or phrase to use in place of *negotiable* on slide 10. Check presentation styles on each slide of the presentation and use your own judgment on how to solve any style problems. Save and close the presentation.

6

Applying and Modifying Design Templates

After completing this lesson, you will be able to:

✔ *Understand and apply design templates.*
✔ *Understand PowerPoint masters.*
✔ *Modify master placeholders.*
✔ *Format master text.*
✔ *Format bullets.*
✔ *Adjust master text indents.*
✔ *Reapply a slide layout.*
✔ *Hide background objects.*
✔ *Save a presentation as a template.*

KEY TERMS

- hanging indent
- indent markers
- margin marker
- masters
- Slide Master
- design template
- Title Master

A **design template** is a presentation file that has a predefined set of color and text characteristics. You can create a presentation from a template, or you can apply a template to an existing presentation. When you apply a template to a presentation, the slides in the presentation take on the characteristics of the template, so you can maintain a uniform design throughout the presentation. PowerPoint uses masters that control the look of the individual parts of the presentation, including formatting, color, graphics, and text placement. Every presentation has a set of masters, one for each view.

As the vice president of sales for the public relations firm Contoso, Ltd, you have been working on a general presentation that can be customized for new clients. After adding and modifying the text in the previous lesson, you are ready to concentrate on the presentation's design.

In this lesson, you will learn how to apply a PowerPoint template, view and switch to various masters, modify and format the master text, reapply a layout from the master, hide the master layout, and save a presentation as a template.

◆ Before you can use the practice files in this lesson, you must install them from the book's companion CD to their default location. See "Using the CD-ROM" at the beginning of this book for more information. To complete the procedures in this lesson, you will need to use files named 06 PPT Lesson and 06 PPT Template in the Lesson06 folder in the PowerPoint Practice folder located on your hard disk.

Understanding and Applying Design Templates

Switching the Design Template

THE BOTTOM LINE

Apply a design template at any time to all or selected slides to give them a consistent, professionally designed appearance that will improve the look of a presentation. To make sure your presentation conveys just the right tone, try out several templates until you find the right one.

PowerPoint comes with a wide variety of professionally designed templates that can help you achieve the look you want. When you apply a template to a presentation, PowerPoint copies the information from each master in the template to the corresponding masters in the presentation. All slides in a presentation will then acquire the look of the template.

You can use one of the many templates that come with PowerPoint, or you can create your own from existing presentations. (You will create a template later in this lesson.) Moreover, you can apply different templates throughout the development process until you find the look you like best. To apply a template to an existing presentation, open the presentation and then use the Slide Design task pane to locate and select the template you want. You can apply a template to all slides in the presentation or to slides you select in the Slides tab.

Apply a design template to an existing presentation

In this exercise, you apply a new design template to the Contoso presentation you have been working with.

◆ Start PowerPoint, if necessary, click the Open button on the Standard toolbar, navigate to the Lesson06 folder in the PowerPoint Practice folder, and then open the 06 PPT Lesson file. Save the file as Contoso Company Pres 06 in the same folder.

1 On the Formatting toolbar, click the Slide Design button.

Design

The Slide Design task pane opens. You won't use one of PowerPoint's design templates; you will use a design template created especially for Contoso presentations. To locate this presentation, you use the Slide Design task pane's Browse option.

ANOTHER METHOD

- On the Format menu, click Slide Design.
- Right-click a blank area of the slide, and then click Slide Design in the shortcut menu.

2 At the bottom of the Slide Design task pane, click Browse.

The Apply Design Template dialog box appears.

3 Navigate to the PowerPoint Practice folder, and then double-click the Lesson06 folder.

4 In the list of file and folder names, click 06 PPT Template.

FIGURE 6-1

Apply Design Template dialog box

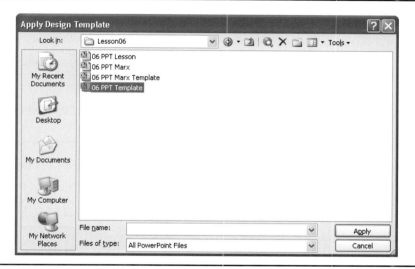

5 Click Apply.

PowerPoint applies, or copies, the information from the template file 06 PPT Template to the masters in the presentation. The text style and format, slide colors, and background objects change to match the template. Your content remains the same.

Your presentation window should look like the following illustration.

FIGURE 6-2

New slide design in place

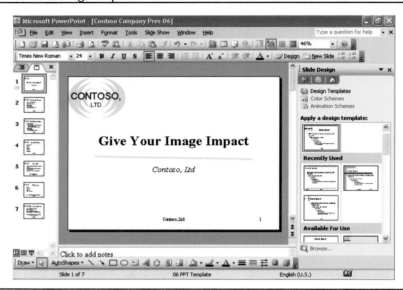

6 In the Slide Design task pane, click the Close button to close the task pane.

◆ Keep this file open for the next exercise.

QUICK REFERENCE ▼

Apply a design template

1 On the Formatting toolbar, click Slide Design.

2 In the Slide Design task pane, click a design template or click Browse.

3 Navigate to the folder that contains the template you want to apply.

4 In the list of file and folder names, click a template.

5 Click Apply.

Understanding PowerPoint Masters

Viewing and Changing Master Slides

THE BOTTOM LINE

PowerPoint's masters control the formats and layout of objects on slides. To make global changes to a presentation's formats quickly and easily, make them on the master slides.

PowerPoint comes with two special slides called **masters**—Slide Master and Title Master. The Slide Master and Title Master for a template are called a slide-title master pair. You can create more than one Slide Master or Title Master within a presentation. This is useful for creating separate sections within the same presentation. To create multiple masters in a presentation, you can insert a new Slide Master and Title Master into a presentation or apply more than one template to your presentation.

> **TIP**
>
> You can allow or prevent multiple masters in a presentation. On the Tools menu, click Options, and then click the Edit tab. Under Disable New Features, clear the Multiple Masters check box to allow multiple design templates to be applied or select the Multiple Masters check box to restrict design templates to one per presentation.

The **Slide Master** controls the properties of every slide in the presentation. All of the characteristics of the Slide Master (background color, text color, font, and font size) appear on every slide in the presentation. When you make a change on the Slide Master, the change affects every slide. For example, if you want to include your company logo, other artwork, or the date on every slide, you can place it on the Slide Master. The Slide Master contains master placeholders for title text, paragraph text, date and time, footer information, and slide numbers. The master title and text placeholders control the text format for every slide in a presentation. If you want to make a change throughout your presentation, you need to change each slide master or pair of masters. For instance, when you change the master title text format to italic, the title on each slide changes to italic to follow the master. If, for a particular slide, you want to override the default settings on the Slide Master, you can use commands on the Format menu. For example, if you want to omit background graphics on a slide, you can use that option in the Background dialog box for the selected slide.

The title slide has its own master, called the **Title Master**. Changes you make to the Title Master affect only slides that have the Title Slide layout. Like the Slide Master, the Title Master contains placeholders. The main difference between the Slide Master and the Title Master is the Title Master's use of a master subtitle style instead of the master text style.

The Slide Master and Title Master appear together in Slide Master view. You can select either master as a slide miniature in Slide Master view to make changes to it. When you view a master, the Slide Master View toolbar appears. This toolbar contains the Close Master View button, which returns you to the view you were in before you opened the master. The Slide Master View toolbar also contains several buttons to insert, delete, rename, duplicate, and preserve masters. When you preserve a master, you protect it from being deleted.

Work with slide masters

In this exercise, you view the Slide Master and the Title Master, switch between them, preserve the original masters, and insert a second slide master and title master.

1 **Display slide 1 if necessary.**

2 **On the View menu, point to Master, and then click Slide Master.**

The Title Master appears along with the Slide Master View toolbar. Slide miniatures of the Title Master and Slide Master appear in the Slides pane on the left side of the presentation window. Your screen should look similar to the following illustration.

FIGURE 6-3

Title Master slide

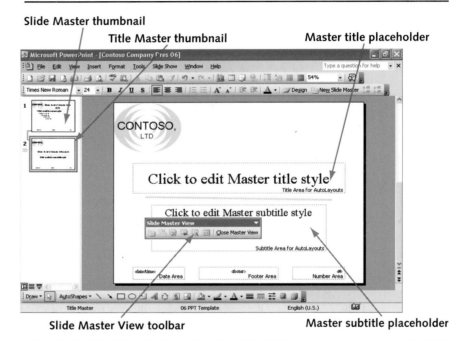

Slide Master thumbnail

Title Master thumbnail

Master title placeholder

Slide Master View toolbar

Master subtitle placeholder

TROUBLESHOOTING

The Title Master displays because you issued the Slide Master command with a title slide selected in Normal view. PowerPoint displays the Title Master or Slide Master according to what kind of slide is selected in Normal view.

3 **In the Slides pane at the left side of the presentation window, click slide 1.**

The Slide Master slide appears, as shown in the following illustration.

FIGURE 6-4

Slide Master slide

Master text placeholder   Master title placeholder

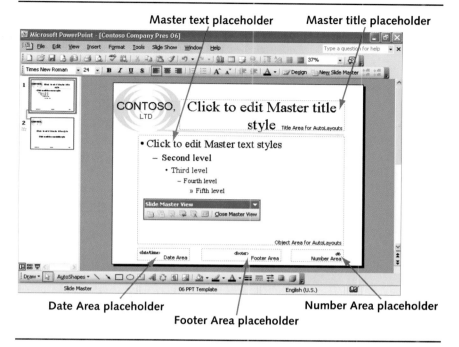

Date Area placeholder   Number Area placeholder

Footer Area placeholder

 4 On the Slide Master View toolbar, click the Preserve Master button.

A gray thumbtack appears next to both slide masters in the Slides pane, protecting them from being deleted or changed by PowerPoint.

ANOTHER METHOD

On the Edit menu, click Preserve Master.

 5 On the Slide Master View toolbar, click the Insert New Slide Master button.

Slide 3 appears below slide 2 with a blank slide design.

ANOTHER METHOD

- Press Ctrl + M.
- On the Insert menu, click New Slide Master.

 6 On the Slide Master View toolbar, click the Insert New Title Master button.

Slide 4 appears below slide 3 with a blank title slide design, and the slide-title master pair is connected together. Notice that the new pair is also preserved from changes or deletion. You need to turn off this protection because you are going to change the new master pair.

 7 On the Slide Master View toolbar, click the Preserve Master button again to allow the new masters to be changed.

An alert message appears, asking if you want to delete these masters since they are currently not used on any slides.

8 **Click No.**

The gray thumbtack next to both new slide masters disappears, and the masters are no longer protected from being deleted or changed.

9 **On the Formatting toolbar, click the Slide Design button to open the Slide Design task pane.**

10 **In the Slide Design task pane, under Apply A Design Template, scroll down to the Clouds design, and then click the design template.**

The new slide masters appear with the Clouds design. Notice that the design is applied automatically only to the new masters because the other masters are protected from change.

FIGURE 6-5

Clouds design applied to the slide master

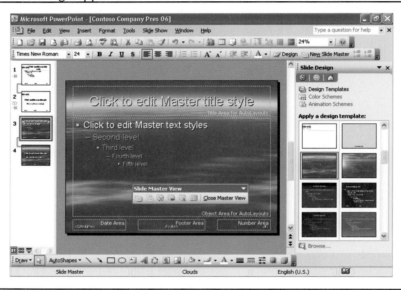

TROUBLESHOOTING

If the Clouds design is not available, scroll to the bottom of the design templates in the Slide Design task pane, and then click Additional Design Templates to install the rest of the PowerPoint design templates.

11 **In the Slide Design task pane, click the Close button to close the task pane.**

◆ **Keep this file open for the next exercise.**

QUICK REFERENCE ▼

View the Title Master and Slide Master

1 On the View menu, point to Master, and then click Slide Master.

2 Click the slide miniature of the Title Master or Slide Master.

Insert another slide or title master

- On the Slide Master View toolbar, click the Insert New Slide Master button.
- On the Slide Master View toolbar, click the Insert New Title Master button.

PowerPoint also comes with a Handout Master and a Notes Master, in which you can add information and data that affect how handouts and notes pages display. You can choose, for example, how many slides to display in the handouts or notes pages and modify the formats and layout of header and footer information.

View the Handout and Notes Masters

Now that you have become somewhat familiar with the Slide and Title Masters, you will switch to Handout Master and Notes Master and view the way information appears on these masters.

1 On the View menu, point to Master, and then click Handout Master.

The Handout Master and Handout Master View toolbar appear.

2 On the Handout Master View toolbar, click the Show Positioning Of 3-Per-Page Handouts button.

The master changes to show three handouts per page.

> **TIP**
>
> Using the Handout Master View toolbar, you can show the positioning of one, two, three, four, six, or nine slides per page.

3 On the View menu, point to Master, and then click Notes Master.

The Notes Master appears, along with the Notes Master View toolbar, showing the slide and speaker note text positioning for the notes pages.

4 On the Notes Master View toolbar, click Close Master View.

PowerPoint returns you to the first slide in the presentation in Normal view.

> **ANOTHER METHOD**
>
> You can also exit a master view and switch back to Normal view by clicking the Normal View button.

5 In the Slide pane, drag the scroll box to slide 7.

To set this slide off from the others in the presentation, you will apply the design template you already applied to the second set of masters in the presentation.

Design
6 On the Formatting toolbar, click the Slide Design button to display the Slide Design task pane.

7 **In the Slide Design task pane, under Used In This Presentation, point to the Clouds design scheme, click the down arrow on the scheme, and then click Apply To Selected Slides.**

PowerPoint applies the Clouds design to slide 7 only. The Clouds design template is listed in the Used In This Presentation section because it has been applied to one set of masters in the presentation.

8 **In the Slide Design task pane, click the Close button to close the task pane.**

◆ **Keep this file open for the next exercise.**

QUICK REFERENCE ▼

View and close Handout Master

1 On the View menu, point to Master, and then click Handout Master.

2 Change the handouts-per-page option if necessary.

3 On the Handout Master View toolbar, click Close Master View.

View and close Notes Master

1 On the View menu, point to Master, and then click Notes Master.

2 On the Notes Master View toolbar, click Close Master View.

Modifying Master Placeholders

THE BOTTOM LINE
You can change the position and formatting of master placeholders to customize the slides in your presentation. Changes you make on the masters affect all slides in the presentation.

Viewing and Changing Master Slides

Each design template specifies how placeholders will appear on the Title and Slide Masters, but you can adjust the default placeholders to suit your needs. You can modify and arrange placeholders on all of the master views for the date and time, footers, and slide numbers, all of which appear on the Slide Master in the default position. You can also customize the position of the title and text placeholders. You can delete the date, footer, or number placeholder from a master.

You can move placeholders anywhere on a slide, but keep in mind that text areas should be clearly defined so the audience will not be confused by the layout of information. It might not be very attractive, for example, to move the footer to the top left of a slide, where it would compete with the slide title for attention.

Modify master placeholders

In this exercise, you edit the master placeholders on the Slide Master.

1 **Display slide 2.**

2 **On the View menu, point to Master, and then click Slide Master.**

The Slide Master view appears.

3 **Click the border of the Date Area placeholder in the bottom-left corner.**

Be sure that you click the placeholder border so that the dotted selection box appears. If the slanted-line selection box appears, click the edge of it.

4 **Press Delete.**

TIP

If you delete a placeholder by mistake, you can click Master Layout on the Slide Master View toolbar, click the appropriate placeholder check box, and then click OK to reapply the placeholder, or you can click the Undo button.

5 **Select the border of the Footer Area placeholder with the dotted selection box.**

6 **Hold down Shift, and then drag the Footer Area placeholder to the left until the edge of the placeholder aligns with the edge of the master text placeholder.**

Holding down Shift while you drag a PowerPoint object constrains the movement of the object horizontally or vertically. That is, the object stays in the same plane. In this case, the footer remains aligned with the Number Area placeholder.

TIP

For more information on moving objects, see Lesson 8, "Drawing and Modifying Objects."

7 **Click a blank area of the slide to deselect the placeholder.**

Your slide master should look like the following illustration.

FIGURE 6-6

Placeholders have been modified

◆ **Keep this file open for the next exercise.**

QUICK REFERENCE ▼

Move master placeholders

1 On the View menu, point to Master, and then click Slide Master.

2 Select with the dotted selection box any placeholders that you want to move.

3 Drag the placeholders to the location where you want the placeholders to go.

4 Click a blank area of the slide to deselect the placeholder.

Formatting Master Text

THE BOTTOM LINE

Formatting placeholders in the slide masters ensures consistency throughout a presentation. This is also a faster way to change formats than to change them on each slide.

Formatting Text and Bullets Throughout a Presentation

Formatting the placeholders in Slide Master view provides consistency to a presentation. For example, changing the title text in the Slide Master to 48 point Times New Roman maroon will format all slide titles in the presentation with this font, size, and color. Making the change once in the Slide Master is both easier and faster than making it on each slide, and also eliminates the possibility of errors that might arise from many manual changes.

The master placeholders for the title, bulleted text, date and time, slide number, and footer determine the style and position of those objects. To format master text, you first select the text placeholder and then alter the format to look the way you want. To format bulleted text, you must place the insertion point in the line of the bulleted text you want to change.

Format master text

You are ready to make some changes to the master formats for your presentation. In this exercise, you format the master text in the Footer Area and Number Area placeholders.

1 Click the Footer Area placeholder, hold down Shift, and then click the Number Area placeholder to select both objects.

18 ▾

2 On the Formatting toolbar, click the Font Size down arrow, and then click 20.

3 Hold down Shift, and then click the Footer Area placeholder.

The Footer Area placeholder is deselected, but the Number Area placeholder stays selected so you can continue to work with it.

B

4 On the Formatting toolbar, click the Bold button.

The Number Area placeholder becomes bold.

ANOTHER METHOD

Press Ctrl + B.

5 Click a blank area outside the Number Area placeholder to deselect it.

To improve alignment on the slide, you will now change text alignment in the footer area to left alignment.

6 Click the Footer Area placeholder to select it. On the Formatting toolbar, click the Align Left button.

ANOTHER METHOD

- Press Ctrl + L.
- On the Format menu, point to Alignment, and then click Align Left.

7 In the master text placeholder, position the I-beam pointer to the right of the text "Second Level," and then click.

The Second Level text is selected.

I

8 On the Formatting toolbar, click the Italic button.

The Second Level text changes to italic.

ANOTHER METHOD

Press Ctrl + I.

9 Click a blank area outside the master text placeholder to deselect it.

Your Slide Master should look like the following illustration.

FIGURE 6-7

Formatting changes made to Slide Master

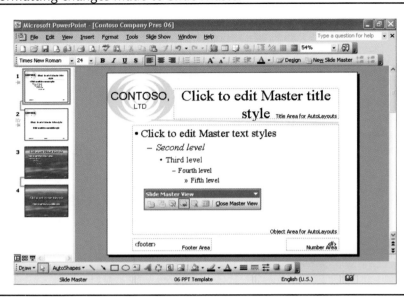

TIP

The changes made to the Contoso master in this exercise apply only to slides that use this master. Changes are not made to slide 7, which is linked to a different master. You can quickly determine which slides use a master by hovering the mouse pointer over a master thumbnail to see a ScreenTip listing the slides that use that master.

◆ **Keep this file open for the next exercise.**

QUICK REFERENCE ▼

Format master text attributes

1 On the View menu, point to Master, and then click Slide Master.

2 Select the master text placeholders that you want to format.

3 On the Formatting toolbar, click a formatting button (such as Bold, Italic, Underline, Shadow, or Font Color).

4 Click a blank area outside the master text placeholder to deselect it.

QUICK CHECK

Q: How do you select more than one object at a time?

A: **Click an object, hold down Shift, and click additional objects.**

Formatting Bullets

Formatting Text and Bullets
Throughout a Presentation

THE BOTTOM LINE

Change bullet formats to customize a presentation. You can use different bullet symbols or insert picture bullets for a special graphical look on the slides.

In addition to formatting text, you can customize the bullets in a presentation for individual paragraphs or entire objects. You can replace a bullet with a different font and color, a picture, or a number. As for text, making these changes on the Slide Master ensures that the same new bullets will display on all slides in the presentation.

The Slide Master provides five levels of bullets for slides. Each design template provides bullet characters for all five levels, and you can change bullet characters for as many levels as you need. In practice, you will probably not need more than two or perhaps three levels of bullets, because using too many levels of bullets may crowd text on a slide and make it difficult to read.

The current font supplies some standard characters that are often used for bullets, such as solid round dots, but you can find many more choices in fonts that are composed solely of symbols, such as Symbol, Windings, and Webdings. After you select a bullet character, you can change its size and color to further customize the look of bulleted text.

Change a bullet character on the Slide Master

To customize your design template, you will change the bullet character for first-level bullets.

1 **On the Slide Master, click the first line of text titled "Click To Edit Master Text Styles" in the master text placeholder.**

The text is selected.

2 **On the Format menu, click Bullets And Numbering.**

The Bullets and Numbering dialog box appears with the current bullet symbol selected.

ANOTHER METHOD

Right-click on a text level in the Slide Master, and then click Bullets And Numbering from the shortcut menu.

3 **Click Customize.**

The Symbol dialog box opens.

4 **Click the Font down arrow, scroll down, and then click Wingdings.**

The display changes to show the symbols available in this font.

5 Click the diamond bullet, as shown in the following illustration.

FIGURE 6-8

Symbol dialog box

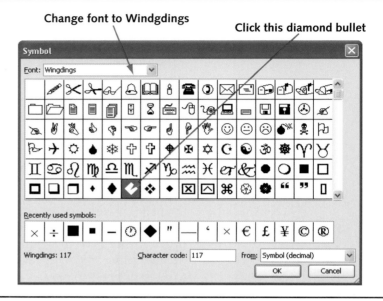

Change font to Windgdings

Click this diamond bullet

> **TIP**
>
> The Recently Used Symbols pane in the Symbol dialog box makes it easy for you to quickly select symbols you have used recently.

6 Click OK to return to the Bullets And Numbering dialog box.

Now that you have selected a symbol, you can customize it further by changing its color and size.

7 Click the Color down arrow, and then click the purple color.

8 Click the Size down arrow until 85 appears.

The new bullet size is reduced by 15 percent on the slide. This size will not overwhelm the text or draw too much attention.

9 Click OK.

The purple diamond bullet appears in the first line of text.

◆ Keep this file open for the next exercise.

QUICK REFERENCE ▼

Format master bullets

1 On the View menu, point to Master, and then click Slide Master.

2 Click the bulleted line of text in the master text placeholder that you want to format.

3 On the Format menu, click Bullets And Numbering.

4 Click Customize.

5 Click the Font down arrow and select a font.

6 Click a bullet and then click OK.

7 Click the Color down arrow, and then click a color.

8 Click the Size down arrow, and then click a size.

9 Click OK.

Besides selecting a new bullet character, you can spice up your slides by inserting picture bullets. Picture bullets are graphics that can be used as bullet symbols. A computer that has Microsoft Office installed offers a good variety of pictures that can be used as bullets.

To insert a picture bullet, take the same steps to open the Bullets And Numbering dialog box and then click the Picture button. The Picture Bullet dialog box appears, displaying pictures you can choose among. You can also search this dialog box if you know the name of a specific picture you want to use.

Insert a picture bullet in the Slide Master

You have changed the bullet character for the first-level bullet. For added interest on your slides, you will insert a picture bullet for the second-level bullet items.

1 Right-click the second line of text titled "Second Level" in the master text placeholder.

PowerPoint selects the text, and a shortcut menu appears.

2 Click Bullets and Numbering on the shortcut menu.

The Bullets And Numbering dialog box opens.

3 Click Picture.

The Picture Bullet dialog box opens. This dialog box is part of the Clip Organizer. It contains pictures you can use as bullets.

4 Click the down scroll arrow until a light blue diamond appears.

Figure 6-9 shows the bullet you should select. If you don't have this bullet, try to find a similar one.

CHECK THIS OUT ▼

Import a Picture for Bullets
You can use any picture as a picture bullet, including scanned images or photographs. For example, you might want to use a company logo or a graphic you have created yourself in an illustration program. Click the Import button in the Picture Bullet dialog box and navigate to the location where you have stored a picture, or view pictures in the Microsoft Clip Organizer. After you have imported the picture, you can resize it, but you can't change its color. Importing pictures for bullets can give your presentation a very special look.

FIGURE 6-9

Picture Bullet dialog box

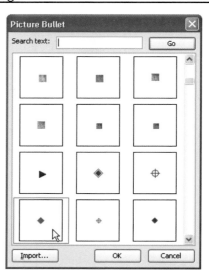

5 **Click the light blue diamond, and then click OK to insert the bullet on the slide.**

6 **Click the Normal View button, and then click the Next Slide button until slide 3 displays.**

The new bullets appear on slide 3, as shown in the following illustration.

FIGURE 6-10

New bullets display in the slide

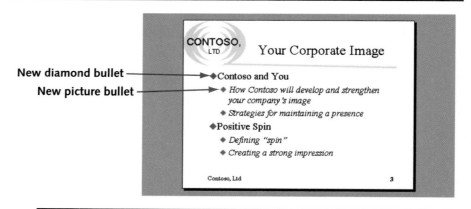

Keep this file open for the next exercise.

QUICK REFERENCE ▼

Format master bullets using a picture

1 On the View menu, point to Master, and then click Slide Master.

2 Click the bulleted line of text in the master text placeholder that you want to format.

Formatting Text and Bullets Throughout a Presentation

3 On the Format menu, click Bullets And Numbering.

4 Click Picture.

5 Click the down scroll arrow until you locate the bullet you want to use, and then click the bullet.

6 Click OK, and then click OK again.

Adjusting Master Text Indents

THE BOTTOM LINE

Change indents to adjust the position of text on a line or adjust space between a bullet character and text. Adjusting indents can make text more readable or give a different look to slides.

PowerPoint uses indent markers to control the distance between bullets and text. Indents can also control the distance between a bullet and the left edge of the placeholder. Adjusting indents in PowerPoint works the same way it does in Microsoft Word.

To change the distance between a bullet and its corresponding text, you first display the ruler, which shows the current bullet and text placement, and then adjust indent markers on the ruler. The indent markers on the ruler control the indent levels of the master text object. Each indent level consists of two triangles, called **indent markers**, and a small box, called a **margin marker**. The upper indent marker controls the first line of the paragraph. The lower indent marker controls the left edge of the paragraph.

Each indent level is set so that the first line extends to the left of the paragraph, with the rest of the paragraph "hanging" below it. This indent setting is called a **hanging indent**. To adjust an indent marker, you move the triangle on the ruler to a new position. You can move the entire level—the bullet and text—by using the margin marker.

Adjust master text indents

In this exercise, you display the ruler, adjust indent markers, and change the margin level.

1 On the View menu, point to Master, and then click Slide Master.

The Slide Master appears.

2 Click the master text placeholder titled "Click To Edit Master Title Style."

3 On the View menu, click Ruler.

Your presentation window should look like the following illustration. If the ruler doesn't match the illustration, make sure you have clicked the title placeholder.

ANOTHER METHOD

Right-click a blank area of the Slide Master, and then click Ruler on the shortcut menu.

FIGURE 6-11

Indent markers on ruler

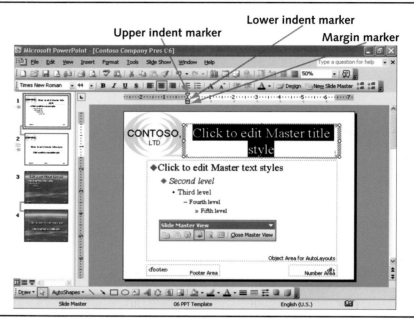

4 **Click the line of text titled "Click To Edit Master Title Style" in the master text placeholder.**

The ruler adds indent markers for each level of text represented in the bulleted list. Five pairs of indent markers appear—upper and lower.

5 **Drag the indent marker of the first indent level to the right so that it is even with the lower indent marker, as shown in the following illustration.**

FIGURE 6-12

Adjust the first indent level

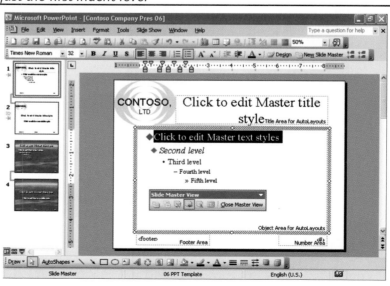

When you release the mouse button, the text for the first indent level moves to the right.

6 Slowly drag the margin marker of the first indent level to the left margin of the ruler.

The bullet, text, and indent markers move to the left margin. Moving the first margin marker repositions the left margin of the master text object.

IMPORTANT

If you drag an indent level or margin marker into another indent level, the first indent level (or marker) pushes the second indent level until you release the mouse button. To move an indent marker back to its original position, drag the indent level's margin marker, or click the Undo button.

TIP

If the indent markers are not aligned over one another, drag one of the markers back to the other. Also, depending on the size of your monitor, indent changes may be subtle and hard to detect.

7 Drag the lower indent marker of the first indent level to the 0.5 inch mark on the ruler.

The first indent level of the ruler is formatted again as a hanging indent. Your presentation window should look like the following illustration.

FIGURE 6-13

Move the lower indent marker

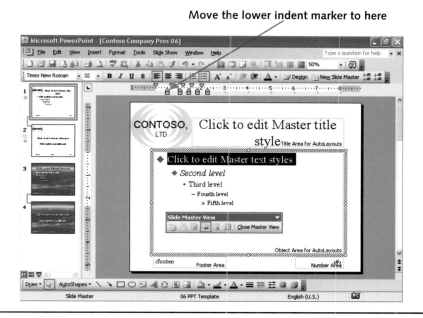

Move the lower indent marker to here

8 Right-click a blank area of the Slide Master, and then click Ruler.

The ruler closes.

9 **Click the Normal View button.**

PowerPoint returns you to slide 3. Notice there is now more space between the first-level bullets and paragraph text.

◆ **Keep this file open for the next exercise.**

Display the ruler

- On the View menu, click Ruler.
- Right-click a blank area of a slide, and then click Ruler.

Adjust indent markers

1 Click to position the insertion point in the text for which you want to adjust indent markers.

2 Display the ruler.

3 Drag the indent markers to adjust.

Adjust the margin level

1 Click to position the insertion point in the text for which you want to adjust the margin marker.

2 Display the ruler.

3 Slowly drag the margin marker of the first indent level to the measurement you want on the ruler.

QUICK CHECK

Q: What does the top, downward-pointing indent marker control?

A: **The top downward-pointing marker controls the first line of the paragraph.**

Reapplying a Slide Layout

Creating Slides and Revising Their Layouts

THE BOTTOM LINE

After you have customized a slide, you can revert to the original slide layout if desired to restore consistency among slides in a presentation.

If you make changes to the layout of a slide but then decide you would rather use the original slide layout, you can reapply the slide layout to that slide using the Slide Layout task pane. You can also change the current layout of a slide by selecting a new layout from the Slide Layout task pane.

Reapply a layout to a slide

1 **On slide 3, select the edge of the title object with the dotted-line selection box.**

2 **Drag the title object to the right edge of the slide.**

FIGURE 6-14

Placeholder has been moved

3 On the Format menu, click Slide Layout to display the Slide Layout task pane.

The Slide Layout task pane appears with the current slide layout style selected.

ANOTHER METHOD

Right-click a blank area of the slide, and then click Slide Layout on the shortcut menu.

4 Click the down arrow next to the Title and Text slide layout.

5 On the menu, click Reapply Layout.

PowerPoint reapplies the slide layout to reposition the title object to its original position on the slide.

✕ **6** In the Slide Design task pane, click the Close button to close the task pane.

◆ Keep this file open for the next exercise.

QUICK CHECK

Q: What do you have to click to access the Reapply Layout command?

A: You have to position the pointer on the layout to display the down arrow to the right, and then click that down arrow.

QUICK REFERENCE ▼

Reapply a slide layout

1 Display the slide to which you want to apply a slide layout.
2 On the Format menu, click Slide Layout.
3 In the Slide Layout task pane, click a slide layout.
4 Click the down arrow next to the layout.
5 Click Reapply Layout.

Hiding Background Objects

THE BOTTOM LINE

Hide background objects when you want a clean or different look for a slide. Hiding background objects also removes useful objects such as slide numbers and footers.

As you have already learned, design templates often include objects such as lines, shapes, and pictures that are used to give slides their graphic appeal. These graphics are stored on the Slide and Title Masters along with the default text, title, and footer placeholders.

For individual slides, you may want to hide background objects, such as date and time, header and footer, slide number placeholders, graphics, shapes, and lines so that they do not appear on the screen. To do so, you use the Background dialog box. However, hiding background items means that *all* master items, such as footer text, slide numbers, and graphics, are hidden.

Hide the background objects on a slide background

In this exercise, you hide background objects on a slide to see how the display changes.

1 Click the Next Slide button to move to slide 4.

2 On the Format menu, click Background.

The Background dialog box appears.

ANOTHER METHOD

Right-click a blank area of the slide, and then click Background.

3 Select the Omit Background Graphics From Master check box.

If you want to see how the slide will look without the background objects, click the Preview button before you click Apply.

4 Click Apply.

The background objects are omitted from the slide.

5 On the Standard toolbar, click the Save button to save your changes.

◆ Keep this file open for the next exercise.

QUICK REFERENCE ▼

Hide background objects

1 Display the slide with the background objects you want to hide.

2 On the Format menu, click Background.

Viewing and Changing Master Slides

3 Select the Omit Background Graphics From Master check box.

4 Click Apply.

Saving a Presentation as a Template

THE BOTTOM LINE

Create your own templates to quickly apply to future presentations
a set of formats you have customized for the current presentation.
You can create a template from scratch or modify an existing design
template.

After customizing masters, you can save the presentation as a new template, which you can apply to other presentations. This can save you a
great deal of time when you know you will be creating a number of presentations that require the same look. For example, you can create a template to be used for all presentations of the Marketing Department, or for
a particular class you are giving or taking.

If you want to create your own custom template, you can do what you've
done in this presentation: modify an existing design template. Or, you can
create a new template from scratch by starting with the blank presentation,
adding graphic elements, and applying formatting as desired.

Save a presentation as a template

You have finished modifying the design template you applied at the
beginning of this lesson. You are now ready to save it for future use in
other Contoso presentations.

1 On the File menu, click Save As.

The Save As dialog box appears. Contoso Company Pres 06 appears in
the File Name box.

2 In the File Name box, type Contoso Company Template.

3 Click the Save As Type down arrow, and then click Design Template.

PowerPoint displays the Templates folder. For the purposes of this
lesson, you save this template with the rest of your practice files.

4 In the Save In box, verify that the Lesson06 folder within the
PowerPoint Practice folder is open.

5 Click Save.

PowerPoint saves the template in the Lesson06 Practice folder.

◆ If you are continuing to other lessons, save the Contoso Company Pres 06 presentation with the current name and then close it. If you are not continuing to other lessons, save and close the Contoso Company Pres 06 presentation, and then click the Close button in the title bar of the PowerPoint window.

QUICK REFERENCE ▼

Save the presentation as a design template

1. On the File menu, click Save As.
2. In the File Name box, type a file name.
3. Click the Save As Type down arrow, and then click Design Template.
4. In the Save In box, navigate to the location where you want to save the presentation as a template.
5. Click Save.

QUICK CHECK

Q: Do you have to use PowerPoint's existing templates for all presentations?

A: **No, you can create your own template from scratch or by modifying an existing template.**

Key Points

- *Apply a design template to format a presentation with colors, graphics, layout, and text formats that have been coordinated by a professional designer. You can use an existing PowerPoint design template or create your own.*
- *The PowerPoint Slide, Title, Handout, and Notes Masters specify layout, text formats, and graphic items that will be included on each slide in a presentation. You can modify placeholder position, text formats, and bullet formats so that they are used on all slides in the presentation.*
- *When modifying master bulleted text, you can insert a new bullet character or choose a picture bullet for a special look.*
- *Adjust space between a bullet character and text by dragging indent markers or the margin marker on the ruler.*
- *If you have made a change to the layout of a slide that you don't like, you can reapply the default slide layout to move placeholders back into position.*
- *If desired, you can hide the background objects that are included on the Slide and Title Masters, such as graphics, lines, shapes, and the placeholders for date, footer, and slide number.*
- *After you have customized a design template, you can save it as a new template to use in future presentations.*

Quick Quiz

True/False

T   F   **1.** Once you have applied a design template to a presentation, you cannot change the template.

T   F   **2.** You could, if desired, move the title placeholder to the bottom of the slide in Slide Master view.

T   F   **3.** If you insert a picture bullet on a slide master, you can change its size but not its color.

T   F   **4.** The ruler shows one set of indent markers for each level of text on a slide.

T   F   **5.** Use the Correct Layout command to revert to a slide's original layout.

Multiple Choice

1. If you want to format a subtitle, you make your changes on the _____.
- **a.** Slide Master
- **b.** Title Master
- **c.** Handouts Master
- **d.** Notes Master

2. A quick way to italicize text is to press _____.
- **a.** Alt + I
- **b.** Alt + F5
- **c.** Ctrl + I
- **d.** Ctrl + T

3. An indent where the first line extends to the left of the paragraph with the rest of the paragraph indented is called a _____ indent.
- **a.** hanging
- **b.** text
- **c.** first-line
- **d.** left

4. If you hide background objects on a slide, you will not see the _____.
- **a.** date and time
- **b.** footer
- **c.** design template graphics
- **d.** all of the above

5. By default, design templates are stored in the _____ folder.
- **a.** Presentation
- **b.** Templates
- **c.** Design Templates
- **d.** AutoContent Wizard

Short Answer

1. How do you apply a template?
2. How do you select a picture as the master bullet?
3. How do you display the ruler?
4. How do you adjust the margin level?
5. How do you save the presentation as a template?
6. How do you view the Title Master?

On Your Own

Exercise 1

Open the Contoso Company Pres 06 in the Lesson06 folder that is located in the PowerPoint Practice folder. Change the title slide to display slide header and footer information, display the date footer on the slide, add the date placeholder to the master layout, move the date placeholder to the bottom middle of the Slide Master, and then save and close the presentation.

Exercise 2

Open the Contoso Company Pres 06 in the Lesson06 folder that is located in the PowerPoint Practice folder. Change the footer and number area placeholder formatting attributes to bold and the font size to 18 points, change the second-level bullet to a picture, hide slide background objects on slide 5, and then save and close the presentation.

One Step Further

Exercise 1

Open Holidays 05 and save it as Holidays 06 in the Lesson06 folder that is located in the PowerPoint Practice folder. Omit background graphics from slides 3 and 6. Change the slide layout on slide 6 to Title Only to match slide 3. Display slide 1 and then open the Title Master. Move the Number Area placeholder to the top right corner of the slide, then move the footer and the date placeholders to the right so that the footer aligns at the right with the subtitle placeholder and the date area aligns at the left with the subtitle placeholder. Right-align the footer. Display the Slide Master and move the number to the top right corner of the slide. Adjust the footer and date area placeholders as on the Title Master, aligning with the main text area on the master. View your presentation and adjust the masters, if necessary. Save and close the presentation.

Exercise 2

Open 06 PPT Marx and save it as Marx 06 in the Lesson06 folder that is located in the PowerPoint Practice folder. Apply to this presentation the 06 PPT Marx Template design template from the Lesson06 folder. Preserve the two masters and add a new slide and title master pair. Apply the Edge design template to the new masters. Apply the Edge master to the title slide and the last slide in the presentation. Save and close the presentation.

Exercise 3

Open Marx 06 from the Lesson06 folder that is located in the PowerPoint Practice folder. Display Slide Master view and select the Edge Slide Master. Change the title text to Book Antiqua, bold, black. Change all bulleted text to Book Antiqua. Display the Title Master and make sure all text on the title slide is Book Antiqua. On both Edge masters, change the other text placeholders to 14 point Arial to match those in the Marx template. On the Edge Slide Master, change the bullet symbols to match those used on the Marx Slide Master. If desired, select a new picture bullet for the main bullet entries. Adjust indents as necessary to display the picture bullets without crowding the text. Make sure the date and slide number display on all slides. Save the presentation as a template with the name Marx New Template 06. Close the presentation.

Using a Color Scheme

After completing this lesson, you will be able to:

✔ *View and choose a color scheme.*
✔ *Change colors in a color scheme.*
✔ *Create a new color scheme.*
✔ *Add new colors to color menus.*
✔ *Add, copy, and change a background.*

KEY TERMS

- background
- color menus
- color scheme

In the previous lesson, you learned how to work with the overall look of a presentation by using templates and masters. In this lesson, you will work with a very important part of a presentation: the color scheme. A **color scheme** is a set of eight colors designed to be used as the primary colors in slide presentations. The color scheme determines the colors for the background, text, lines, shadows, fills, and accents of slides. Using Microsoft PowerPoint's color scheme capabilities, you can experiment with different colors and schemes until you find the combination of colors that you like for an aesthetically pleasing design.

As vice president of sales at Contoso, Ltd, you have been working on a company presentation. After modifying the master in the previous lesson, you are ready to change the presentation colors to match the company colors.

In this lesson, you will learn how to view and choose a color scheme, change colors in a color scheme, create a color scheme, add other colors to color menus, add a shaded or textured background to a slide, and copy a color scheme to other slides.

◆ Before you can use the practice files in this lesson, you must install them from the book's companion CD to their default location. See "Using the CD-ROM" at the beginning of this book for more information. To complete the procedures in this lesson, you will need to use a file named 07 PPT Lesson in the Lesson07 folder in the PowerPoint Practice folder located on your hard disk.

Viewing and Choosing a Color Scheme

Working with Color Schemes and Other Colors

THE BOTTOM LINE

Every design template offers a number of color schemes you can choose from to give your presentation a distinctive look. Color schemes consist of eight coordinated colors that are used for all slide objects to ensure consistency throughout a presentation.

Every presentation, even a blank one, has a color scheme. The color scheme can be a set of custom colors that you choose, or it can be the default color scheme. Understanding color schemes helps you create professional-looking presentations that use an appropriate balance of color for your presentation content.

To view your presentation's color scheme, click Color Schemes in the Slide Design task pane. The Slide Design task pane displays all of the custom color schemes you can apply to your presentation. The currently active color scheme is highlighted with a black selection box. To edit a color scheme, click Edit Color Schemes at the bottom of the task pane. The Edit Color Scheme dialog box allows you to change the colors in your color scheme, choose a different color scheme, or create your own color scheme. Once you find the look that you want, you can apply the color scheme to one or all slides in a presentation.

The default color schemes in PowerPoint are made up of a palette of eight colors. These colors appear on the menu when you click the Fill Color or Font Color down arrow on the Drawing toolbar. These eight colors correspond to the following elements in a presentation:

- Background—This color is the color of the canvas, or drawing area, of the slide.
- Text And Lines—This color contrasts with the background color. It is used for typing text and drawing lines.
- Shadows—This color is generally a darker shade of the background.
- Title Text—This color, like the Text And Lines color, contrasts with the background.
- Fills—This color contrasts with both the Background color and the Text And Lines color.
- Accent—This color is designed to work as a complementary color for objects in the presentation.
- Accent And Hyperlink—This color is designed to work as a complementary color for objects and hyperlinks.
- Accent And Followed Hyperlink—This color is designed to work as a complementary color for objects and visited hyperlinks.

By default, the color scheme is applied to all slides in the presentation. To apply a color scheme to selected slides, first select slides in the Slides tab or Slide Sorter view, then click the down arrow on the color scheme in the Slide Design task pane and click Apply To Selected Slides.

View and choose a color scheme

In this exercise, you examine the current color scheme applied to a presentation and then choose another color scheme.

◆ **Start PowerPoint, if necessary, click the Open button on the Standard toolbar, navigate to the Lesson07 folder in the PowerPoint Practice folder, and then open the 07 PPT Lesson file. Save the file as Contoso Company Pres 07 in the same folder.**

1 **In the Slide pane, drag the scroll box to slide 7.**

2 **On the Formatting toolbar, click the Slide Design button, and in the Slide Design task pane, click Color Schemes.**

All available Color Scheme choices appear in the task pane. The current color scheme is indicated by the black selection box surrounding it.

ANOTHER METHOD

- On the Format menu, click Slide Design.
- Right-click a blank area of the slide, and then click Slide Design on the shortcut menu.

3 **Click the color scheme in the last row.**

The color scheme is applied to all slides, as shown in the following illustration. Next you will view the Edit Color Scheme dialog box for this scheme.

Figure 7-1

Click the new color scheme

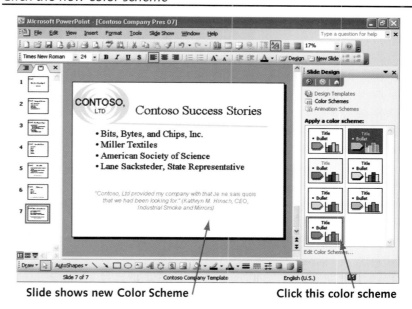

Slide shows new Color Scheme   Click this color scheme

4 **Click Edit Color Schemes at the bottom of the Slide Design task pane.**

The Edit Color Scheme dialog box appears, showing the Custom tab. The Custom tab displays a grid of eight colored boxes that correspond to the selected color scheme and a Preview box that shows the colors in use. These eight colors make up the presentation's current color scheme.

Figure 7-2

Edit Color Scheme dialog box

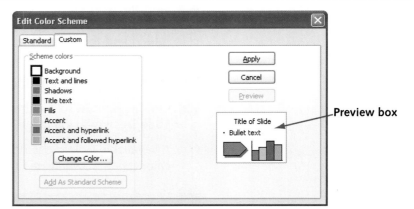

Preview box

5 **Click Apply to return to slide 7.**

Even though you didn't make any changes in this dialog box, you can click Apply to close it.

◆ **Keep this file open for the next exercise.**

QUICK REFERENCE ▼

View and choose a color scheme

1 On the Formatting toolbar, click the Slide Design button, and in the Slide Design task pane, click Color Schemes.

2 Click a color scheme.

Changing Colors in a Color Scheme

Creating a New Color Scheme

THE BOTTOM LINE

Though color scheme colors have been selected to complement one another, you may want to change one or more of the scheme colors to customize a presentation or create a fresh look for the scheme.

You can modify any or all of the colors within a color scheme to create your own color combinations. You can apply changes you make to a color scheme to the current slide or to the entire presentation. For example, you might want to create a customized color scheme that complements your company's logo.

To change colors, open the Edit Color Scheme dialog box and then use the Change Color feature available on the Custom tab. This button opens a Color dialog box for the selected element. The Standard tab in this dialog box lets you select colors from a color palette simply by clicking. If you don't see a color you like, you can create your own color using the Custom tab in the Color dialog box. On the Custom tab, drag a pointer to select a color or specify a color based on RGB (Red, Green, and Blue) values. A large percentage of the visible spectrum is represented by mixing red, green, and blue colors. When you specify values for red, green, and blue, the mixing of the shades creates a color.

Change colors in a color scheme

Now that you have applied a new color scheme, you will customize it by changing a color in the color scheme.

1 **In the Slide Design task pane, click Edit Color Schemes at the bottom of the task pane.**

The Edit Color Scheme dialog box appears, showing the Custom tab.

2 **In the Scheme Colors area, click the Title Text color box.**

PowerPoint will apply any color change you make to that selected color.

Figure 7-3

Select a scheme color to change it

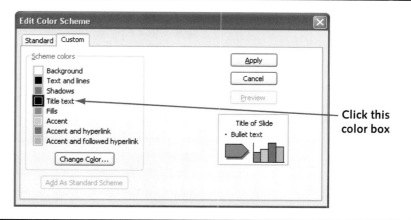

3 **Click Change Color.**

The Title Text Color dialog box appears, showing the Standard tab. The Standard tab displays a color palette of standard colors from which to choose.

ANOTHER METHOD

You can double-click a color scheme color box to go directly to the Color dialog box for that element.

4 **In the color palette, click the dark violet color, as shown in the following illustration.**

The New/Current window at the bottom right of the dialog box shows a preview of the selected new color compared to the currently applied color.

Figure 7-4

Click the violet color shown here

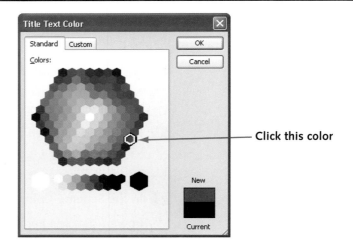

──────── Click this color

5 **Click OK.**

The Title Text color box changes to violet in the color scheme.

6 **Click Apply.**

Slide titles throughout the presentation are now violet.

◆ **Keep this file open for the next exercise.**

QUICK REFERENCE ▼

Change colors in a color scheme

1 On the Formatting toolbar, click the Slide Design button, and in the Slide Design task pane, click Color Schemes.

2 Click Edit Color Schemes in the Slide Design task pane.

3 In the Scheme Colors area, click an element color box.

4 Click Change Color.

5 In the color palette, click a color.

6 Click OK.

7 Click Apply.

Creating a New Color Scheme

Creating a New Color Scheme

THE BOTTOM LINE

When you have customized a color scheme, you can save it so that it will appear in the Slide Design pane and be available for use in future presentations. This can save you a lot of time if you intend to use a color scheme over and over.

You may spend quite a while tweaking colors in a presentation to get them exactly right. If you know you will use the color scheme for future presentations—such as for all the presentations you create for a class, a client, or a department of your company—you can add your color scheme to the standard color schemes for the current design template. Your color scheme will then be available on the Slide Design task pane and the Standard tab of the Edit Color Scheme dialog box.

Create a new color scheme

In this exercise, you make a few more changes to the current color scheme to create a new scheme and then add your modified color scheme to the list of standard schemes for this design template.

1 In the Slide Design task pane, click Edit Color Schemes at the bottom of the task pane.

2 Double-click the Accent And Hyperlink color box.

The Accent And Hyperlink Color dialog box appears, showing the Standard tab.

3 In the color palette, click the purple color, as shown in the following illustration.

Figure 7-5

Click the purple color shown here

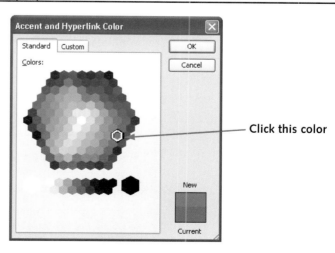

4 **Click OK.**

The accent color changes in the Edit Color Scheme dialog box.

5 **Click Add As Standard Scheme in the Edit Color Scheme dialog box.**

The Add As Standard Scheme button turns gray, indicating that the color scheme has been added to the color scheme list.

6 **Click the Standard tab.**

The new color scheme appears with a selection box around it, as shown in the following illustration.

Figure 7-6

New color scheme appears in Edit Color Scheme dialog box

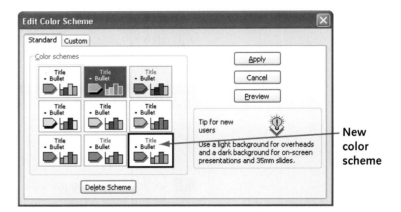

New color scheme

TIP

You can delete a color scheme from the list of Standard schemes by selecting the color scheme and clicking Delete Scheme in the Edit Color Scheme dialog box.

7 **Click Apply.**

The new accent color changes the text objects on all slides to the shade of purple you selected. The newly added color scheme appears on the Slide Design task pane with other color schemes.

8 **In the Slide Design task pane, click the Close button to close the task pane.**

◆ **Keep this file open for the next exercise.**

QUICK REFERENCE ▼

Add a new standard color scheme

1 On the Formatting toolbar, click the Slide Design button, and in the Slide Design task pane, click Color Schemes.

2 Click Edit Color Schemes on the Slide Design task pane.

QUICK CHECK

Q: What change in the Add As Standard Scheme button lets you know your color scheme has been successfully added to the color scheme list?

A: **The Add As Standard Scheme button turns gray when the scheme has been added.**

3 Double-click a Scheme Colors box.

4 In the color palette, click a color.

5 Click OK.

6 Repeat for other scheme color boxes as necessary.

7 In the Edit Color Scheme dialog box, click Add As Standard Scheme.

8 Click Apply.

Adding New Colors to Color Menus

Working with Color Schemes and Other Colors

THE BOTTOM LINE

Add new colors to a presentation's color menus when you want colors available for use in addition to the color scheme colors. Adding colors to the color menus lets you maintain consistency throughout a presentation.

In addition to the eight basic color scheme colors, PowerPoint allows you to add more colors to your presentation. You might add a color when the color scheme doesn't have quite the color you need or when you need to match a specific color, such as a business or school logo color.

When you select a new color from the PowerPoint color palette, it is automatically added to each of the toolbar button **color menus**—the Font Color button menu, for example. Adding colors in this way makes them available to apply to text or objects throughout the presentation. Colors you add to a specific color menu appear in all color menus and remain in the menu even if the color scheme changes.

Add new colors to color menus

Your presentation would benefit from having an additional color available to use to emphasize text. In this exercise, you will add a new color that will then be available on all color menus.

1 On slide 7, move the pointer to the edge of the bulleted paragraph text object so that the pointer changes to the selection pointer, and then select the text object with the dotted selection box.

2 On the Drawing toolbar, click the Font Color button down arrow.

A menu appears, showing the eight colors for the current color scheme, with the currently selected color highlighted by a selection box. The Font Color menu should look like Figure 7-7.

Figure 7-7

Font color menu

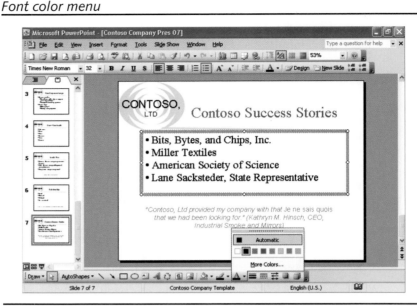

3 **On the menu, click More Colors.**

The Colors dialog box opens, displaying the PowerPoint standard color palette.

4 **In the color palette, click the dark blue color, as shown in the following illustration.**

Figure 7-8

Click the dark blue color shown here

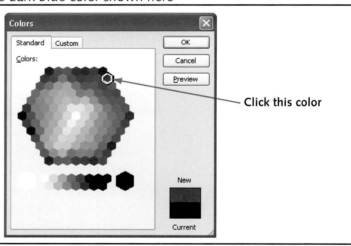

Click this color

5 **Click OK.**

The selected text changes to the dark blue color, and the colored bar on the Font Color button appears with the currently selected color—in this case, dark blue.

6 **On the Drawing toolbar, click the Font Color button down arrow.**

The color you just added appears on the second line, below the standard color scheme colors, and is now available for use throughout the presentation. The Font Color menu should look like the following illustration.

Figure 7-9

Font color menu shows new color

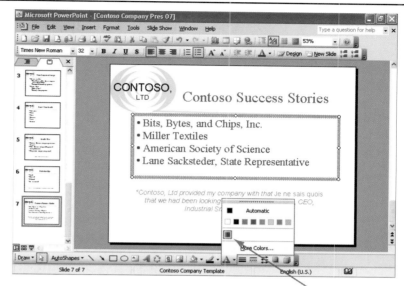

Added color appears here in all color menus

7 Click anywhere in the presentation window to close the menu.

◆ Keep this file open for the next exercise.

QUICK REFERENCE ▼

Add a color and view the new color in color menus

1 Select a text box.

2 On the Drawing toolbar, click the Font Color button down arrow.

3 On the menu, click More Colors.

4 In the color palette, click a color.

5 Click OK.

Adding a Background

THE BOTTOM LINE

Besides a plain color background, you can specify a shaded, textured, patterned, or picture background to add graphic impact to a presentation.

Coloring and Shading the Slide Background

In PowerPoint, you can create a special **background** by adding a shade, a texture, a pattern, or even a picture to slides. These background options give your presentation graphic impact that can make your slides really stand out.

To choose a background option, open the Background dialog box and click the Background Fill down arrow to display options. Besides using one of the scheme colors, or adding a new color, you can click Fill Effects to open the Fill Effects dialog box and choose a background fill effect.

You can apply a background to a single slide or to all slides in a presentation. To save time, you can also copy background formatting from one slide to others.

Apply a Shaded Background

A shaded background is a visual effect in which a solid color gradually changes from light to dark or dark to light. The Gradient tab lets you choose from one-color and two-color shaded backgrounds with six styles: horizontal, vertical, diagonal up, diagonal down, from corner, and from center. For a one-color shaded background, the shading color can be adjusted lighter or darker, depending on your needs. You can also choose a preset color background, one of 24 professionally designed backgrounds in which the color shading changes direction according to the shading style selected.

Add a background

To improve the graphic appeal of your presentation, you will apply a shaded background in this exercise.

1 **On the Format menu, click Background.**

The Background dialog box appears.

ANOTHER METHOD

Right-click a blank area of the slide, and then click Background on the shortcut menu.

2 **Click the Background Fill down arrow, as shown in the following illustration.**

Figure 7-10

Display background fill options

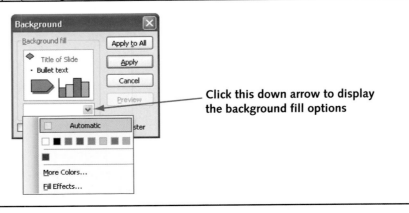

Click this down arrow to display the background fill options

3 **On the Background Fill list, click Fill Effects.**

The Fill Effects dialog box appears, showing four tabs: Gradient, Texture, Pattern, and Picture, with the Gradient tab on top. This tab shows three color options, six shading styles, and four variants for the selected colors. Currently, no colors or shading styles are selected.

Figure 7-11

Shading background fill options

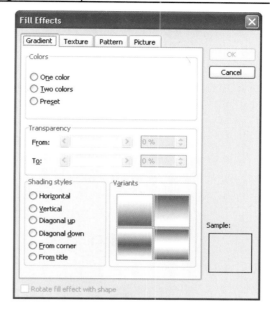

4 **In the Colors area, click the Preset option.**

The Preset colors list appears.

5 **Click the Preset Colors down arrow, and then click Daybreak.**

The Daybreak gradient displays in the Variants and Sample boxes toward the bottom of the dialog box.

6 **In the Shading Styles area, click the Diagonal Up option, and then click the top left variant.**

The Sample box shows you a preview of your selection, as shown in Figure 7-12.

Figure 7-12

Create a gradient fill

Click the Preset button . . .

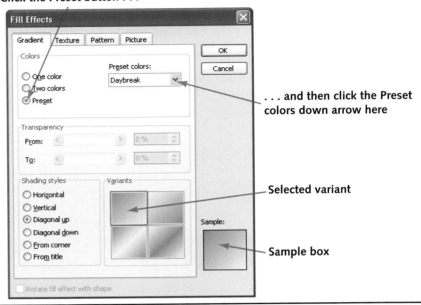

. . . and then click the Preset colors down arrow here

Selected variant

Sample box

7   **Click OK.**

The Background dialog box appears. Notice that the new shaded background displays in the sample slide area of the dialog box.

8   **Click Apply.**

The shaded background is applied only to the currently selected slide in the presentation.

◆   **Keep this file open for the next exercise.**

QUICK REFERENCE ▼

Create and apply a shaded background

1   On the Format menu, click Background.

2   Click the Background Fill down arrow, and then click Fill Effects.

3   In the Colors area, click an option.

4   In the Shading Styles area, click an option, and then click a variant.

5   Click OK.

6   Click Apply or Apply To All.

Copying a Background and Color Scheme

An alternative to storing a color scheme as a standard scheme is to simply copy it to additional slides in the current presentation or in other presentations. You select the slide in the Slides tab or Slide Sorter view with the color scheme you want to reuse, click the Format Painter button on the

Standard toolbar to copy or pick up the color scheme, and then click the slide to apply the color scheme. Copying in this way helps to ensure consistency within a presentation or among presentations.

Copy a background and color scheme

In the last exercise, you applied the shaded background to one slide. Now that you have inspected the design, you decide to apply it to the remaining slides in the presentation. In this exercise, you copy the color scheme to other selected slides.

1 Click the Slide Sorter View button.

2 If necessary, select slide 7.

3 On the Standard toolbar, click the Format Painter button.

The color scheme for slide 7 is picked up and is now ready for you to apply to other slides in the current presentation or in any other open presentation.

4 On the Edit menu, click Select All.

All slides are selected.

ANOTHER METHOD

Press Ctrl + A.

5 Click any of the selected slides, except slide 7.

PowerPoint applies the color scheme to all the slides in the presentation, as shown in the illustration below.

Figure 7-13

The background has been copied to all other slides

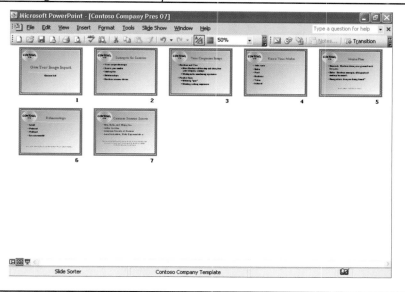

QUICK CHECK

Q: Besides Slide Sorter view, what other view can you use for copying slide formats?

A: You can use the Slides tab in the Outline/Slides pane in Normal view.

6 **Double-click slide 1.**

PowerPoint returns to Normal view.

◆ **Keep this file open for the next exercise.**

QUICK REFERENCE ▼

Copy a color scheme

1 Click the Slide Sorter View button (or the Slides tab on the Outline/Slides pane).

2 Select the slide with the format you want to pick up.

3 On the Standard toolbar, click the Format Painter button.

4 On the Edit menu, click Select All if you want to apply the copied background to all slides in the presentation.

5 Click any of the selected slides to apply the color scheme.

Applying a Textured Background

In addition to a shaded background, you can also have a background with a texture, a pattern, or a picture. PowerPoint has several different textures that you can apply to a presentation. You can find the textures on the Texture tab in the Fill Effects dialog box.

Be sure to use care when applying a texture, pattern, or picture background. These backgrounds can easily overwhelm slide text and make it difficult to read. You may need to adjust text formats for the text to show up clearly against the background.

Create a textured background

In this exercise, you change the background from shaded to textured.

1 **On the Format menu, click Background.**

The Background dialog box appears.

2 **Click the Background Fill down arrow, and then click Fill Effects.**

The Fill Effects dialog box appears.

3 **Click the Texture tab.**

The available textures display in the dialog box.

4 **Click the Newsprint textured fill in the upper-left corner.**

The Newsprint name appears at the bottom of the dialog box, as shown in the following illustration.

Figure 7-14

Select the Newsprint texture

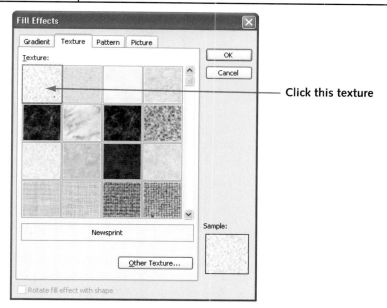

Click this texture

5 **Click OK.**

The Background dialog box appears, displaying a preview of the Newsprint texture in the sample slide.

6 **Click Apply To All.**

PowerPoint applies the textured background to all the slides in the presentation. Notice that it overrides the previously selected background color.

◆ **If you are continuing to other lessons, save the Contoso Company Pres 07 presentation with the current name and then close it. If you are not continuing to other lessons, save and close the Contoso Company Pres 07 presentation, and then click the Close button in the title bar of the PowerPoint window.**

QUICK REFERENCE ▼

Create a texture background

1 On the Format menu, click Background.

2 Click the Background Fill down arrow, and then click Fill Effects.

3 Click the Texture tab.

4 Click a texture option.

5 Click OK.

6 Click Apply or Apply To All.

QUICK CHECK

Q: What is one precaution you must consider when choosing a textured background?

A: You should consider whether the slide text can be read easily against the background.

Key Points

✔ *All design templates offer a number of different color schemes that can be applied to change the look of the presentation. Each color scheme consists of eight colors chosen to complement each other.*

✔ *You can change one or more colors in a color scheme at any time to customize the scheme and give your presentation a fresh look.*

✔ *Create a new color scheme by changing the colors in an existing color scheme. You can then add the new color scheme to the standard color scheme list for the current design template to make it available for future presentations.*

✔ *If the color scheme doesn't offer all the colors you need for a presentation, you can add colors to the color menus by selecting them from PowerPoint's color palette. They are then available for use throughout the presentation.*

✔ *You can create dramatic impact in your presentation by applying a background. Use shading to create a gradual color shift or a texture to add depth and visual interest. A background can be applied to one, selected, or all slides and may be copied from one slide to another using the Format Painter.*

Quick Quiz

True/False

T   F   **1.** The default blank presentation has no color scheme.

T   F   **2.** You can open the Color dialog box for a color element by right-clicking the element's color box in the Edit Color Scheme dialog box.

T   F   **3.** A new color scheme that you create and add as a standard scheme will be available in the Slide Design task pane.

T   F   **4.** By default, PowerPoint applies a slide background to all slides.

T   F   **5.** The quickest way to copy a background to another slide is to use the Copy and Paste buttons.

Multiple Choice

1. The element that controls the color of hyperlinks you have already visited is _____.
   a. Title And Text
   b. Fills
   c. Accent And Hyperlink
   d. Accent And Followed Hyperlink

2. If you choose to create your own color, you can do so by clicking the
    _____ tab in the Colors dialog box.
    a. Create Color
    b. Custom
    c. Standard
    d. New

3. To add a new color to a color menu, click _____ on the color
    menu.
    a. More Colors
    b. New Color
    c. Color Palette
    d. More Options

4. To save time, you can choose a _____ color background, one of
    24 professionally designed backgrounds.
    a. standard
    b. patterned
    c. preset
    d. one-color

5. Besides the shading option, you can create a background using a
    _____.
    a. texture
    b. pattern
    c. picture
    d. all of the above

Short Answer

1. How do you apply a color scheme to the first and last slides in a
    presentation?

2. How do you delete a standard color scheme?

3. How do you change colors in a color scheme and apply the new
    scheme to the current slide?

4. How do you add a two-color gradient with a band of vertical color to
    a slide background?

5. How do you choose a color scheme?

On Your Own

Exercise 1

Open the Contoso Company Pres 07 file in the Lesson07 folder that is located in the PowerPoint Practice folder. Change the color scheme to the
one with the blue, red, and green accent colors; change the Fills color to
light blue; add the color scheme as a standard; apply the color scheme to
all the slides; and then save and close the presentation.

Exercise 2

Open the Contoso Company Pres 07 file in the Lesson07 folder that is located in the PowerPoint Practice folder. Add a purple color to the color menus, change the background to purple with a light shade from the left corner, apply the background changes to the current slide, and then save and close the presentation.

One Step Further

Exercise 1

Open Holidays 06 from the Lesson06 folder that is located in the PowerPoint Practice folder. Save the presentation as **Holidays 07** in the Lesson07 folder. View the color schemes for the design you applied to this presentation. Choose a new color scheme. Scroll through the slides to see how the new scheme changes colors. If any elements such as bullets or numbers do not show up well in the new scheme, edit the scheme to modify colors. (You can use the Preview button in the Edit Color Scheme dialog box to check your changes before applying them.) Apply changes to all slides. Save and close the presentation.

Exercise 2

Open Marx 06 from the Lesson06 folder that is located in the PowerPoint Practice folder. Save the presentation as **Marx 07** in the Lesson07 folder. With slide 1 active, display the Slide Design task pane and choose a new color scheme for this master. Choose the third scheme in the right column, with a slate blue background. Both slide 1 and slide 8, which are controlled by the same master, change to display the new color scheme. View the Edit Color Scheme dialog box for this scheme and determine the background color. Display slide 2 and change the background shading to use the blue background color you determined for the darker color and a very light blue for the lighter color. Save and close the presentation.

Exercise 3

Open Marx 07 from the Lesson07 folder that is located in the PowerPoint Practice folder. Copy the color scheme from slide 2 to the other brown-shaded slides. Choose a new color for the slide 2 title, such as dark rust. Display Slide Master view and change the title text color to the color you just added to the presentation to apply the same color to all slide titles. Display the color scheme for slide 1 and change the Fills color to the same light blue you used to create the two-color shading for slide 2 in Exercise 2. Save the current color scheme as a new standard scheme. Apply the Cork texture to slide 1 only, and adjust font styles, as necessary, so that the text shows up well against this background. Save and close the presentation.

LESSON

Drawing and Modifying Objects

After completing this lesson, you will be able to:

✔ Draw and edit an object.
✔ Copy and move an object.
✔ Replace an AutoShape and add text to a shape.
✔ Modify object attributes.
✔ Align and connect objects.
✔ Change object stacking order.
✔ Rotate and flip objects.
✔ Group and ungroup objects.

KEY TERMS

- Adjustable objects
- Connection sites
- Office Clipboard
- Offset

In addition to meaningful text, an effective presentation includes shapes and pictures that complement and enhance the message. You have already seen how to create text objects. Now you will draw objects and modify their attributes, which include size, line style, color, and effects such as shadows or 3-D.

As vice president of sales at Contoso, Ltd, you have been working on a company presentation. After applying a template and changing masters in previous lessons, you are ready to draw and modify shapes to enhance the text.

In this lesson, you will learn how to draw and edit shapes; copy and move shapes; replace one AutoShape with another and add text to it; change object attributes such as line, fill color, text color and style, and shadows and 3-D effects; align and connect shapes; change the stacking order of shapes; rotate and flip shapes; and group and ungroup objects.

◆ Before you can use the practice files in this lesson, you must install them from the book's companion CD to their default location. See "Using the CD-ROM" at the beginning of this book for more information. To complete the procedures in this lesson, you will need to use a file named 08 PPT Lesson in the Lesson08 folder in the PowerPoint Practice folder located on your hard disk.

Drawing an Object

Drawing and Modifying Shapes

THE BOTTOM LINE

Use the Drawing toolbar to create basic shapes such as rectangles and ovals or more complex AutoShapes. These shapes enhance slides by adding graphic interest.

PowerPoint's Drawing toolbar gives you access to a number of tools for creating and formatting graphic shapes. Use the Rectangle tool, for example, to draw rectangles and squares on your slides, or use the Oval tool to draw ellipses and circles. You can use the Line or Arrow tool to draw straight lines you can use for labeling or as parts of more complicated drawings. Shapes such as these not only add graphic interest to a slide but can also help to convey information to the audience.

In addition to the basic drawing tools on the Drawing toolbar, you can use PowerPoint's AutoShapes to draw more complex shapes, such as flow chart symbols, stars and banners, various geometric shapes, block arrows, and many types of lines and connectors. These shapes would be difficult or impossible to create using the basic drawing tools.

You draw all objects in PowerPoint using the same techniques, except for freeform objects, which are made up of multiple lines and curves. To draw an object, select a drawing tool from the Drawing toolbar or AutoShapes menu, and then drag the pointer to create the object. Turn off a drawing tool by clicking its button on the Drawing toolbar or by pressing Esc.

TIP

You can draw a proportional object by holding down Shift or Ctrl while you draw. Holding down Shift maintains the proportions of the object, while holding down Ctrl draws the object from its center outward.

Draw an AutoShape object

You are ready to start adding graphic interest to your presentation. In this exercise, you draw an AutoShape from PowerPoint's AutoShapes menu.

◆ **Start PowerPoint, if necessary, click the Open button on the Standard toolbar, navigate to the Lesson08 folder in the PowerPoint Practice folder, and then open the 08 PPT Lesson file. Save the file as Contoso Company Pres 08 in the same folder.**

1 **Drag the scroll box to advance to slide 2.**

AutoShapes ▾

2 **On the Drawing toolbar, click the AutoShapes button.**

A menu pops up giving you access to a number of AutoShapes categories. You will use a drawing tool from the Basic Shapes category.

ANOTHER METHOD

On the Insert menu, point to Picture, and then click AutoShapes to open an AutoShapes toolbar.

3 Point to Basic Shapes, and then point to the sun in the middle of the sixth row, as shown in the following illustration.

Figure 8-1

AutoShapes Basic Shapes palette

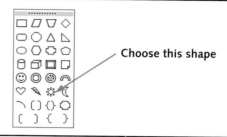

4 Click the Sun button.

In the presentation window, the pointer changes to the cross-hair pointer.

5 Position the cross-hair pointer to the right of the bulleted text, hold down Shift (which maintains the proportions of the object), and then drag to draw a sun shape, as shown in the following illustration.

The sun shape appears with white circles on each corner and side of the object, indicating the object is selected. You use the white circles, called resize handles, or sizing handles, to resize the object. The shape is filled with the default fill color for this color scheme, but you can change the fill at any time.

Figure 8-2

Draw the sun shape

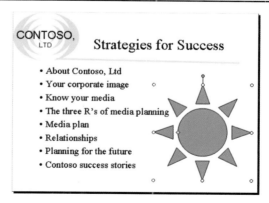

◆ Keep this file open for the next exercise.

QUICK **CHECK**

Q: To draw a shape from the center outward, what key do you hold down while drawing?

A: Hold down the Ctrl key to draw a shape from the center outward.

QUICK REFERENCE ▼

Draw an AutoShape object

1 On the Drawing toolbar, click the AutoShapes button.

2 Point to a category, and then Click an AutoShape.

3 Position the cross-hair pointer in the slide, and then drag to draw a shape.

Editing an Object's Size or Shape

THE BOTTOM LINE

Edit an object's size or shape to make it more attractive or useful. Before you can edit a shape, you must select the object.

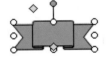

Drawing and Modifying Shapes

Unless you are very adept with the drawing tools, you will most likely need to adjust an object's size and shape before it exactly suits your needs. You can change the size of an object by dragging its resize handles. Drag a side handle in or out to adjust width or height, or drag a corner handle to adjust both width and height at the same time.

Some PowerPoint objects—such as triangles, parallelograms, rounded rectangles, arrows, and other AutoShape objects—are adjustable. **Adjustable objects** have an adjustment handle (a small, yellow diamond) positioned on one side of the object next to a resize handle. This handle allows you to alter the appearance of the object without changing its width or height. Some objects have more than one adjustment handle so you can reshape the object in various ways. The banner in the margin illustrates an object with two adjustment handles.

Before you can adjust an object's size or shape, you must select it. When you draw an object, it is automatically selected. To select an object that isn't already selected, click a visible part of the object. To deselect an object, move the pointer off the object and click in a blank area of the slide.

Edit an object's size and shape

In this exercise, you work with an object on another slide. After you practice selecting and deselecting, you will resize the object and adjust its shape.

1 In the Slides tab of the Outline/Slides pane, click slide 5.

2 Click the arrow object.

The arrow object is selected. Note the white circle resize handles that display around the object and the yellow diamond adjustment handle.

3 **Click outside the arrow object in a blank area of the slide.**

The arrow object is deselected.

4 **Select the arrow object.**

Resize handles reappear around the edges of the object. When you position the pointer over a resize handle, the pointer changes to a small two-headed arrow, indicating the directions in which you can resize the object.

5 **Drag the arrow's right-middle resize handle to match the following illustration and then release the mouse button.**

As the object is resized, a dotted outline of the object appears, indicating what the object will look like when you release the mouse button.

Figure 8-3

Resize the arrow as shown here

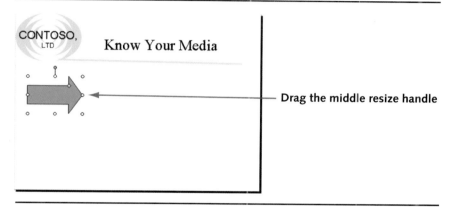

6 **Position the pointer on the arrow object's adjustment handle (yellow diamond).**

The pointer changes to the adjustment pointer.

7 **Drag the adjustment handle to the left, but do not release the mouse button.**

Notice that dragging the adjustment handle changes the shape of the arrowhead but leaves the overall size of the arrow the same. As you adjust the object, a dotted outline of the object appears, indicating what the object will look like when you release the mouse button.

8 **Drag the adjustment handle back to its approximate original position and release the mouse button.**

◆ **Keep this file open for the next exercise.**

QUICK **REFERENCE** ▼

Select or deselect an object

- Click an object to select it.
- Click outside the object in a blank area of the slide to deselect it.

QUICK **CHECK**

Q: What does the adjustment handle look like?

A: The adjustment handle looks like a small, yellow diamond.

Resize or adjust an object

1 Select the object.

2 Drag the object's resize handle or adjustment handle and release the mouse button to complete the shape.

Copying and Moving an Object

Drawing and Modifying Shapes

THE BOTTOM LINE

Move an object easily by dragging it to position it exactly where you want it. If a slide or presentation uses the same shape more than once, copying is a quick way to create multiple versions.

When a slide or presentation uses an object more than once, you can save yourself considerable time and effort by copying the shape and then pasting as many duplicates as you need. You can then modify individual objects if necessary.

Like all Office applications, PowerPoint offers several methods for copying objects. You can use the Copy and Paste commands or buttons to copy an object or group and then paste it as many times as you like. You can use the Office Clipboard to store copied items and then paste them as desired. (You'll learn more about the Office Clipboard later in this section.)

You can also copy an object to another location in a single movement by using the Ctrl key or by using the Duplicate command on the Edit menu. To use the Ctrl key, select the object you want to copy, hold down Ctrl, and then drag. As you drag, a copy of the original object follows the mouse pointer.

To save time, you can copy a group of objects, rather than copy them singly. To select multiple objects for copying or formatting, click the first object, hold down Shift, and then click additional objects. Or, you can use the pointer to draw a selection box that encloses all the objects.

Pasted items by default overlap the original copied item. You will usually need to move the pasted item to position it where you want it. Moving is easy in PowerPoint: point to an object, hold down the mouse button, and drag it to its new location.

Copy and move an object

Now that you have resized the arrow, you're ready to make some copies of it to add information to the slide. In this exercise, you copy and move an object and select, deselect, and copy multiple objects.

1 **With the arrow still selected, click the Copy button on the Standard toolbar.**

A copy of the arrow is stored on the Office Clipboard. If you have already copied an item, the Office Clipboard may open at this point.

2 **On the Standard toolbar, click the Paste button.**

A copy of the arrow is pasted on the slide and overlaps the original arrow.

Your slide should look like the following illustration.

Figure 8-4

Copied arrow overlaps original arrow

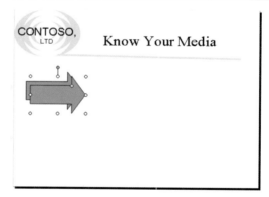

3 **Drag the new arrow about half an inch to the right of the original arrow.**

As the object moves, a dotted outline of the arrow appears, indicating where the new location will be when you release the mouse button.

 4 **Hold down Ctrl, position the mouse pointer over the second arrow, and then hold down the mouse button.**

The pointer changes to the Copy pointer.

5 **While still holding down Ctrl, drag the arrow about a half an inch to the right of the second arrow and release the mouse button.**

A copy of the object appears to the right of the other two, as shown in the following illustration.

Figure 8-5

Arrow has been copied by dragging

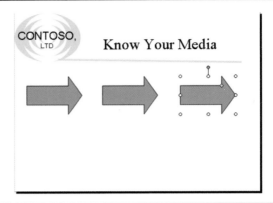

> **TIP**
>
> To constrain an object's movement horizontally or vertically, hold down Shift while you drag the object.

6 **With the third arrow still selected, hold down Shift, and then click the first two arrows.**

The initially selected object remains selected, and the first two objects are added to the selection

QUICK CHECK

Q: Besides the Copy command, what command on the Edit menu can you use to copy an item?

A: You can use the Duplicate command to copy an item.

> **TIP**
>
> To deselect one object in a group, hold down Shift, and then click the object.

7 **Hold down Shift, and then click the middle object again.**

The object is removed from the selection.

8 **Click a blank area of the slide to deselect the arrow objects.**

◆ **Keep this file open for the next exercise.**

QUICK REFERENCE ▼

Copy an object

1 Select the object.

2 On the Standard toolbar, click the Copy button.

3 On the Standard toolbar, click the Paste button.

Move an object

Drag the new object to another area of the slide.

Copy and move an object in one step

Hold down Ctrl, and then drag the object.

You can use the **Office Clipboard** in the Clipboard task pane to store multiple pieces of information from several different sources in one storage area shared by all Office programs. Unlike the Windows Clipboard, which stores only a single piece of information at a time, the Office Clipboard allows you to copy multiple pieces of text or pictures from one or more presentations, up to 24 items. When you copy multiple items, the Office Clipboard appears and shows all the items you stored there. You can paste these pieces of information into any Office program, either individually or all at once.

Use the Office Clipboard to copy and paste items

You now have three arrows on the slide. In this exercise, you'll use the Office Clipboard to copy the arrows and paste them so you have six arrows.

1 Position the pointer near the top left corner of the slide, just below the Contoso logo.

2 Drag a selection box to the bottom-right corner and then release the mouse button to enclose and select all three objects within the marquee.

TROUBLESHOOTING

If all three objects aren't selected, you didn't make the selection box large enough to include every bit of the three objects.

3 With the three arrow objects still selected, click the Copy button on the Standard toolbar.

The Office Clipboard appears in the Clipboard task pane showing all objects currently on the Clipboard and available for pasting. If the Office Clipboard doesn't appear, click the Edit menu, and then click Office Clipboard.

4 On the Clipboard task pane, click the item with the three arrows.

A copy of the three arrows is pasted on the slide, overlapping the original arrows.

5 With all three copied arrows still selected, position the pointer over one of the arrows so that the pointer changes to the selection pointer, and then drag the copied arrows down and to the right, as shown in the following illustration.

Figure 8-6

Slide now shows six arrows

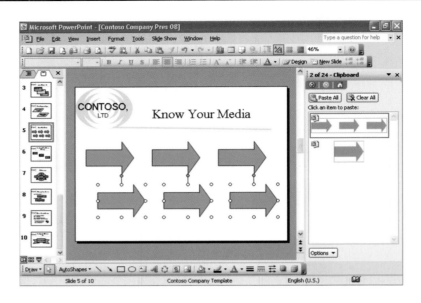

6 In the Clipboard task pane, click Clear All to remove all of the items in the Office Clipboard.

All items disappear from the Clipboard task pane. The Office Clipboard is now empty.

7 In the Clipboard task pane, click the Close button to close the task pane.

◆ Keep this file open for the next exercise.

QUICK REFERENCE ▼

Select multiple objects

■ Hold down Shift, and then click the objects you want to select.

■ Position the pointer on the left of the top-left object, and then drag a selection box to the bottom-right corner, enclosing and selecting all objects within the marquee.

Copy multiple objects using the Office Clipboard

1 Select an object.

2 On the Standard toolbar, click the Copy button.

3 Select another object.

4 On the Standard toolbar, click the Copy button.

5 On the Clipboard task pane, click an item to paste it on the slide.

QUICK CHECK

Q: How many items can the Office Clipboard hold?

A: The Office Clipboard can hold 24 items.

Replace an AutoShape and Add Text to a Shape

Drawing and Modifying Shapes

> **THE BOTTOM LINE**
>
> You can easily replace one AutoShape with another that better suits your purpose. To make any shape more useful, you can add text to the shape that becomes part of the shape.

If you created an object using an AutoShape, PowerPoint allows you to change the shape to another shape with one easy command. With the shape selected, click the Change AutoShape command on the Draw menu on the Drawing toolbar. One advantage of replacing a shape rather than redrawing it is that the shape will maintain the same size and attributes as the original shape.

You can add text to an object to supply more information about it or about the slide's content. When you add text to an object, PowerPoint centers the text as you type, and the text becomes part of the object. You can add text to only one object at a time. To add text, simply select the object and start typing. PowerPoint uses the default text font for text you add to objects, but this font can be changed at any time.

Replace an AutoShape and add text to shapes

You now have the right number of arrows on the slide, but you've decided to replace the arrows with another shape. After you replace the shape, you'll add text to all shapes.

1 **With the bottom three arrows still selected, hold down Shift, and then click each of the top three arrows.**

All six arrows are selected.

Draw ▾

2 **On the Drawing toolbar, click the Draw button, point to Change AutoShape, and then point to Stars and Banners.**

The AutoShape Stars and Banners submenu appears.

3 **On the submenu, click the Horizontal Scroll shape in the fourth row, as shown in the following illustration.**

Figure 8-7

Select a new AutoShape

The selected arrow shapes change to the scroll shape. The new scroll shape fits in the same area and keeps the same attributes as the original arrow shape. Your slide should look like Figure 8-8.

Figure 8-8

AutoShapes replaced with new shapes

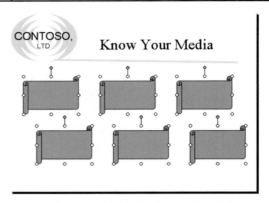

4 Click a blank area of the slide to deselect the objects.

5 Click the top-left object, and then type Television.

As you type, a slanted-line selection box appears around the object, indicating that the object is ready for you to enter or edit text, as shown in the following illustration.

Figure 8-9

Add text to a shape

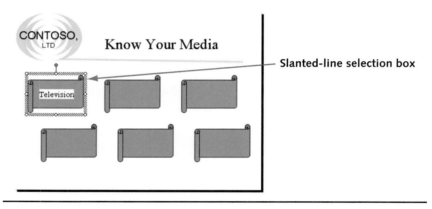

Slanted-line selection box

6 Click the top-middle object, and then type Print.

7 Click the top-right object, and then type Video.

8 In the bottom-left object, type Radio; in the bottom-middle object, type Outdoor; and then in the bottom-right object, type Internet.

9 Click a blank area of the slide to deselect the object.

You have added important information to all six AutoShapes.

◆ Keep this file open for the next exercise.

QUICK CHECK

Q: Why is it more efficient to replace an AutoShape than to draw a new one?

A: **The replacement AutoShape maintains the same size and attributes as the original shape.**

QUICK REFERENCE ▼

Replace one AutoShape with another

1 Select an object.

2 On the Drawing toolbar, click the Draw button, point to Change AutoShape, and then point to a category.

3 On the submenu, click a shape.

Add text to an object

1 Select an object.

2 Type the text.

Modifying Object Attributes

Drawing and Modifying Shapes

THE BOTTOM LINE

PowerPoint's formatting options let you change object attributes such as fill color, line style, text font and style and add special shadow and 3-D effects. These formatting options improve the look of your objects and make them stand out on the slide.

Objects have attributes that define how they appear on the slide. An object has graphic attributes (such as fill, line, shape, and shadow) and may also have text attributes (such as style, font, color, and shadow). Before you can modify these attributes, you must select the objects that you want to change.

Changing Fill and Line Attributes

Objects that you draw usually have a fill and a border or frame. The fill is the area inside a closed shape such as a rectangle or star. The border is the outline of the shape.

You control the fill using the Fill Color button on the Drawing toolbar. You can fill a shape with a color, texture, pattern, or even a picture. To format an object's border, you can use several tools on the Drawing toolbar: the Line Color button (to change or remove the border color), the Line Style button (to change the line's weight or thickness), or the Dash Style button (to make a border dotted or dashed). All of these formatting options can also be made by clicking AutoShape on the Format menu.

Modify fill and line attributes

In this exercise, you modify an object's fill and frame.

1 Drag the scroll box to slide 10.

2 Select the ribbon object.

The ribbon object is selected with the dotted selection box.

3 **On the Drawing toolbar, click the Fill Color button down arrow.**

A drop-down menu appears with a number of fill options. If you clicked the button itself rather than the down arrow, the shape fills with the color currently shown on the button.

4 **Click Fill Effects on the Fill Color menu.**

The Fill Effects dialog box appears.

5 **Click the Texture tab.**

6 **Click the Blue Tissue Paper textured fill (the first box in the third row), as shown in the following illustration.**

Figure 8-10

Fill Effects dialog box

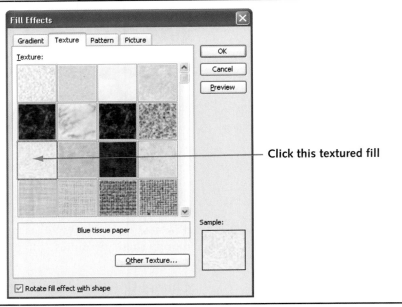

Click this textured fill

TIP

You can click Other Texture to import new textures to the list of current textured fills.

7 **Click OK.**

The ribbon is filled with the new texture. Because the black border now looks a little harsh against the new fill, you will change the line color.

8 **With the ribbon object still selected, on the Drawing toolbar, click the Line Color button down arrow.**

A drop-down menu appears with a selection of line colors.

9 **On the Line Color menu, click in the light blue Follow Accent And Hyperlink Scheme Color box.**

The new line color is applied to the object.

◆ **Keep this file open for the next exercise.**

QUICK REFERENCE ▼

Modify an object's fill

1 Select an object.

2 On the Drawing toolbar, click the Fill Color button down arrow.

3 Click a new color, or click More Fill Colors, or click Fill Effects.

4 Select a new color or fill effect.

5 Click OK.

Modify an object's border

1 Select an object.

2 On the Drawing toolbar, click the Line Color button down arrow, and then click a color box.

Applying Shadow Attributes

You can give an object a shadow to help create a three-dimensional appearance. When you give an object a shadow, you choose from a menu the shadow's **offset**, the direction in which it falls from the object.

To further refine a shadow affect, click Shadow Settings on the Shadow menu to display the Shadow Settings toolbar. Tools on this toolbar let you nudge a shadow in any direction, turn the shadow off or on, and select the color of the shadow.

TIP

You can click the Shadow Style button on the Drawing toolbar to add a shadow to any selected text (not in an object) in PowerPoint.

Apply shadow effects to an object

You have changed fill and line attributes for the ribbon object. In this exercise, you improve its look by applying a shadow.

1 With the ribbon object still selected, on the Drawing toolbar, click the Shadow Style button.

The Shadow popup menu appears with a selection of shadow styles.

2 On the Shadow menu, click the Shadow Style 6 button (the second box in the second row), as shown in the following illustration.

The shadow is applied to the object.

Figure 8-11

Shadow menu

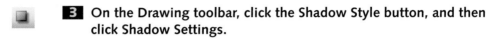

3 **On the Drawing toolbar, click the Shadow Style button, and then click Shadow Settings.**

The Shadow Settings toolbar appears.

4 **On the Shadow Settings toolbar, click the Nudge Shadow Down button five times.**

The shadow moves down below the object.

5 **On the Shadow Settings toolbar, click the Shadow Color button down arrow, and click the Follow Accent Scheme Color blue color.**

The shadow changes color.

TIP

You can click the Shadow On/Off button on the Shadow Settings toolbar or click No Shadow on the Shadow popup menu to turn off a shadow.

---

6 **Click the Close button on the Shadow Settings toolbar.**

The Shadow Settings toolbar closes.

◆ **Keep this file open for the next exercise.**

QUICK REFERENCE ▼

Add and modify an object's shadow

1 Select an object.

2 On the Drawing toolbar, click the Shadow Style button, and then click a style.

3 On the Drawing toolbar, click the Shadow Style button, and then click Shadow Settings.

4 Select the settings you want to customize the object.

5 Click the Close button on the Shadow Settings toolbar.

QUICK CHECK

Q: What would happen if you clicked the Nudge Left button on the Shadow Settings toolbar?

A: **The shadow would move to the left of the object.**

Changing Text Color and Style

You can format the text you have added to an object by selecting the object and then using formatting buttons to achieve the look you want. Formatting text in an object is the same process as formatting text in a slide.

To speed the process of applying new text attributes, you can use the Format Painter. This feature lets you copy a set of styles from selected text and objects and apply them to other selected text and objects.

Change text color and style

In this exercise, you change the text color and style of the ribbon object and format title text using the Format Painter button.

1 Verify that the ribbon object is still selected.

2 On the Drawing toolbar, click the Font Color button down arrow, and then click in the dark blue Follow Accent Scheme Color box.

The text inside the object turns blue.

3 On the Formatting toolbar, click the Bold button.

The text inside the object becomes bold.

4 On the Formatting toolbar, click the Font down arrow, scroll down the font list, and then click Comic Sans MS.

The text inside the object changes to the Comic Sans MS font.

5 Drag the top adjustment handle for the ribbon object about one-quarter inch to the left to increase the center area of the ribbon.

Adjusting the shape gives more room for the text to display in the center area of the ribbon, improving its look.

6 Click outside the ribbon object in a blank area of the slide.

Your slide should look like the following illustration.

Figure 8-12

Text and style changes in object

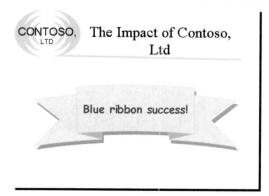

7 Select the ribbon object.

8 On the Standard toolbar, click the Format Painter button.

PowerPoint copies and stores the specific text and object styles (but not the text itself) of the selected object. The standard pointer changes to the Format Painter pointer, as shown in the left margin.

9 Click the title text object to copy the format to the object.

PowerPoint applies all the formats from the ribbon object to the title object.

10 Click a blank area of the slide to deselect the object.

Your slide should look like the following illustration.

Figure 8-13

Formats have been copied to title object

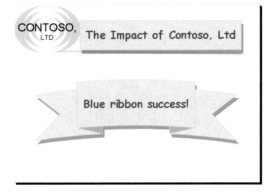

QUICK CHECK

Q: What does the Format Painter pointer look like?

A: **The Format Painter pointer looks like a paintbrush next to a pointer.**

◆ **Keep this file open for the next exercise.**

QUICK REFERENCE ▼

Change text color

1 Select an object.
2 On the Drawing toolbar, click the Font Color button down arrow, and then click a color box.

Change text style

1 Select an object.
2 On the Formatting toolbar, click a formatting option such as Bold, Italic, or Underline.

Format text with the Format Painter command

1 Select the object with the format you want to copy.
2 On the Standard toolbar, click the Format Painter button.
3 Click the object to copy the format to the object.

Adding 3-D Effects to Objects

Once you draw an object, you can change the object to look three-dimensional. Three-dimensional effects can emphasize shapes so they really stand out on the slide. With PowerPoint's 3-D options, you can change the depth of the object and its color, rotation, angle, direction of lighting, and surface texture.

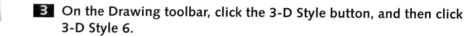

Add 3-D effects to objects

In this exercise, you modify objects on another slide to look three-dimensional and then change the 3-D settings for a custom look.

1 Scroll up to slide 4.

2 Click the top object, hold down Shift, and then click the bottom object.

Both objects are selected and can be formatted at the same time.

3 On the Drawing toolbar, click the 3-D Style button, and then click 3-D Style 6.

The selected 3-D style is applied to both objects.

4 On the Drawing toolbar, click the 3-D button, and then click 3-D Settings.

The 3-D Settings toolbar appears.

5 On the 3-D Settings toolbar, click the Lighting button, and then click the third Lighting Direction button.

The brightness on the objects changes because the "lighting" on them is coming from a different direction.

6 On the 3-D Settings toolbar, click the Tilt Left button five times.

The objects change orientation and become flatter on the slide.

7 On the 3-D Settings toolbar, click the Depth button, and then click 144 pt.

The depth of the objects is increased, making them look like pedestals.

8 Click the Close button on the 3-D Setting toolbar to close the toolbar.

9 Click a blank area of the slide to deselect the objects.

Your slide should look like the following illustration.

Figure 8-14

Objects display 3-D effects

◆ **Keep this file open for the next exercise.**

QUICK REFERENCE ▼

Change an object to look 3-D

1 Select an object.

2 On the Drawing toolbar, click the 3-D Style button, and then click a style.

Change an object's 3-D settings

1 Select an object.

2 On the Drawing toolbar, click the 3-D Style button, then click 3-D Settings.

3 Select the settings you want to customize the object.

4 Click the Close button on the 3-D Settings toolbar to close the toolbar.

Aligning Objects

Aligning and Connecting Shapes

THE BOTTOM LINE

Use PowerPoint's alignment options to make sure objects on a slide line up with each other and are distributed attractively on a slide. Use the PowerPoint grid and guides to help you align objects.

When you have multiple objects on a slide, you can use PowerPoint's alignment and distribution options to make sure the objects line up with each other and are positioned equal distances apart.

The Align or Distribute command aligns two or more objects relative to each other vertically to the left, center, or right. You can also align objects horizontally to the top, middle, or bottom. To align several objects to each other, you select them and then choose an alignment option. To distribute objects, select them and choose to distribute either vertically or horizontally. You can also choose to distribute them relative to each other or to the slide.

Besides aligning objects relative to each other, you can align them to a vertical or horizontal guide. Turning on the visible grid or visible guides option makes it easier to create, modify, and align an object. Within the Grid And Guides dialog box, you can select from a variety of options, such as snapping objects to the grid or to other objects and displaying drawing guides on-screen.

Align objects

One slide in your presentation has two objects that would look better if aligned. You will align them with each other and then align them to a guide line.

1 In the Slides tab, click slide 8.

2 In the Slide pane, hold down Shift, and then select both shapes.

Both shapes must be selected before you can align them with each other.

Draw ▾   **3** On the Drawing toolbar, click the Draw menu button, point to Align Or Distribute, and then click Align Center.

The objects align vertically to each other at their centers.

   4 On the Standard toolbar, click the Show/Hide Grid button.

A grid of regularly spaced dots appears on screen. You can use this grid to gauge the size of objects as you create them or align existing objects.

ANOTHER METHOD

On the View menu, click Grid And Guides.

5 If necessary, reselect the two objects, hold down Shift, and then drag the selected objects to the left until their left edges touch or snap to the nearest vertical grid line.

6 On the View menu, click Grid And Guides.

The Grid And Guides dialog box appears.

Figure 8-15

Grid And Guides dialog box

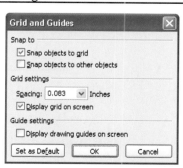

7 Clear the Display Grid On Screen check box, select the Display Drawing Guides On Screen check box, and then click OK to close the dialog box.

Vertical and horizontal dotted guidelines appear in the center of the slide, indicating that the guides are turned on.

> **TIP**
>
> You can press Alt + F9 to quickly turn the guides on and off and press Shift + F9 to quickly turn the grid on and off.

8 Position the pointer on the vertical guide in a blank area of the slide, and then drag the guide toward the left.

As you drag the pointer (which changes to a Guide indicator), a number (shown in inches) appears, indicating how far you are from the center of the slide.

9 Drag the vertical guide left until the Guide indicator reaches 1.75.

> **TIP**
>
> If the Guide indicator skips numbers as you drag the guides across the slide, you can clear the Snap Objects To Grid check box in the Grid And Guides dialog box. This option automatically aligns objects to an invisible grid on the slide.

10 If necessary, reselect the two objects, and then drag the selected objects to the right until their left edges touch or snap to the vertical guide.

Your slide should look like the following illustration.

Figure 8-16

Objects aligned to guideline

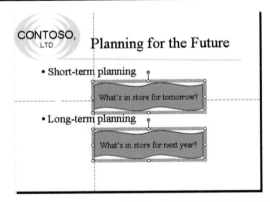

11 Press Alt + F9 to turn off the guides.

◆ Keep this file open for the next exercise.

QUICK REFERENCE ▼

Align objects

1 Select the objects you want to align.

2 On the Drawing toolbar, click the Draw button, point to Align Or Distribute, and then click an alignment.

Turn on the visible grid and guides to align objects

1 On the View menu, click Grid And Guides.

2 Select desired display options for grid and guides and then click OK.

3 Position the pointer on the vertical or horizontal guide in a blank area of the slide, and then drag the guide to where you want to align the objects.

4 Click Alt + F9 or Shift + F9 to turn off the guides or grid.

Connecting Objects

Aligning and Connecting Shapes

THE BOTTOM LINE

To make some shapes such as flowchart objects look more professional, you can connect them with a variety of connector types. Making connections visible helps your audience understand the relationship between objects on a slide.

PowerPoint makes it easy to draw and modify flowcharts and diagrams. Flowcharts and diagrams consist of shapes connected together to indicate a sequence of events. PowerPoint includes a number of connector styles you can use to connect objects.

Use the Connectors submenu on the AutoShapes menu to select one of nine different connector styles. After you choose a connector, you use the connection pointer to identify special **connection sites** on the objects. You can drag a connection endpoint to another connection point to change the line or drag the adjustment handle to change the shape of the connection line. Once two objects are joined, the connecting line moves when either of the objects is moved.

Connect objects

In this exercise, you connect two objects and then change and format a connector line.

1 In the Slides tab, click slide 6.

2 On the Drawing toolbar, click the AutoShapes menu button, point to Connectors, and then click the Elbow Double-Arrow Connector button in the second row.

The pointer changes to a cross-hair.

3 **Position the pointer over the top object.**

Small blue handles called connection sites appear on each side of the object, and the pointer changes to a small box called the connection pointer, shown in the left margin.

4 **Position the center of the pointer halfway up the right side of the top object (over the outer blue handle), and then click the object.**

One end of the connector anchors to the outer blue handle.

5 **Position the pointer halfway up the left side of the middle object (over the outer blue handle), and then click the object.**

Red circle handles appear at each end of the line, indicating the objects are connected. A yellow diamond adjustment handle appears in the middle of the connector lines so that you can resize the curve of the line.

Figure 8-17

First two objects are connected

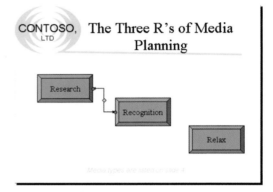

TROUBLESHOOTING

If green square handles appear at the end, the objects are not connected.

6 **On the Drawing toolbar, click the AutoShapes menu button, point to Connectors, and then click the Elbow Double-Arrow Connector button in the second row.**

7 **Draw a connection line between the right, outer blue handle on the middle object and the left, outer blue handle on the bottom object.**

A double-arrow line connects the objects.

TIP

After you connect objects, you can change the connector line at any time.

8 **Drag the red connection handle on the right side of the middle object to the connection site on the bottom center of the middle object.**

The line reconnects to a different connection site on the object.

9 Select the connector line that connects the top and middle objects.

10 Drag the red handle on the left side of the middle object to the connection site at the top center of the middle object.

The line reconnects to a different connection site.

11 With the top connector line still selected, hold down Shift, and then click the bottom connector line.

The two connector lines are selected.

 12 On the Drawing toolbar, click the Dash Style button, and then click the second line from the top.

The dash style is applied to the two connectors.

 13 On the Drawing toolbar, click the Line Style button, and then click the 3 pt line style.

The connector lines are now dotted and 3 points in size.

◆ Keep this file open for the next exercise.

QUICK REFERENCE ▼

Connect two objects

1 On the Drawing toolbar, click AutoShapes, point to Connectors, and then click a connector.

2 Position the pointer over an object handle, and then click the object to select a connection point.

3 Position the pointer over the object handle on another object, and then click the object to select another connection point.

Change a connector line

1 Select a connector line.

2 Drag the connector line handle to another object handle.

Changing Object Stacking Order

THE BOTTOM LINE

Objects may need to be "restacked" to display information properly. Changing the stacking order can improve the appearance and usefulness of shapes on a slide.

Stacking and Grouping Shapes

As you draw objects on a slide, they are "stacked" in layers from bottom (or back) to top (or front). For example, the first object you draw is on the bottom layer, and the last object you draw is on the top layer.

In some cases, objects you draw later might obscure objects you drew earlier. To change the stacking order, you can use the Bring To Front, Send To Back, Bring Forward, and Send Backward commands on the Order submenu of the Draw menu on the Drawing toolbar. Bring To Front moves an object to the top or front of a stack, and Send To Back moves an object to the bottom or back of the stack. Bring Forward and Send Backward move an object one layer toward the front or back of the stack.

Change object stacking order

A slide in your presentation has objects improperly stacked. You will change the stacking order so all information in the shapes is clearly visible.

1 **Scroll up to slide 3.**

Notice that the objects have been drawn so that text in two of shapes is obscured.

2 **Click the top rectangle object.**

Because this object was drawn last, it is on the top (or in the front) of the stack.

Draw ▾

3 **On the Drawing toolbar, click the Draw button, point to Order, and then click Send To Back.**

The top object moves behind the middle rectangle.

ANOTHER METHOD

Right-click the object, point to Order on the shortcut menu, and then click Send to Back.

4 **Click the bottom rectangle.**

Draw ▾

5 **On the Drawing toolbar, click the Draw button, point to Order, and then click Bring To Front.**

The bottom rectangle is now in front of the middle rectangle, so the objects are correctly organized.

6 **Click a blank area of the slide to deselect the object.**

Your slide should look like the following illustration.

Figure 8-18

Objects have been reordered

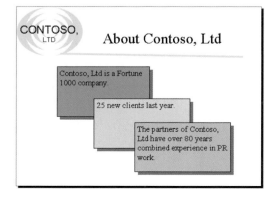

◆ **Keep this file open for the next exercise.**

QUICK REFERENCE ▼

Change object stacking order

1 Select an object.

2 On the Drawing toolbar, click the Draw button, point to Order, and then click a stacking order option.

Rotating and Flipping Objects

Drawing and Modifying Shapes

THE BOTTOM LINE

Enhance the appearance of an object by rotating it or flipping it to change its orientation on the slide.

Once you create an object, you can change its orientation on the slide by rotating or flipping it. Rotating turns an object 90 degrees to the right or left. Flipping turns an object 180 degrees horizontally or vertically. To quickly rotate or flip an object, use the commands on the Rotate Or Flip submenu, which you can display from the Draw menu.

If you need a more exact rotation that you cannot achieve in 90- or 180-degree increments, you can drag the green rotate lever at the top of an object to rotate it to any position. You can also rotate and flip any type of picture—including bitmaps—in a presentation. This is useful when you want to change the orientation of an object or image, such as changing the direction of an arrow.

Rotate and flip objects

In this exercise, you rotate and flip an object to make it more useful on the slide.

1 **Scroll down to slide 9.**

The arrow on this slide should be pointing at the quote in the text box at the bottom of the slide.

2 **Select the arrow shape.**

3 **On the Drawing toolbar, click the Draw button, point to Rotate Or Flip, and then click Flip Horizontal.**

The object flips horizontally. It is now pointing in the right direction, but it could be rotated to give its appearance more impact.

4 **Position the pointer (which changes to the Free Rotate pointer) over the green rotate lever at the top of the object, and then drag slightly to the left to rotate the arrow as shown in the following illustration.**

Figure 8-19

Object has been rotated and flipped

ANOTHER METHOD

You can also use the Free Rotate command on the Rotate Or Flip submenu on the Draw menu to rotate an object to any angle. The Free Rotate command changes the resize handles to green rotate levers, which allows you to drag any of the green rotate levers to rotate the object to any position.

QUICK CHECK

Q: What command on the Flip Or Rotate submenu changes resize handles to green rotate levers, allowing you to change the angle of rotation in free-form?

A: The Free Rotate command changes resize handles to green rotate levers.

◆ **Keep this file open for the next exercise.**

QUICK REFERENCE ▼

Flip an object

1 Select an object.
2 On the Drawing toolbar, click the Draw button, point to Rotate Or Flip, and click a flip option.

Rotate an object

1 Select an object.
2 Point to the Draw menu, select Rotate or Flip, and select a Rotate option, or drag the green rotate lever left or right to rotate the object.

Grouping and Ungrouping Objects

THE BOTTOM LINE

Working with a grouped object is much easier than working with a number of separate images. After you group shapes, you can work with the group as a unit to resize or apply formats.

Stacking and Grouping Shapes

Objects can be grouped together, ungrouped, and regrouped in PowerPoint to make editing and moving information easier. Rather than moving several objects one at a time, you can group the objects and move them all together. Grouped objects appear as one object, but each object in the group maintains its individual attributes.

You can change an individual object within a group without ungrouping. This is useful when you need to make only a small change to a group, such as changing the color of a single shape in the group. You can also format specific AutoShapes, drawings, or pictures within a group without ungrouping. Simply select the object within the group, change the object or edit text within the object, and then deselect the object.

However, if you need to move an object in a group, you need to first ungroup the object, make the change, and then group the objects together again. After you ungroup a set of objects, PowerPoint remembers each object in the group and in one step regroups those objects when you use the Regroup command. Before you regroup a set of objects, make sure that at least one of the grouped objects is selected.

Group and ungroup objects

In this exercise, you group, ungroup, and regroup objects.

1 Scroll up to slide 4.

2 Drag a selection marquee around the two objects.

Each object has its own dotted selection box.

Draw ▾

3 On the Drawing toolbar, click the Draw button, and then click Group.

The objects are grouped together as one object with one set of resize handles around the edge of the grouped object.

ANOTHER METHOD

Right-click one of the selected objects, point to Grouping on the shortcut menu, and click Group.

4 Click the upper object to select it.

The resize handles around the object change to gray circles with x's inside, indicating that an individual object in a group is selected.

5 On the Drawing toolbar, click the Fill Color button down arrow, click More Fill Colors, select a new light blue color for the fill, and then click OK.

The object changes to the color blue without ungrouping.

Draw ▾

6 On the Drawing toolbar, click the Draw button, and then click Ungroup.

Separate dotted selection boxes appear for the objects.

7 Click a blank area of the slide to deselect the objects.

Until you deselect the objects, they still function as a group.

8 Drag the upper object to the right about half an inch.

Make sure this object stays selected.

9 On the Draw menu, click Regroup to regroup the objects.

The selection handles reappear around the group.

◆ If you are continuing to other lessons, save the Contoso Company Pres 08 presentation with the current name and then close it. If you are not continuing to other lessons, save and close the Contoso Company Pres 08 presentation, and then click the Close button in the title bar of the PowerPoint window.

QUICK REFERENCE ▼

Group objects

1 Select the objects you want to group.

2 On the Drawing toolbar, click the Draw button, and then click Group.

Ungroup objects

1 Select the object you want to ungroup.

2 On the Drawing toolbar, click the Draw button, and then click Ungroup.

Regroup objects

1 Select one of the objects in the set of previously grouped objects.

2 On the Drawing toolbar, click the Draw button, and then click Regroup.

QUICK CHECK

Q: How do you know you have selected an object within a group?

A: **The resize handles are gray circles with x's inside.**

Key Points

- ✔ Use PowerPoint's basic shapes or AutoShapes to create drawing objects that enhance or add information to a slide. You can easily resize shapes by dragging a resize handle or adjust the shape of an AutoShape by dragging an adjustment handle.

- ✔ To speed work, use the Copy and Paste commands or the Office Clipboard to duplicate shapes and paste them where needed. The Office Clipboard can hold up to 24 items.

- ✔ If you have drawn an AutoShape, you can quickly replace it with another AutoShape that will take on the same size and attributes. Add text to any shape to make it more useful on a slide.

- ✔ Enhance a shape's appearance by changing line and fill attributes, formatting text, or adding a shadow or 3-D effect.

- ✔ Use the Align Or Distribute commands to line up and position objects relative to each other or to the slide. You can also use PowerPoint's grid or drawing guides to align objects.

- ✔ When creating shapes that need to show connections, use the AutoShape connectors to draw connections between the objects. Once a connection has been inserted, it can be moved or formatted as desired.

- ✔ Adjust the position of objects on stacking layers from front to back to make sure each object is clearly visible.

- ✔ Rotate an object to change its orientation around a specified axis. Flip an object to change its orientation from right to left or top to bottom.

- ✔ Group objects so you can work with them as a unit. After objects have been grouped, you can still work with a single member of the group without having to ungroup. If you do want to ungroup, you can easily regroup the objects.

Quick Quiz

True/False

T F   1. You can turn off a drawing tool by pressing Esc.

T F   2. Once you have copied an object, you can paste it from the Clipboard as many times as you like.

T F   3. The direction in which a shadow falls from its object is called the setoff.

T F   4. PowerPoint's grid consists of dashed lines at regular intervals on the slide.

T F   5. The second object you draw on a slide will be on top of the first object, in terms of stacking order.

Multiple Choice

1. You can copy and move an object at the same time by dragging while you hold down the _____ key.
   a. Alt
   b. Ctrl
   c. Shift
   d. Insert

2. You can fill an object with a _____.
   a. color
   b. texture
   c. shadow
   d. either A or B

3. With PowerPoint's 3-D options, you can change the _____ of the object.
   a. depth
   b. line style
   c. fill color
   d. size

4. Connection sites are _____ that appear on each side of an object when a connection pointer is over the object.
   a. small yellow diamonds
   b. gray circle handles
   c. open circle handles
   d. small blue handles

5. The default Rotate option turns an object _____ degrees to the right or left.
   a. 45
   b. 90
   c. 120
   d. 180

Short Answer

1. How do you modify an object's fill?
2. How do you vertically flip an object?
3. How do you select and copy multiple objects?
4. How do you align objects?
5. How do you add text to an object?
6. How do you group multiple objects?
7. How do you draw and then adjust an object?
8. How do you move a layer in a stack all the way to the back?

On Your Own

Exercise 1

Open Contoso Company Pres 08 in the Lesson08 folder that is located in the PowerPoint Practice folder. Insert a new slide at the end of the presentation with the Blank layout, draw a cube object, copy the cube two times, stack the cubes on top of each other, and then save and close the presentation.

Exercise 2

Open Contoso Company Pres 08 in the Lesson08 folder that is located in the PowerPoint Practice folder. Insert a new slide at the end of the presentation with the Blank layout, draw a flowchart document object, copy the flowchart document two times, align the objects horizontally in the middle of the slide, connect the objects together with connector lines, and then save and close the presentation.

One Step Further

Exercise 1

Open Holidays 07 from the Lesson07 folder that is located in the PowerPoint Practice folder and save it as Holidays 08 in the Lesson08 folder. Display slide 3. Using the Explosion AutoShape, create a graphic of Independence Day fireworks on the slide. Change the AutoShape's colors and shape so that it resembles fireworks explosions. Rotate and flip the explosions as necessary to vary the look of the shapes. Use the Arc tool from the AutoShapes Basic Shapes submenu to show the path of the fireworks from the "ground" to the explosion in the air. Change the arc to a dashed line to better resemble a firework's path through the air. Save and close the presentation.

Exercise 2

Open Marx 07 from the Lesson07 folder that is located in the PowerPoint Practice folder and save it as Marx 08 in the Lesson08 folder. Display slide 1. Use the Horizontal Scroll AutoShape to draw a scroll below the subtitle on the slide. Type the following text in the scroll: Convenient, Fast . . . and Delicious! Change the color of the scroll to another scheme color, or a color of your choice that shows up well against the slide background. Change the text font, color, and style to display the message attractively. Adjust the scroll size as necessary to accommodate the text. Save the presentation and close it.

Exercise 3

Open Marx 08 from the Lesson08 folder that is located in the PowerPoint Practice folder. Display the last slide. In the empty space below the text, use the 5-Point Star AutoShape to draw a star. Apply a 3-D effect to the star and adjust 3-D settings as desired. Copy the star and paste it five times for a total of six stars. Delete one of the stars. Adjust the position of the five stars so that they overlap slightly, and give each a different color if you like. Change stacking order as desired to display the group of stars attractively. Group the stars, and then change the color or position of one star without ungrouping. Move the group of stars to the left of the slide beneath the text. At the right of the stars, draw a shape of your choice and insert the text Five-Star Cuisine! Modify text properties as you wish, and then add a shadow effect to the shape. Save and close the presentation.

LESSON

Adding Graphics to PowerPoint

After completing this lesson, you will be able to:

✔ *Change the layout of a slide.*
✔ *Insert a clip art image.*
✔ *Scale an image.*
✔ *Recolor a clip art image.*
✔ *Insert and modify a picture.*
✔ *Insert and modify WordArt.*

KEY TERMS

▪ clip art   ▪ scaling

Adding graphics to a Microsoft PowerPoint presentation can help you communicate your message as well as enhance the appearance of slides. Clip art pictures and photographs can act as illustrations for the slide content or impart the tone you wish to set for the presentation. For a light-hearted presentation topic, for example, humorous clip art pictures can amuse your audience. A travel presentation can be greatly improved with photographs illustrating the destination under discussion.

You use commands on the Insert menu and the Drawing toolbar to insert graphic objects such as clip art pictures, photographs, and stylized text. Once you have a graphic object on the slide, tools from the Picture toolbar and other specialized toolbars help you modify and customize your graphics.

As vice president of sales at Contoso, Ltd, you have been working on a company presentation. Now you are ready to add clip art, pictures, and stylized text to enhance your message.

In this lesson, you will learn how to change a slide layout; insert, modify, and resize clip art images; scale an image; recolor a clip art image; insert and modify a picture; and insert and modify WordArt.

◆ Before you can use the practice files in this lesson, you must install them from the book's companion CD to their default location. See "Using the CD-ROM" at the beginning of this book for more information. To complete the procedures in this lesson, you will need to use files named 09 PPT Lesson and 09 Future Picture in the Lesson09 folder in the PowerPoint Practice folder located on your hard disk.

Changing the Layout of a Slide

THE BOTTOM LINE

Change a slide layout at any time to one that better suits the slide content. Existing content reflows into the new placeholders.

As you work with the content of a slide, you may realize that you need a different slide layout. Suppose you have decided to add a clip art picture to a Title and Text slide, for example. Although you can insert a clip art picture anywhere on any slide layout, using a Title, Text, and Content or Title, Text and Clip Art layout can make it easier to size and position the clip art.

When you change a slide layout after you have already added content, you don't lose the existing content. Instead, it is repositioned in the placeholders of the new layout. You have considerable flexibility in adjusting layouts at any time during the creation of a presentation.

Change the layout of a slide

You begin this lesson by changing the layout of a slide to which you want to add a graphic image. The new layout will make it easy to position the image.

◆ Start PowerPoint, if necessary, click the Open button on the Standard toolbar, navigate to the Lesson09 folder in the PowerPoint Practice folder, and then open the 09 PPT Lesson file. Save the file as Contoso Company Pres 09 in the same folder.

1 In the Slides tab, click slide 4.

2 On the Format menu, click Slide Layout.

The Slide Layout task pane opens with the current slide layout style selected.

ANOTHER METHOD

Right-click a blank area of the slide, and then click Slide Layout on the shortcut menu.

3 In the Slide Layout task pane, scroll down until you reach the Text and Content Layouts heading.

The layouts in this section make it easy for you to add both text and graphic content to a slide.

4 Under the Text and Content Layouts heading, click the Title, Text, and Content slide layout.

The layout of slide 4 changes. The bulleted list now occupies only the left half of the screen. A content placeholder occupies the right half. The slide is now ready for you to insert content such as a table, a chart, a piece of clip art, a picture, a diagram or organization chart, or a media clip. Your presentation window should look like the following illustration.

Figure 9-1

Text fits to the new placeholder

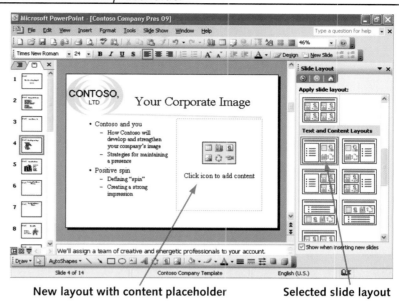

New layout with content placeholder | Selected slide layout

TROUBLESHOOTING

If the bulleted text doesn't automatically fit to the text placeholder, click the AutoFit button at the lower left corner of the text place-holder and choose to fit the text to the placeholder.

5 In the Slide Layout task pane, click the Close button to close the task pane.

◆ Keep this file open for the next exercise.

QUICK CHECK

Q: What kinds of objects can you insert into a content placeholder?

A: You can insert a table, a chart, a clip art image, a picture, a diagram or or-ganization chart, or a media clip.

QUICK REFERENCE ▼

Change the layout of a slide

1 Display the slide to which you want to apply a different slide layout.

2 On the Format menu, click Slide Layout to display the Slide Layout task pane.

3 Click a new slide layout.

Inserting a Clip Art Image

THE BOTTOM LINE

Inserting Clip Art and Pictures

Use clip art to add graphic interest to a slide or to help illustrate the slide content. Use the Clip Art task pane to specify what kind of graphic content to insert and to search for images by keyword.

PowerPoint provides access to hundreds of professionally designed pieces of **clip art**. Clip art images include illustrations, symbols, borders, and other graphic images that can add impact to your slides. While it isn't necessary to illustrate every slide in a presentation, inserting clip art judiciously can provide "eye relief" for your audience.

In PowerPoint, as in all Microsoft Office applications, clip art is stored in the Microsoft Clip Organizer. The Clip Organizer organizes clips by category, and each clip is identified by several keywords. A picture of an eagle, for example, might be identified by the keywords *animals, bald eagles, birds*. Keywords that apply to multiple categories make it easy for you to search for an image.

You have several options for adding a clip art image to a slide. In a slide with a content placeholder, click the Insert Clip Art icon to open the Select Picture dialog box. This dialog box shows you all clip art on your system, as well as any other graphic images that the Clip Organizer has organized for you. You can search in the Select Picture dialog box to find images.

To have more control over the process of searching, you can display the Clip Art task pane. To do so, click the Insert Clip Art button on the Drawing toolbar or point to Picture on the Insert menu and then click Clip Art. The Clip Art task pane has a Search For box where you type a keyword to identify the type of clip you want to find, such as clips that show *clients* or *doctors*. The Search In box lets you select which collections to search in: your personal collections, the standard Office collections, collections on the Web, or all collections. The Results Should Be box lets you choose what type of media to search: clip art images, photographs, movies, or sounds. You can select any one of these, or select multiple options. After you have typed a keyword and selected options for the search, click Go to complete the search and display images that match your search criteria in the pane. You can then simply click the image to insert it on the slide.

If you don't find an image you like when you search in the Clip Art task pane, you can click Clip Art On Office Online at the bottom of the Clip Art task pane to connect to Microsoft's Clip Art And Media Web page. This Web page gives you access to many more clip art images.

You can also work directly in the Clip Organizer to locate images. Click Organize Clips to open the Clip Organizer. You can then browse through the categories for each collection. If you find a clip you want to use, you can copy it and paste it onto the slide.

Insert a clip art image

Now that you have changed the slide layout, you are ready to insert a clip art image in the content placeholder. You will use the Clip Art task pane to locate and insert the clip.

1 **With slide 4 displayed, click in a blank area inside the content placeholder to select the placeholder.**

Selecting the placeholder before you insert the clip art will ensure that the clip art uses the placeholder size and position.

2 **On the Insert menu, point to Picture, and then click Clip Art.**

The Clip Art task pane appears with search options.

ANOTHER METHOD

On the Drawing toolbar, click the Insert Clip Art button.

3 **Click the Results Should Be down arrow and make sure only the Clip Art check box is selected.**

The search will be restricted to clip art images, which will save time in searching and in evaluating the results of the search.

4 **In the Search For text box, type** peak, **and then click Go.**

All clip art pertaining to *peak* appears.

TIP

Clip art from the Clip Organizer appears with a small globe icon in the lower-left corner of the image.

5 **Scroll down, if necessary, and then click a clip art picture similar to the one shown in the following illustration. (You may find it faster to scroll up from the bottom of the pane to locate this illustration.)**

PowerPoint inserts the clip art in the placeholder. The picture is selected on the slide, and the Picture toolbar opens. When a picture is selected, PowerPoint automatically opens the Picture toolbar.

Figure 9-2

Select picture similar to this one

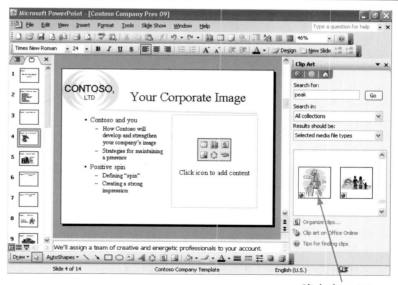

Click this picture

6 **Click outside the image to deselect it.**

The Picture toolbar is hidden.

✕

7 **In the Clip Art task pane, click the Close button to close the task pane.**

◆ **Keep this file open for the next exercise.**

QUICK REFERENCE ▼

Insert a clip art image using the Clip Art task pane

1 On the Insert menu, point to Picture, and then click Clip Art.

2 In the Clip Art task pane, in the Search For text box, type what you want to search for.

3 Make any necessary adjustments in Search In and Results Should Be boxes.

4 Click Go.

5 Click a clip art image to insert it into the placeholder or on the slide.

Scaling an Image

Modifying Clip Art and Pictures

THE BOTTOM LINE

If a graphic isn't exactly the right size on the slide, you can scale it to resize it precisely by percentage or by measurement.

Graphics that you insert on slides may not be the right size for the area where you want to place them. You can adjust image size by scaling. **Scaling** changes the size of an entire object by a set percentage. Scaling differs from simply dragging a resize handle in that you can specify an exact measurement for width or height or type a percentage to enlarge or reduce the image.

Use the Picture command on the Format menu to open the Format Picture dialog box, or right-click the picture and select Format Picture from the shortcut menu. The Size tab in this dialog box gives you access to several measurement boxes for scaling. By default, a change to one dimension of the picture will automatically change the other dimension so that the current ratio of width to height is maintained. The Size tab also displays the original dimensions of the image so you can reset the original size if you don't like the result of your scaling.

If you create a presentation specifically for giving a slide show, you can also optimize the size of an image for the size of the slide show screen by selecting the Best Scale For Slide Show check box on the Size tab.

Scale an object

An image you have already inserted in the presentation could be scaled for greater impact on the slide.

1 Scroll down to slide 8.

2 Select the clip art image.

The Picture toolbar appears.

TROUBLESHOOTING

If the Picture toolbar doesn't appear, click the View menu, point to Toolbars, and then click Picture.

3 On the Picture toolbar, click the Format Picture button, or click Picture on the Format menu.

The Format Picture dialog box appears.

ANOTHER METHOD

Right-click the picture, and then click Format Picture on the shortcut menu.

4 Click the Size tab.

The Size tab displays a number of options for changing the scale of the image.

5 In the Scale area, select the number in the Height box.

6 Type 120.

Because the Lock Aspect Ratio check box is selected, the Width option setting will also automatically change to 120% when you click OK. If you are not sure about the new scale size, you can click Preview (next to Cancel) to view the object before you close the dialog box.

7 Click OK, and then deselect the object.

The dialog box closes, and you should see that the picture is larger. Your slide should look like the following illustration.

ANOTHER METHOD

You can also press Esc to deselect an object.

Figure 9-3

Image has been scaled

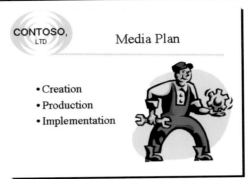

CONTOSO, LTD   Media Plan

- Creation
- Production
- Implementation

◆ **Keep this file open for the next exercise.**

QUICK REFERENCE ▼

Scale an object

1. Select the clip art image.
2. On the Picture toolbar, click the Format Picture button, or click Picture on the Format menu.
3. Click the Size tab.
4. In the Scale area, select the number in the Height box.
5. Type a number.
6. Click OK.

Recoloring a Clip Art Image

Modifying Clip Art and Pictures

THE BOTTOM LINE

Recolor clip art images to make them coordinate with the color scheme of your current design template. This gives a custom look to the image.

You can change the color of clip art images to create a different look or to match the current color scheme. Recoloring customizes the image so it looks as if it were created specifically for the current presentation.

The Recolor Picture command displays a dialog box with a preview of the picture and a list of all the colors in the picture. You can change any color in the list. By default, when you select a color to change, the color menu displays the current color scheme colors. Choose one of these colors to have the image blend in with slide colors already in use. You can also click More Colors to select any other color from the PowerPoint color palette.

Recolor an image

You have already inserted a clip art image on slide 5, but it would be improved by recoloring. You will change both image colors to colors that coordinate with the color scheme.

1 Scroll up to slide 5.

2 Select the clip art object.

3 On the Picture toolbar, click the Recolor Picture button.

The Recolor Picture dialog box appears with the Colors option selected in the Change section. This image has only two colors, black and white.

4 Under New, click the down arrow next to the black color.

A color menu appears, showing the current color scheme colors.

5 Click in the dark blue color box.

The color swatch changes to dark blue, and the preview box on the right shows that all the parts of the image that were black—the lines— are now blue. Now you will choose a new color from the PowerPoint color palette to replace the white color.

6 Under New, click the down arrow next to the white color, click More Colors, and then click the first gray cell in the bottom row, as shown in the following illustration.

Figure 9-4

Select the light gray shown here

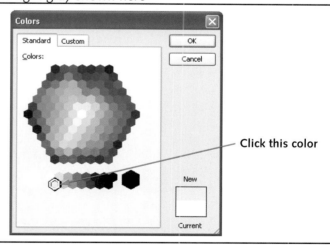

7 Click OK, and then click OK in the Recolor Picture dialog box.

PowerPoint recolors the clip art image so all white areas are light gray.

8 Deselect the object.

The Picture toolbar closes.

◆ Keep this file open for the next exercise.

QUICK CHECK

Q: How does PowerPoint determine which colors are shown in the drop-down menu of the New box?

A: The colors shown are the current color scheme colors.

QUICK REFERENCE ▼

Recolor a clip art image

1 Select a clip art object.

2 On the Picture toolbar, click the Recolor Picture button.

3 Under New, click the down arrow next to a color.

4 Click a color box or click More Colors, click a color, and then click OK.

5 Click OK.

Inserting a Picture

Inserting Clip Art and Pictures

THE BOTTOM LINE

Pictures stored on your system, network, or removable media give you a great deal of flexibility for locating and inserting pictures to illustrate your slides. You can also save time by inserting pictures directly from your scanner or camera.

Besides using PowerPoint's broad collection of clip art and photographs, you can insert pictures that are stored anywhere on your system, on a network, or on removable media such as disk or CD-ROM. You can also insert a picture directly from a scanner or digital camera to a slide, without having to first save it to a location on your system. Using the Picture submenu on the Insert menu gives you access to an almost limitless number of pictures that can add visual impact to your slides.

You already know that the Picture submenu gives you access to the Clip Art command that opens the Clip Art task pane. This submenu also offers the From File command, which you can use to locate a picture stored on any local or network drive, and From Scanner or Camera, which you can use to download a picture directly from either of these devices.

You do not have to use a placeholder to contain a picture. You can insert a picture on any slide and then adjust its size as desired.

TIP

You can also find the New Photo Album command on the Picture submenu. Use a photo album to display a collection of photos in a presentation using special layout options such as oval frames and captions under the pictures.

When you insert pictures from files on your hard disk drive, scanner, digital camera, or Web camera, PowerPoint allows you to select multiple pictures, view thumbnails of them, and insert them all at once.

Insert a picture

You have available a photograph that you think will illustrate the excitement of working with Contoso. In this exercise, you will insert the picture on a slide.

1 In the Slides tab, click slide 10.

2 On the Insert menu, point to Picture, and then click From File.

The Insert Picture dialog box appears.

ANOTHER METHOD

- Click the Insert Picture button on the Drawing toolbar.
- Click the Insert Picture button in any content placeholder.

3 Navigate to the Lesson09 folder in the PowerPoint Practice folder.

A thumbnail of the picture stored in the folder displays. (You may need to change the View option to see the thumbnail view.)

4 Click 09 Future Picture, and then click Insert.

The picture and the Picture toolbar appear. The picture is inserted at a very small size, as shown in the following illustration. You will adjust the size in the next exercise.

Figure 9-5

Picture inserted on slide

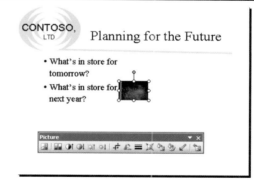

◆ Keep this file open for the next exercise.

QUICK REFERENCE ▼

Insert a picture

1 On the Insert menu, point to Picture, and then click From File.

2 In the Look In box, navigate to the location from which you want to insert a picture.

3 In the list of file names, click the picture you want to insert.

4 Click Insert.

QUICK CHECK

Q: Besides inserting clip art from the Picture submenu, what other options do you have for inserting graphics?

A: You can insert a picture from a file, insert a picture from a scanner or digital camera, or create a new photo album.

Modifying a Picture

Modifying Clip Art and Pictures

THE BOTTOM LINE

Change attributes such as size, brightness, and contrast to improve the look of a picture. Cropping can eliminate unnecessary parts of the picture, and compressing can help to keep file size reasonable.

You can enhance a photograph or scanned image by using tools on the Picture toolbar to control brightness, contrast, and color. Modifying a picture using these controls ensures that it will look its best on the slide. If you find that your changes don't improve the picture as you wanted, you can click the Reset Picture button on the Picture toolbar to reverse all changes.

Sometimes you need only a portion of a picture in the presentation. With the Crop command, you can mask portions of a picture so you do not see all of it on the screen. The picture is not altered, just covered up.

You can also compress pictures with PowerPoint to minimize the file size of the image. In doing so, however, you may lose some visual quality, depending on the compression setting. You can pick the resolution that you want for the pictures in a presentation based on where or how they'll be viewed (for example, on the Web or printed), and you can set other options, such as deleting cropped areas of a picture, to get the best balance between picture quality and file size.

Modify a picture

As you have already seen, the picture you inserted is too small. In this exercise, you will resize it as well as make other modifications to improve its appearance on the slide.

1 Click the picture on slide 10 to select it if necessary and display the Picture toolbar.

2 Hold down Shift, and then drag the corner resize handles on the picture to enlarge the picture on the slide.

Holding Shift as you drag maintains the current ratio of width to height so the picture doesn't become distorted.

IMPORTANT

If you are having trouble resizing the picture, you can press the Alt key while dragging the resize handles to turn off the Snap Objects To Grid feature.

3 On the Picture toolbar, click the Color button, and then click Washout.

The picture is converted to a watermark, which is a grayed version of the image.

4 On the Picture toolbar, click the Less Brightness button twice.

The picture brightness decreases to enhance the look of the picture.

 5 On the Picture toolbar, click the More Contrast button twice.

The picture contrast increases to enhance the look of the picture.

6 Drag the picture up until it is aligned to the top of the text box on the slide.

For fine positioning of the picture, nudge it using the keyboard arrow keys.

7 On the Picture toolbar, click the Crop button.

The pointer changes to the cropping tool.

8 Position the center of the cropping tool over the left-middle resize handle, and then drag right to crop the left side of the picture to cover the pole.

While you are dragging, a dotted outline appears to show you the area that remains after cropping. The cropping tool also changes to a constrain pointer, indicating the direction in which you are cropping.

9 Position the center of the cropping tool over the right-middle resize handle, and then drag left to crop the right side of the picture to cover the pole.

 10 On the Picture toolbar, click the Crop button, or click a blank portion of the slide.

The cropping tool changes back to the pointer.

11 Drag the corner and side resize handles to resize the picture so that it covers the right side of the slide.

12 On the Picture toolbar, click the Compress Pictures button.

The Compress Pictures dialog box appears. The current settings, shown in the illustration below, fit your needs.

Figure 9-6

Compress Pictures dialog box

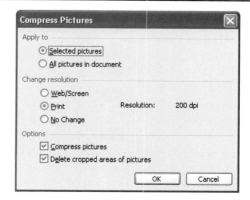

13 Click OK.

A warning box appears, letting you know that compressing pictures may reduce the quality of your images.

14 **Click Apply to compress the image.**

15 **Deselect the picture.**

Your presentation window should look like the following illustration.

Figure 9-7

Modified picture

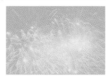

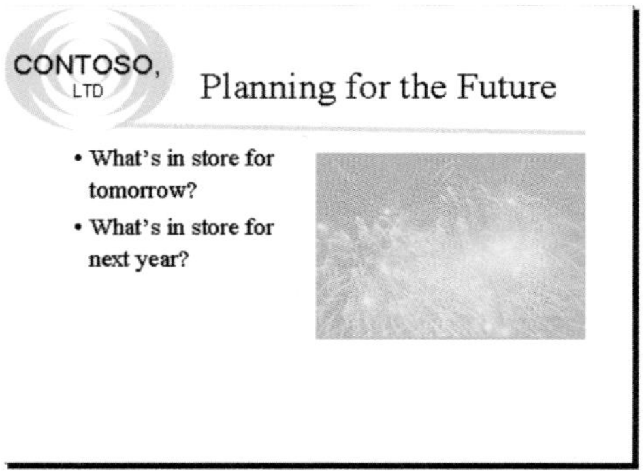

CONTOSO,
LTD
Planning for the Future
• What's in store for tomorrow?
• What's in store for next year?

QUICK CHECK

Q: What Picture toolbar button allows you to convert a color picture to grayscale?

A: **The Color button offers an option to convert a color picture to grayscale.**

◆ **Keep this file open for the next exercise.**

QUICK REFERENCE ▼

Resize a picture

Select the picture, hold down Shift, and then drag the corner resize handles on the picture to enlarge the picture on the slide.

Move a picture

Drag the picture until it is properly aligned.

Enhance a picture

1. Select the picture.
2. On the Picture toolbar, click formatting buttons such as Color, Less Brightness, or More Contrast until you reach the effect you want.

Crop a picture

1. Select the clip art image.
2. On the Picture toolbar, click the Crop button.
3. Position the center of the cropping tool over a resize handle and drag to crop the picture.
4. On the Picture toolbar, click the Crop button or click a blank portion of the slide to deselect the Crop button.

Compress a picture

1 Select the picture.

2 On the Picture toolbar, click the Compress Pictures button.

3 Click the compression options that you want.

4 Click OK, and then click Apply.

Inserting and Modifying WordArt

Inserting and Modifying Stylized Text

THE BOTTOM LINE

WordArt creates a graphic from text and thus can add both information and visual appeal to a slide. Use the WordArt toolbar options to
further customize a WordArt graphic for the presentation.

You can insert fancy or stylized text into a presentation with Microsoft's
WordArt feature. WordArt allows you to add visual enhancements to your
text that go beyond changing a font or font size. Most users apply
WordArt to emphasize short phrases, such as *Our Customers Come First*,
or to a single word, such as *Welcome*. You do not have to be an artist to
create stylized text—WordArt provides you with a gallery of choices. You
can insert stylized text by clicking the Insert WordArt button on the
Drawing toolbar (or by clicking Picture on the Insert menu and then
clicking WordArt) and then selecting a style.

Insert and modify WordArt

Your final enhancement to the presentation will be adding a WordArt
graphic to the last slide.

1 Scroll down to slide 14.

2 On the Drawing toolbar, click the Insert WordArt button.

The WordArt Gallery dialog box appears, displaying a list of styles.

ANOTHER METHOD

On the Insert menu, point to Picture and then click WordArt.

3 Click the style in the third column, third row, as shown in the following illustration.

Figure 9-8

WordArt Gallery dialog box

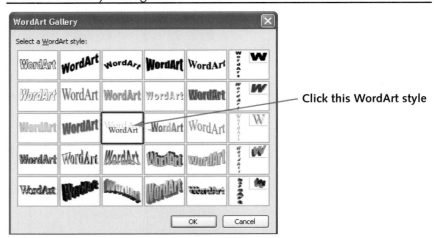

Click this WordArt style

4 **Click OK.**

The Edit WordArt Text dialog box appears.

5 **In the Text box, type** We bask in the glow of your image!

The WordArt text defaults to the Times New Roman font at 36 points. You can change this text at any time using the Edit Text button on the WordArt toolbar.

6 **Click OK.**

The text you typed and the WordArt toolbar appear. Notice that the shadow extends almost off the slide at the right.

7 **Drag the lower-right resize handle to the left to decrease the size of the WordArt object so it fits on the slide.**

 8 **On the WordArt toolbar, click the WordArt Shape button, and then click the Double Wave 2 symbol, as shown in the following illustration.**

The new shape is applied to the WordArt, adding even more visual interest.

Figure 9-9

WordArt Shape menu

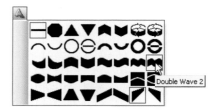

 9 **On the WordArt toolbar, click the WordArt Character Spacing button.**

A submenu appears with character spacing types. Character spacing options increase or decrease the space between the letters in the words.

10 On the Character Spacing submenu, click Loose.

Space between letters increases slightly.

 11 On the WordArt toolbar, click the Format WordArt button.

The Format WordArt dialog box opens.

12 Click the Colors and Lines tab, click the Color down arrow in the Fill section at the top of the dialog box, and then click in the dark blue box in the top row of color boxes (Follow Accent Scheme Color box).

The fill color changes from a green marble texture to the color scheme dark blue.

13 Click the Color down arrow in the Line section, and then click in the dark blue box in the top row of color boxes (Follow Accent Scheme Color box).

The line color now matches the fill color.

14 Click OK.

The text now coordinates better with the color scheme, but the shadow behind the text still has a greenish tint that can be modified to improve the graphic.

 15 On the Drawing toolbar, click the Shadow Style button, and then click Shadow Settings.

The Shadow Settings toolbar appears.

 16 On the Shadow Settings toolbar, click the Shadow Color button down arrow, and then click in the light blue box (Follow Accent And Hyperlink Scheme Color box).

17 Click the Close button on the Shadow Settings toolbar.

The shadow now coordinates with the text.

18 Drag the WordArt text object to the center of the slide, and then click a blank area of the presentation window to quit WordArt.

The WordArt toolbar closes.

◆ If you are continuing to other lessons, save the Contoso Company Pres 09 presentation with the current name and then close it. If you are not continuing to other lessons, save and close the Contoso Company Pres 09 presentation, and then click the Close button in the title bar of the PowerPoint window.

QUICK CHECK

Q: What WordArt toolbar button can help you tighten up the space between letters?

A: **The WordArt Character Spacing button adjusts space between letters.**

QUICK REFERENCE ▼

Insert WordArt in a slide

1 On the Drawing toolbar, click the Insert WordArt button.

2 Click a style, and then click OK.

3 In the Text box, type text.

4 Click OK.

Format the WordArt text

1 Click the WordArt text.

2 On the WordArt toolbar, click formatting buttons to adjust the graphic as desired.

3 To adjust a WordArt shadow, on the Drawing toolbar, click the Shadow Style button, and then click Shadow Settings.

4 On the Shadow Settings toolbar, click the Shadow Color button down arrow, and then click a color box.

5 Click the Close button on the Shadow Settings toolbar.

Key Points

✓ *Change the layout of a slide at any time to adjust the way content appears on the slide. Existing content reformats into the new placeholders.*

✓ *Use the Select Picture dialog box or Clip Art task pane to search for and insert clip art stored on your system. The Clip Art task pane gives you greater flexibility in searching for particular types of clip art.*

✓ *When you want to adjust an image's size precisely, use the scaling options in the Format Picture dialog box.*

✓ *Make a clip art image match your color scheme more closely by recoloring portions of it.*

✓ *You can insert a picture such as a photograph or illustration from any drive on your system, from a scanner, or from a digital camera. You can then modify the picture using the tools on PowerPoint's Picture toolbar.*

✓ *WordArt creates stylized text that can add visual impact as well as information to your slides. Format a WordArt graphic using the tools on the WordArt toolbar.*

Quick Quiz

True/False

T   F   1. After you change a slide layout, you have to manually move information into the new placeholders.

T   F   2. To search for clip art on a particular subject, you type a keyword in the Search For box in the Clip Art task pane.

T   F   3. Most clip art images are created using only one or two colors.

T   F   4. A picture must be inserted into a placeholder.

T   F   5. It is probably best to limit WordArt graphics to short phrases or single words.

Multiple Choice

1. Clip art images can include _____.
   a. illustrations
   b. symbols
   c. borders
   d. all of the above

2. To scale an image, you use the _____ tab in the Format Picture dialog box.
   a. Scale
   b. Size
   c. Format
   d. Layout

3. To insert a picture from your digital camera, click Insert, _____.
   a. point to Import, and then click From Scanner or Camera
   b. point to Camera, and then click Insert Picture
   c. point to Picture, and then click From Scanner or Camera
   d. point to New, and then click Digital Image

4. To remove a portion of a picture you don't need, you use the _____ tool.
   a. Trim
   b. Reset
   c. Compress
   d. Crop

5. To change the color of a WordArt graphic, click the _____ button on the WordArt toolbar.
   a. Format WordArt
   b. Recolor
   c. WordArt Color
   d. Shadow Color

Short Answer

1. How do you scale an object disproportionately?
2. How do you recolor an image?
3. How do you search for a photograph using the Clip Art task pane?
4. How do you insert a picture stored on a CD-ROM?
5. How do you make an image into a watermark?
6. How do you crop a picture?
7. How do you insert WordArt?

On Your Own

Exercise 1

Open Contoso Company Pres 09 in the Lesson09 folder that is located in the PowerPoint Practice folder. Insert a new slide at the end of the presentation with the Title, Text, and Content layout, search for clip art with the keyword *communication*, and insert a clip art image into the content placeholder. Scale the image by 50 percent, recolor the image, and then save and close the presentation.

Exercise 2

Open Contoso Company Pres 09 in the Lesson09 folder that is located in the PowerPoint Practice folder. Insert a new slide at the end of the presentation with the Blank layout, insert WordArt in the slide with any style and the text Any Questions? with the Inflate shape, and then save and close the presentation.

One Step Further

Exercise 1

Start a new presentation for A. Datum Corporation, using any design template or the one you have been using in other lessons. Save the presentation as AD Sales 09 in the Lesson09 folder that is located in the PowerPoint Practice folder. In the title area of the title slide, insert a WordArt object using the text A. Datum Corporation, and modify styles and formats as desired. Add the subtitle Annual Sales Conference. Save and close the presentation.

Exercise 2

Open the AD Sales 09 presentation in the Lesson09 folder. In the Clip Art task pane, search for photographs only using the keyword *presentation*. Insert an appropriate picture on the slide. Scale the image as necessary to fit on the slide (you may want to move the title and subtitle to make room for the picture). Modify the picture properties and crop as necessary. Compress the picture. Save and close the presentation.

Exercise 3

Open the AD Sales 09 presentation in the Lesson09 folder. Add a new slide using the Title and Text layout. Type the title Focus on Clients and then insert in the text area the names of five clients (you can make up these names). Insert an appropriate clip art graphic (use the keyword *client*, for example) on this slide to the right of the bulleted list. Scale the clip art appropriately. Recolor the clip art to match the current design template colors. Save and close the presentation.

Inserting Information into PowerPoint

After completing this lesson, you will be able to:

✓ *Insert and format a table.*
✓ *Insert a Microsoft Excel chart.*
✓ *Insert and format a Microsoft Graph chart.*
✓ *Insert and modify an organization chart.*
✓ *Insert and modify a diagram.*

KEY TERMS

- Cell
- Embedded object
- Linked object

- Source document
- Source program

You can use several features in Microsoft PowerPoint to insert and organize information that can help you communicate your message. Tables organize information in a grid that your audience will find easy to read. Charts and diagrams present numerical data and information in a graphical format that makes the data simple to understand. If you have created information or data tables in another program such as Word or Excel, you can import the information directly into PowerPoint without having to retype it on the slides.

As vice president of sales at Contoso, Ltd, you have been working on a company presentation. Now you are ready to add a table, charts, and diagrams to enhance the message.

In this lesson, you will learn how to insert and modify a table, a Microsoft Excel chart, a Microsoft Graph chart, an organization chart, and a diagram.

◆ Before you can use the practice files in this lesson, you must install them from the book's companion CD to their default location. See "Using the CD-ROM" at the beginning of this book for more information. To complete the procedures in this lesson, you will need to use files named 10 PPT Lesson, 10 Company Performance, and 10 PR Budget in the Lesson10 folder in the PowerPoint Practice folder located on your hard disk.

Inserting and Formatting a Table

Inserting and Formatting a Table

THE BOTTOM LINE

Use a table to organize information in rows and columns that make data easy to understand. Table formatting can emphasize parts of the table to improve comprehension.

A table organizes information neatly into rows and columns. The intersection of a row and a column is called a **cell**. The regular grid structure of a table makes tabular or numerical information easy to comprehend.

Create a table by clicking the Insert Table button in any content placeholder, by double-clicking the table placeholder in a Title and Table slide layout, or by clicking Table on the Insert menu. You can then choose how many columns and rows the table will have. If you click the Insert Table button on the Standard toolbar, you can select columns and rows from a drop-down grid.

TIP

You can also use the Draw Table tool on the Tables And Borders toolbar to draw your table structure. This is a good way to create a table that has cells of various sizes.

Enter text into the cells by typing just as you would in a paragraph. You can use the Tab key to move the insertion point from cell to cell. The first row in the table is commonly used for column headings. The leftmost column is ideal for row labels.

You can customize and format individual cells as well as the entire table. To accommodate the text that you enter in the table, you can merge, or combine, cells to form a larger cell. This is useful when you want to spread the text across the top of a table. You can also split, or divide, a cell into two. With the Formatting and Tables and Borders toolbars, you can add color to cells and borders and change the text alignment in a table.

Insert and format a table

Begin this lesson by inserting and formatting a table that presents some Contoso successes.

◆ **Start PowerPoint, if necessary, click the Open button on the Standard toolbar, navigate to the Lesson10 folder in the PowerPoint Practice folder, and then open the 10 PPT Lesson file. Save the file as Contoso Company Pres 10 in the same folder.**

1 Scroll down to slide 11.

Slide 11 has a Title and Table layout already applied.

2 Double-click the table placeholder.

The Insert Table dialog box appears.

ANOTHER METHOD

- On the Insert menu, click Table.
- On the Standard toolbar, click the Insert Table button.

---

3 Click the Number Of Rows up arrow until the number reaches 4.

You do not need to change the Number Of Columns option.

4 Click OK.

PowerPoint inserts a blank table of two columns and four rows that you can fill with text. The Tables And Borders toolbar also appears in the presentation window.

5 Type the following text in the table, using Tab to move from cell to cell.

Don't worry if the table runs off the bottom of the slide. You'll fix the layout in a later step.

Figure 10-1

Type text as shown

Company	Success
Bits, Bytes, and Chips, Inc.	Landed a $20 million contract
Miller Textiles	Improved community presence through local sponsorships
American Society of Science	Increased membership by 33% by modernizing their image

6 Select the column titles "Company" and "Success" in the table, and then click the Bold button on the Formatting toolbar.

7 On the Formatting toolbar, click the Center button, and then click Center Vertically on the Tables And Borders toolbar.

The column titles now stand out more in the table because of their bold, centered formatting.

8 With the column titles still selected, on the Tables And Borders toolbar, click the Fill Color button down arrow, and then click the light gray color box on the right.

Adding a fill to the first row helps to differentiate it from the rest of the table.

ANOTHER METHOD

Click the Fill Color button on the Drawing toolbar.

9 Click the Draw Table button on the Tables and Borders toolbar, and then draw a line under "Miller Textiles."

You have added a cell border to the table. Your slide should look like the following illustration.

Figure 10-2

Cell border added to table

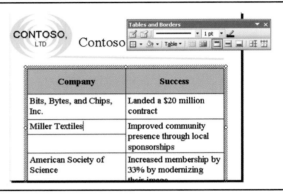

10 Click the Eraser button on the Tables And Borders toolbar, and then click the line under "Miller Textiles."

You have erased the border you just drew. Use this tool to erase any cell border in a table.

11 Click the Eraser button again to turn it off.

12 Click on the vertical line between the two columns and drag to the left until the right-hand column text fits on the slide.

The table now fits properly on the slide, as shown in the following illustration.

Figure 10-3

Table formatting is complete

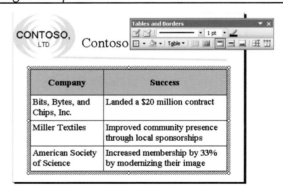

13 Click outside the table to deselect it.

◆ Keep this file open for the next exercise.

QUICK CHECK

Q: What button on the Tables and Borders toolbar allows you to re-move any cell border?

A: **Use the Eraser button to remove any cell border.**

QUICK REFERENCE ▼

Insert a table

1 On the Insert menu, click Table, or in the content placeholder, click the Insert Table icon, or double-click the table placeholder on a Title and Table slide.

2 Click the Number Of Rows and Number Of Columns arrows to select the number of rows and columns you want.

3 Click OK.

4 Type text in the table, using Tab to move from cell to cell.

Format a table

1 Select the cells in the table that you want to format.

2 Click buttons on the Formatting, Drawing, and Tables and Borders toolbars to modify the table formats as desired.

Inserting a Microsoft Word Table

You may already have created a table in Microsoft Word whose data you want to use on a slide. Instead of creating a table in PowerPoint and re-typing the information, you can import the Word table into PowerPoint as an embedded object. (See "Inserting a Microsoft Excel Chart" in this lesson for more information about embedded objects.)

To insert an existing Word table on a PowerPoint slide:

1. In PowerPoint, on the Insert menu, click Object.

2. In the Insert Object dialog box, click Create From File.

3. Click the Browse button and navigate to the location of the Word file. Select the file and click OK.

4. Click OK in the Insert Object dialog box.

5. Resize the object by dragging a resize handle and edit it by double-clicking on it.

Inserting a Microsoft Excel Chart

Inserting and Formatting a Table

THE BOTTOM LINE

If you have an Excel worksheet that contains numerical information or a chart you want to use on a slide, you can import the worksheet into PowerPoint as an embedded object. Embedding the Excel work-sheet lets you work with it using Excel's tools.

Microsoft Excel is a spreadsheet program that allows users to manipulate numerical data in many ways. One of its most useful features is its charting capability. If you have already created a chart in Excel, you can very easily import the worksheet with its chart into PowerPoint so that you don't have to recreate the chart on a slide.

PowerPoint simplifies the process of inserting a Microsoft Excel chart into a presentation by embedding the chart as an object in the slide. An **embedded object** is an object that maintains a direct connection to its original program, known as the **source program**. After you insert an embedded object, you can easily edit it by double-clicking it, which opens the program in which it was originally created.

Use the Insert Object dialog box to insert an object such as an Excel chart. In this dialog box, you can choose to create an object from a file that already exists or create a new object. After you locate the correct file, PowerPoint embeds the object on the slide.

One advantage to embedding an object is that you can edit it using the tools of the source program. Double-click an embedded object to open it in its source program. The source program's toolbars and menu commands become available in PowerPoint so that you can edit the object from within PowerPoint.

Embedding objects greatly increases the file size of a presentation because the embedded object is stored in the presentation. To reduce the file size of the presentation, you can link an object instead of embedding it. A **linked object** appears in the slide, but it actually is just a "link" back to the original document, known as the **source document**. When you link an object, the original object is stored in the source document where it was created. The presentation stores only a representation of the original. The source program will update the object when you modify the source document.

CHECK THIS OUT ▼

Create New Object in PowerPoint

You can create a new object such as a Word document or Excel worksheet from right inside PowerPoint by using the Create New option in the Insert Object dialog box. In fact, as long as you have the proper program available, you can create any object in the Object Type list. For example, try clicking Bitmap Image in the Object Type list, and then click OK. PowerPoint opens a drawing program in which you can create an image that you can then embed on the slide.

Insert a Microsoft Excel Chart

You have chart data already created in Excel that you can add to the presentation. In this exercise, you insert an Excel chart object in a slide and then edit the embedded object.

1 Scroll up to slide 7.

2 On the Insert menu, click Object.

The Insert Object dialog box appears.

3 Click the Create From File option.

This option tells PowerPoint you already have a file to insert on the slide.

4 Click Browse.

The Browse dialog box appears. It is similar to the Open dialog box.

5 Navigate to the Lesson10 folder in the PowerPoint Practice folder.

6 **In the list of file and folder names, click 10 PR Budget, and then click OK to close the Browse dialog box.**

The Insert Object dialog box shows the complete path to the file you want to insert, as shown in the following illustration. Note the Link check box, which would allow you to link the object rather than embed it.

Figure 10-4

Path to the file to be inserted

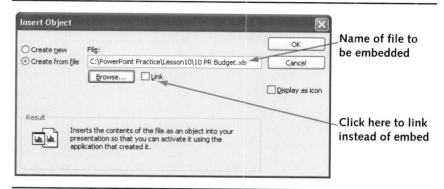

Name of file to be embedded

Click here to link instead of embed

7 **Click OK.**

PowerPoint embeds the chart (a bar chart) into the new slide.

8 **Double-click the embedded Excel chart.**

Excel opens and displays the Chart1 worksheet. The Standard and Formatting toolbars change to the Excel toolbars, and the Excel Chart toolbar appears.

9 **Click the Chart2 worksheet tab.**

You have edited the Excel object to show a different chart. Your embedded object should look like the following illustration.

Figure 10-5

Chart2 displays in the embedded object

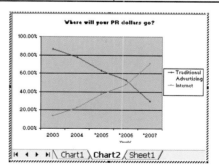

10 Click twice on a blank area of the slide to exit Excel and deselect the embedded Excel object.

The PowerPoint toolbars and menus return, and the embedded Excel object is updated on the slide, as shown in the following illustration.

Figure 10-6

Updated embedded object

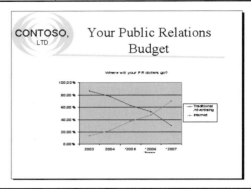

TIP

You may need to resize the Excel object on the slide by dragging its side handles to make it resemble the object in the illustration above.

◆ Keep this file open for the next exercise.

QUICK REFERENCE ▼

Insert an existing Excel chart

1 On the Insert menu, click Object.

2 Click the Create From File option.

3 Click Browse.

4 In the Look In box, navigate to the location of the Excel file that you want to insert.

5 In the list of file names, click the Excel file that you want to insert.

6 Click OK to close the Browse dialog box.

7 Click OK.

Edit an embedded Excel object

1 Double-click the embedded Excel chart.

2 Edit the Excel chart or worksheet.

3 Click twice on a blank area of the slide to exit Microsoft Excel and deselect the embedded Excel object.

Inserting and Formatting a Microsoft Graph Chart

Inserting and Formatting a Chart

THE BOTTOM LINE

You can create a variety of charts right in PowerPoint using the Microsoft Graph feature. Graph's options and features let you modify and format charts to present data attractively and accurately.

Microsoft Graph is a program that PowerPoint uses to insert a chart in a presentation slide. When you start Graph, create a chart, and return to the presentation slide, the chart becomes an embedded object in the slide. You can start Graph by double-clicking a chart placeholder, clicking the Insert Chart button on the Standard toolbar, or clicking Chart on the Insert menu.

In Graph, data is displayed in a datasheet and represented in a chart. The *datasheet* is composed of individual cells that form rows and columns, which, in turn, make up a group of related data points called a *data series*. A *data series marker* is a graphical representation in the chart of the information in the data series. Along the left and top edges of the datasheet are gray boxes, called control boxes. *Control boxes* correspond to the different data series in the datasheet. The first row and column of the datasheet contain names or labels for each data series. The data series labels appear in the chart.

The chart is made up of different elements that help display the data from the datasheet. The following chart has an X-axis (horizontal axis) and a Y-axis (vertical axis), which serve as reference lines for the plotted data. (In a 3-D chart, the third axis is the Z-axis.) Along each axis are labels, called *tick-mark labels*, that identify the data plotted in the chart. There is also a *legend* in the chart that identifies each data series in the datasheet.

Figure 10-7

Datasheet and sample chart

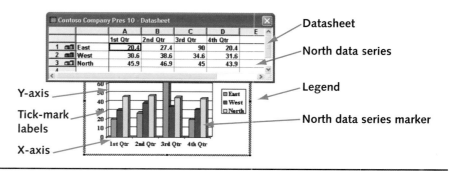

In a datasheet, you can use the mouse or keyboard commands to work with selected data by selecting an individual cell, a range of cells, or an entire row or column. A cell is identified by its row and column location in the datasheet. A selected cell, called the *active cell,* has a heavy border around it. When more than one cell is selected, the active cell is highlighted with a heavy border, and all other selected cells are highlighted in black. To perform most tasks on the datasheet, you must first select a specific cell or range of cells.

Figure 10-8

Parts of the datasheet

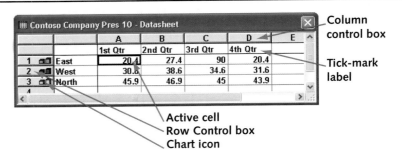

To enter data into the datasheet, you can type your own data into the datasheet, import information directly from Microsoft Excel, or copy and paste a specified range of data or a complete worksheet into Graph. By default, Graph creates a column chart, but you can change the chart type at any time. There are 14 chart categories, including both two-dimensional and three-dimensional charts.

Insert a Microsoft Graph chart

You are ready to create your own chart in the presentation. For this task, you can use the data in an existing Excel worksheet.

1 **In the Slides tab, click slide 12, and then double-click the chart placeholder.**

When you double-click the chart placeholder, PowerPoint launches Microsoft Graph. The Graph Standard and Formatting toolbars and menus replace the PowerPoint toolbars and menus. The datasheet and chart windows appear with default data that you can replace with your own data.

ANOTHER METHOD

On the Insert menu, click Chart.

2 **On the Graph Standard toolbar, click the Import File button.**

The Import File dialog box appears. This dialog box functions just like the Open dialog box.

3 **Navigate to the Lesson10 folder in the PowerPoint Practice folder, click 10 Company Performance, and then click Open.**

The Import Data Options dialog box appears, giving you options for selecting a worksheet and importing an entire sheet or only a range of cells. You will import the entire sheet and overwrite existing cells in the datasheet.

4 **Click OK to overwrite the current data in the datasheet.**

Graph inserts the worksheet data in the datasheet and also creates a graph associated with the data. A blank row appears at the top of the datasheet.

5 Right-click the blank row's control box and click Delete to remove the blank row.

The blank row is removed so all data displays correctly in the chart behind the datasheet.

6 Double-click cell C5, select the number, type .20, and then press Enter.

You have edited an existing value in the datasheet. Graph accepts the new entry and moves the selection down to cell C6.

> **TIP**
>
> You can adjust the datasheet size by dragging the lower-right corner of the datasheet window. If the datasheet obstructs the chart, move the datasheet window out of the way by dragging its title bar.

7 In cell C6, type .16, and then press Enter.

You have added a new entry in the datasheet, and the chart displays the change. Your datasheet window should look like the following illustration.

Figure 10-9

Completed datasheet

		A	B	C	
		2003	2004	2005	
1	Alpine Ski (	0.08	0.05	0.07	
2	Solomon W	0.18	0.2	0.22	
3	The Wine C	0.22	0.17	0.15	
4	Five Lakes	0.15	0.21	0.23	
5	Coho Winer	0.16	0.18	0.2	
6	Mightyfligh	0.25	0.15	0.16	
7					

Contoso Company Pres 10 - Datasheet

8 On the Graph Standard toolbar, click the Chart Type button down arrow, and then click the 3-D Bar Chart (the second chart down in the center column).

The chart changes to the 3-D Bar Chart type. This is not quite the look you want, however, so you will look at other chart types.

> **TIP**
>
> By default, Graph plots the chart so that the chart gives you information about the rows in the datasheet. In other words, the columns in the column chart represent the row names. You can change this to plot the data by the column names instead.

9 On the Chart menu, click Chart Type.

The Chart Type dialog box appears with standard and custom chart types and formats.

10 **Click the Custom Types tab.**

The Custom Types settings appear.

11 **Click Columns With Depth in the Chart Type list, and then click OK.**

The chart is now a column chart with deep, three-dimensional columns.

 12 **Click the Close button on the Datasheet window to close the window.**

The datasheet closes so you can see the chart.

TIP

To close and open the datasheet window, click the View Datasheet button on the Graph Standard toolbar.

◆ **Keep this file open for the next exercise.**

QUICK REFERENCE ▼

Insert a Microsoft Graph object

On the Insert menu, click Chart, or in the content placeholder, click the Insert Chart icon, or double-click the chart placeholder on a slide.

Import data into a chart

1 Double-click the Microsoft Graph chart and display the datasheet.

2 On the Graph Standard toolbar, click the Import File button.

3 Navigate to the location of the file that you want to insert, and then double-click the file.

4 Click OK to overwrite the current data in the datasheet.

Once the data is entered into the datasheet, you can easily modify and format the associated chart. If the chart is not selected, double-click it to open the chart in Microsoft Graph so you can make changes. Use the tools on the Graph Standard and Formatting toolbars to modify and format the chart objects. You can double-click almost any object in the chart window to edit its attributes. For example, you can double-click the Y-axis to display the Format Axis dialog box.

Format a Microsoft Graph chart

Now that you have entered data and settled on a chart type, you're ready to do some fine-tuning of the chart's formats.

Chart Area ▾

1 **On the Graph Standard toolbar, click the Chart Objects down arrow, and then click Chart Area, if necessary.**

The entire chart area is selected.

2 On the Graph Formatting toolbar, click the Font Size down arrow, and then click 18.

Because the entire chart area is selected, all text within the area, including the X-axis and Y-axis data labels and the legend, changes to 18 points.

3 On the Chart menu, click Chart Options, and then click the Gridlines tab.

The Chart Options dialog box appears with the Gridlines settings.

4 In the Value (Z) Axis section, select the Major Gridlines check box, and then click OK.

Gridlines appear on the chart.

5 In the chart, click the Y-axis with the percent values.

Black handles appear at the end of the Y-axis.

6 On the Graph Formatting toolbar, click the Italic button, and then click the Percent Style button.

The values on the Y-axis are italicized and the number format changes to percents.

ANOTHER METHOD

Press Ctrl + I.

---

7 Click the X-axis with the category values.

Black handles appear at the end of the X-axis.

8 On the Graph Formatting toolbar, click the Angle Counterclockwise button.

The X-axis text angle changes to a 45-degree angle.

9 Click a blank area of the presentation window outside the Graph chart to quit Graph. Click again to deselect the chart.

The PowerPoint toolbars and menus replace the Graph toolbar and menus, and the chart is embedded in the presentation slide. Your Graph chart should look like the following illustration.

Figure 10-10

Completed chart

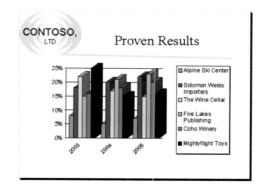

◆ Keep this file open for the next exercise.

QUICK CHECK

Q: What button on the Graph Standard toolbar lets you select any part of the chart from a drop-down list?

A: **The Chart Objects button displays a list of chart objects from which you can select.**

QUICK REFERENCE ▼

Format a Microsoft Graph chart

1 Double-click the Graph chart.

2 On the Chart menu, click Chart Type, and then click a chart type tab.

3 Click a chart type, click a chart subtype if desired, and then click OK.

4 Use the options on the Graph Standard toolbar, Graph Formatting toolbar, and Chart Options on the Chart menu to format the chart.

5 Click a blank area of the slide to exit Microsoft Graph.

Inserting and Modifying an Organization Chart

Inserting and Formatting an Organization Chart

THE BOTTOM LINE

Insert an organization chart to depict in graphical fashion the relationships among members of an organization. You can modify an organization chart to make it more attractive and keep it up to date.

An organization chart shows the relationship between individuals in an organization. For example, you can show the relationship between a manager and employees within a company. An organization chart can also be used in any situation where a hierarchy needs to be displayed, such as the departments in a large company or a family tree.

You create an organization chart by double-clicking the organization chart placeholder, by clicking the Insert Diagram or Organization Chart button on the Drawing toolbar or in a content placeholder, or by clicking Diagram on the Insert menu. When you create an organization chart, a sample chart appears. Type directly in the chart boxes to add information to the chart.

The default organization chart has a single box at the top for the head of the organization and three boxes below the top box for subordinates. If your organization requires more boxes, you must add shapes to the chart. Select the chart box above or next to the place where you want to add the new chart box, click the arrow on the Insert Shape button on the Organization Chart toolbar, and click one or more of the following:

- Subordinate—to place the new shape below the selected shape and to connect it to the selected shape
- Coworker—to place the shape next to the selected shape and connect it to the same manager shape
- Assistant—to place the new shape below the selected shape with an elbow connector

If you add a chart box in the wrong place, you can delete it by first selecting the chart box and then pressing the Delete key.

Other options on the Organization Chart toolbar let you change the chart layout, select portions of the chart, or fit text that is too long for a box. You can also zoom in or out on the chart to make it easier to see text as you add it.

Format an organization chart's box color, shadow, border style and color, or border line style using Drawing toolbar tools. You can use the Autoformat button on the Organization Chart toolbar to change the chart style. When you're finished working with the organization chart, you simply deselect the object to see it on the slide. To make further edits, click the chart to reopen it.

Insert and modify an organization chart

In this exercise, you insert an organization chart, enter text, add chart boxes, and then change the chart style.

1 **Scroll up to slide 3.**

This slide has the Title and Diagram or Organization Chart layout already applied.

2 **Double-click the organization chart placeholder.**

The Diagram Gallery dialog box appears with the Organization Chart selected.

ANOTHER METHOD

- On the Insert menu, click Diagram.
- On the Drawing menu, click Insert Diagram or Organization Chart.

3 **Click OK.**

PowerPoint displays a default chart of four boxes, one at the top and three below the top box. The Organization Chart toolbar is also displayed.

4 **Click in the top box and type** Wendy Beth Kahn.

5 **Press Enter, and then type** CEO.

You have completed the top box.

6 **Select the lower-left chart box and enter text in this and the other two subordinate boxes to match Figure 10-11.**

Figure 10-11

Enter text in the chart as shown

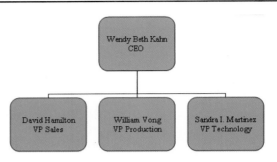

You have used up the default boxes, and you need to add more boxes to show other employees.

7 **Click in the lower-left chart box.**

Because you're going to add subordinates for David Hamilton, you need to select his box before adding a shape.

8 **On the Organization Chart toolbar, click the Insert Shape down arrow, and then click Subordinate.**

A subordinate chart box is placed below the left chart box. The Organization chart boxes are automatically resized to accommodate the new box.

9 **Type your name in the new chart box.**

10 **Click the David Hamilton box again. On the Organization Chart toolbar, click the Layout down arrow, and then click Right Hanging.**

The layout style changes so that subordinates will "hang" below the selected chart box in a column.

11 **Add chart boxes, change the layout, and enter text to match the following illustration.**

Figure 10-12

Complete the chart as shown

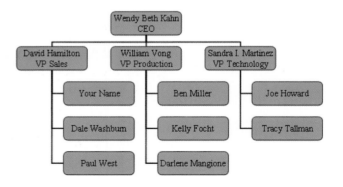

You have entered all of the names. Now you can modify the chart's format to improve its look.

TROUBLESHOOTING

For best results, insert the first subordinate, change the layout, and then add other subordinates.

12 On the Organization Chart toolbar, click the Autoformat button.

The Organization Chart Style Gallery dialog box appears.

13 Under Select A Diagram Style, click 3-D Color, and then click OK.

The style of the organization chart changes to show 3-D boxes that display shaded colors. Note that each level has a different color.

TIP

To format individual chart boxes or entire levels of chart boxes, select the chart boxes you want to format using an option from the Select menu on the Organization Chart toolbar, and then apply formats from the Formatting toolbar or the Drawing toolbar.

14 On the Formatting toolbar, click the Font Size down arrow, and then click 16.

All text in the organization chart is resized to 16 points.

15 Click outside the organization chart to deselect it.

The chart is embedded into PowerPoint, as shown in the following illustration.

Figure 10-13

Completed chart on slide

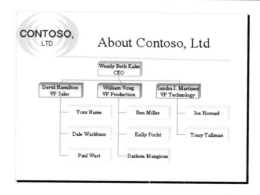

◆ Keep this file open for the next exercise.

QUICK CHECK

Q: What three organization chart levels can you add from the Insert Shapes list?

A: **You can add a subordinate, a coworker, or an assistant.**

QUICK REFERENCE ▼

Insert an organization chart

1 On the Insert menu, click Diagram, or in the content placeholder or Drawing toolbar, click the Insert Diagram or Organization Chart icon, or double-click the organization chart placeholder on a slide.

2 Select Organization Chart, and then click OK.

3 Click each chart box, and then type new text.

4 On the Organization Chart toolbar, click the Insert Shape down arrow, and then click an option to insert a chart box, if necessary.

5 Click a blank area of the presentation to quit Organization Chart.

Inserting and Modifying a Diagram

Inserting and Formatting
an Organization Chart

THE BOTTOM LINE

Diagrams deliver information using a variety of graphic formats. Their visual impact draws audience attention to the information on the slide.

A diagram can help a viewer to better understand information on a slide because of its visual cues. In a pyramid diagram, for example, the most important piece of information is at the top, with supporting information in the steps below. PowerPoint's diagrams include pyramid, cycle, radial, Venn, and target diagrams, as well as organization charts. Using built-in diagrams makes it easy for you to create special types of illustrations without having to draw them from scratch.

To use the built-in diagrams, click the Insert Diagram or Organization Chart button on the Drawing toolbar or in a content placeholder, click Diagram on the Insert menu, or double-click the Diagram or Organization Chart placeholder and then select a diagram. The diagram displays on the slide with text boxes where you need to add information.

As for an organization chart, you can add (or remove) shapes from a diagram to suit your topic. Use tools on the Diagram toolbar to add shapes, adjust the order of shapes in the diagram, and modify its layout. You can also choose to change the current diagram to another diagram type. Format the diagram text using Formatting toolbar buttons. Use Drawing toolbar buttons to format the diagram's shapes and lines. The Autoformat button on the Diagram toolbar lets you apply custom formats to the diagram, just as you did for the organization chart in the last exercise.

Insert and modify a diagram

To punch home the message of your presentation, you will create and format a Venn diagram in this exercise.

1 **In the Slides tab, click slide 6.**

2 **In the content placeholder, click the Insert Diagram or Organization Chart button.**

The Diagram Gallery dialog box appears.

ANOTHER METHOD

- On the Insert menu, click Diagram.
- On the Drawing toolbar, click the Insert Diagram or Organization Chart button.

3 **Select the Venn diagram in the middle of the second row of objects, and then click OK.**

A Venn diagram appears on your slide with text boxes next to each circle.

4 **Click the top text box, and then type** Research.

5 **Click the right text box, and then type** Recognition.

6 **Click the left text box, and then type** Relax.

7 **Click a blank area of the diagram to deselect the text box.**

You deselect this text box so that the formatting change you make in the next step will apply to the entire chart, not just this text box.

8 **On the Formatting toolbar, click the Font Size down arrow, and then click 28.**

All text in the chart changes to 28-point size.

B　**9** **On the Formatting toolbar, click the Bold button.**

All text in the chart becomes bold.

ANOTHER METHOD

Press Ctrl + B.

10 **On the Diagram toolbar, click the Autoformat button.**

The Diagram Style Gallery dialog box appears.

11 **Under Select A Diagram Style, click 3-D Color, and then click OK.**

Applying 3-D Color to this diagram makes it consistent in appearance with the organization chart formatting.

12 **Click outside the diagram.**

The diagram should resemble the illustration below.

Figure 10-14

Completed diagram

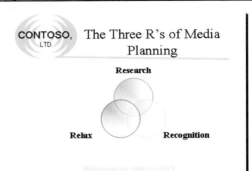

◆ **If you are continuing to other lessons, save the Contoso Company Pres 10 presentation with the current name and then close it. If you are not continuing to other lessons, save and close the Contoso Company Pres 10 presentation, and then click the Close button in the title bar of the PowerPoint window.**

QUICK REFERENCE ▼

Insert a diagram

1 Click the Insert Diagram or Organization Chart button in a content placeholder or on the Drawing toolbar, or select Diagram from the Insert menu.

2 Select a diagram, and then click OK.

3 Click a text box, select the current text, and then type new text.

4 Click a blank area of the presentation window to quit Diagram.

QUICK **CHECK**

Q: Besides organization charts, what other types of diagrams can you create?

A: **You can create pyramid, cycle, radial, Venn, and target diagrams.**

Key Points

✔ *A table organizes information in rows and columns for easy comprehension. Enter text in a table by typing and then pressing Tab to move to the next cell. Format a table to emphasize portions of the table.*

✔ *When you have already created a chart or inserted data in an Excel worksheet, you can import the worksheet and embed it on a PowerPoint slide. Edit an embedded object by double-clicking it to display the source program's menus and toolbars.*

✔ *To create charts right in PowerPoint, use the Microsoft Graph feature. Enter or import data into the datasheet to create the chart series, and then use Graph's menus and toolbars to modify and format the chart.*

✔ *Add an organization chart to a slide to show how the members of an organization relate to one another. Add or remove boxes from the default organization chart to represent all members of the organization, and then format the chart using tools from the Formatting, Drawing, or Organization Chart toolbars.*

✔ *Use a diagram to show specialized chart information in a striking visual format. Built-in diagrams eliminate the necessity of drawing a complex illustration from scratch.*

Quick Quiz

True/False

T F **1.** Merging combines two or more cells into a single larger cell.

T F **2.** Linking objects on a slide greatly increases the file size of the presentation.

T F **3.** In a Microsoft Graph chart, the Y-axis is the vertical axis.

T F **4.** If you add a coworker to an organization chart, the new box appears next to the currently selected box.

T F **5.** A diagram displays text boxes in which you type the diagram information.

Multiple Choice

1. If you want to create a table with various-sized cells, you can use the _____ tool to insert cell borders where you want them.
   a. Insert Border
   b. Draw Cell
   c. Draw Table
   d. Cell Border

2. The original application for an embedded document is known as the
   _____.
   a. source program
   b. source object
   c. embedded program
   d. none of the above

3. The selected cell in a datasheet is called the _____.
   a. main cell
   b. current cell
   c. data cell
   d. active cell

4. To change the way subordinate boxes in an organization chart "hang"
   under a higher-level box, you would make a selection from the
   _____ menu on the Organization Chart toolbar.
   a. Setup
   b. Fit Text
   c. Layout
   d. Insert Shape

5. If you wanted to change the fill color of a single shape in a diagram,
   you would use the Fill Color button on the _____ toolbar.
   a. Formatting
   b. Drawing
   c. Diagram
   d. Standard

Short Answer

1. How do you shade the last row of a table?

2. How do you insert an existing Excel chart object?

3. How do you import an Excel file for use in Graph?

4. How do you change the chart type?

5. How do you add an assistant in an organization chart?

6. How do you change the style of a diagram?

On Your Own

Exercise 1

Open Contoso Company Pres 10 in the Lesson10 folder that is located in
the PowerPoint Practice folder. Display slide 11, select all the text in the
table and change the font to Arial (adjust font size as necessary), change
the column titles shading color in the table to light purple, and then save
and close the presentation.

Exercise 2

Open Contoso Company Pres 10 in the Lesson10 folder that is located in
the PowerPoint Practice folder. Display slide 7, open the embedded
Microsoft Excel object, display Sheet1, exit Microsoft Excel, and then save
and close the presentation.

One Step Further

Exercise 1

Open AD Sales 09 from the Lesson09 folder that is located in the PowerPoint Practice folder. Save the presentation as AD Sales 10 in the Lesson10 folder. Add a slide after slide 1 using the Title and Table layout and type the title Agenda. Insert the following table:

Speaker	Date	Time
Dave Richards	April 28	9:00 a.m.
Annette Hill	April 28	10:00 a.m.
Luis Bonifaz	April 29	9:00 a.m.

Format the table as desired to make it stand out on the slide. Save and close the presentation.

Exercise 2

Open the AD Sales 10 presentation in the Lesson10 folder and add a new slide at the end of the presentation using the Title and Chart layout. Type the title First Quarter Sales. Open the chart datasheet and insert the names of the clients you listed on slide 3 as row titles. Insert January, February, and March as the column headers and delete the 4th Quarter sample text. Add data to the datasheet to represent sales for all five clients. Modify the graph as desired to make it more attractive and useful. Save and close the presentation.

Exercise 3

Open the AD Sales 10 presentation in the Lesson10 folder, and add a new slide at the end of the presentation with the Title and Diagram or Organization Chart layout. Type the title Gaining New Clients. Insert a cycle diagram in the diagram placeholder and add text to the diagram as follows, starting in the top right text box:

Identify New Clients
Visit New Client
Ask for the Job

Add a new shape and insert the final text, Do the Job!

Adjust the diagram's formats as desired to make it appear attractive on the slide. Save and close the presentation.

LESSON 11

Producing a Slide Show

After completing this lesson, you will be able to:

✔ *Navigate in Slide Show view.*
✔ *Annotate slides during a slide show.*
✔ *Set slide transitions.*
✔ *Animate slides.*
✔ *Hide a slide.*
✔ *Create and edit a custom show.*

KEY TERMS

- Animation Schemes
- Custom shows

In Microsoft PowerPoint, you can display presentations on your computer monitor using Slide Show view. Slide Show uses your computer like a projector to display a presentation on one or two monitors using the full screen or, using special hardware, on an overhead screen. To make your slide shows more exciting and engaging, you can add animation to text and graphics on the slide to display during a slide show. As you present a slide show, you can also take notes to document discussion points that members of your audience express during the presentation.

As vice president of sales at Contoso, Ltd, you have been working on a company presentation. You are ready to rehearse the slide show for Wendy Beth Kahn, the CEO, who wants to see it before you give the presentation at next month's meeting of department heads.

In this lesson, you will learn how to navigate through a slide show, draw on a slide during a slide show, add slide transitions, animate text and objects, hide a slide, and create and edit a custom slide show.

◆ Before you can use the practice files in this lesson, you must install them from the book's companion CD to their default location. See "Using the CD-ROM" on at the beginning of this book for more information. To complete the procedures in this lesson, you will need to use a file named 11 PPT Lesson in the Lesson11 folder in the PowerPoint Practice folder located on your hard disk.

Navigating in Slide Show View

THE BOTTOM LINE

Delivering a Slide Show

Knowing how to get around in Slide Show view will make you a more comfortable and professional presenter. Use PowerPoint's keyboard and popup menu options to move from slide to slide.

In earlier lessons, you learned to click the mouse to advance to the next slide in a slide show. PowerPoint has several additional options for navigating through a slide show presentation, as shown in the table below. Mastering these options will help you navigate with ease and confidence during a presentation.

Table 11-1

Presentation navigation methods

Action	Mouse Options	Keyboard Options
Go to next slide	Click the slide	Press Spacebar
	Click Next button on popup toolbar	Press →
	Right-click and click Next	Press Enter
		Press Page Down
		Press N
Go to previous slide	Click Previous button on popup toolbar	Press ←
	Right-click and click Previous	Press Page Up
	Right-click and click Last Viewed	Press P
End show	Right-click and click End Show	Press Esc

You may have noticed a small toolbar in the bottom-left corner of slides when you used Slide Show view in previous lessons. This is the popup toolbar, which displays when you move the mouse pointer on the screen in Slide Show view. The popup toolbar is new in PowerPoint 2003. Its options streamline the process of navigating a presentation in Slide Show view. The popup toolbar has four buttons, as shown in the illustration at left.

As mentioned in Table 11-1, you can use the Previous and Next buttons on this toolbar to move forward and backward among the slides. Click the Pointer button to display a menu of pointer and annotation options. (You learn more about annotating in the "Annotating Slides During a Slide Show" section of this lesson.) Click the Navigation button to display a menu of additional options for moving to the next or previous slide, to the slide last viewed, or to a specific slide or custom show. You'll also find options on this menu for changing the screen color and ending the show.

As you fine-tune your presentation, you will often want to check a slide in Slide Show view. You don't have to start with slide 1 each time you check slides in Slide Show view. You can start a slide show with any slide by selecting the slide in the current view and then clicking the Slide Show button.

Figure 11-1

Popup toolbar

Previous   Next

Pointer   Navigation

Navigate in Slide Show view

In this exercise, you use various keyboard and mouse techniques to navigate your slide show.

◆ **Start PowerPoint, if necessary, click the Open button on the Standard toolbar, navigate to the Lesson11 folder in the PowerPoint Practice folder, and then open the 11 PPT Lesson file. Save the file as Contoso Company Pres 11 in the same folder.**

1 Click the Slide Show button.

PowerPoint displays the first slide in the presentation.

2 **Click anywhere on the screen, or press the Spacebar.**

The slide show advances to the next slide.

3 **Move the mouse to display the pointer.**

The popup toolbar displays in the bottom-left corner of the slide.

4 **Click the Next button on the popup toolbar.**

The slide show advances to slide 3.

5 **On the popup toolbar, click the Navigation button.**

A shortcut menu displays, as shown in the following illustration, giving you multiple options for navigating in the presentation.

Figure 11-2

Navigation shortcut menu

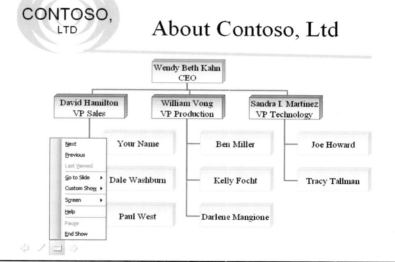

6 **On the shortcut menu, point to Go To Slide, and then click 9 Relationships.**

Slide 9 appears in Slide Show view.

7 **Right-click anywhere on the screen, point to Go To Slide, and then click 14 Contoso, Ltd.**

Right-clicking displays the same navigation shortcut menu that you open when you click the Navigation button on the popup toolbar. You have now displayed the last slide in the presentation.

8 **Click the screen.**

Slide 1 appears in Normal view. Now you will start the slide show from a slide other than slide 1.

> **TROUBLESHOOTING**
>
> If you see a black screen after the last slide, click to exit this screen and return to Normal view.

9 Click slide 3 in the Slides tab of the Outline/Slides pane.

10 Click the Slide Show button.

The slide show starts by displaying slide 3.

> **IMPORTANT**
>
> Pressing the F5 Shortcut key or clicking Slide Show on the View menu always displays the first slide in the presentation. To start a slide show with another slide in the presentation, use the Slide Show button.

11 On the popup toolbar, click the Previous button.

Slide 2 displays.

12 Right-click anywhere on the screen, and then click End Show or press Esc.

Slide 2, the current slide in the slide show, appears in Normal view.

◆ Keep this file open for the next exercise.

QUICK CHECK

Q: What will happen if you click the left arrow key during a slide show?

A: **Pressing this key moves you to the previous slide.**

QUICK REFERENCE ▼

Navigate through a slide show

1 Click the Slide Show button.

2 Use keyboard or mouse options to move forward or back through the slides.

3 To go to a specific slide, click the Navigation button on the popup toolbar, point to Go To Slide, and click a slide title.

Start a show on a specific slide

1 Select a slide in the Slide pane, Slides tab, or Slide Sorter view.

2 Click the Slide Show button.

Using Presenter View with Multiple Monitors

If your computer is connected to two monitors, you can view a slide show on one monitor while you control it from another. This is useful when you want to control a slide show and run other programs that you don't want the audience to see. You can set up your presentation to use multiple monitors by choosing options in the Multiple Monitors area in the Set Up Show dialog box (you learn more about this dialog box in the next lesson). When you display your slide show on multiple monitors, you can present it using PowerPoint's presenter tools in the Presenter view, which allows presenters to have their own view not visible to the audience. In addition to including details about what bullet or slide is coming next, this view enables you to see your speaker notes and lets you jump directly to any slide.

> **IMPORTANT**
>
> In order to use multiple monitors, you must first install the proper hardware and software.

To use presenter tools in Presenter view, select the Show Presenter View check box in the Set Up Show dialog box. If you clear the Show Presenter View check box, the slide show runs as it would on a single monitor.

To present a slide show on two monitors:

1. Connect the two computers as instructed by the manufacturer.

2. On the Slide Show menu, click Set Up Show.

3. In the Multiple Monitors area, click the Display Slide Show On down arrow.

4. Click the name of the monitor on which you want to project the slide show.

5. Select the Show Presenter View check box under the Multiple Monitors options.

6. Click OK.

7. Click the Slide Show button to start the slide show.

8. In Presenter view, use the navigation tools to deliver the presentation on multiple monitors.

Annotating Slides During a Slide Show

Delivering a Slide Show

> **THE BOTTOM LINE**
>
> To help your audience grasp a point, you can highlight text or write or draw on a slide during a presentation.

During a slide show presentation, you can annotate slides by drawing freehand lines and shapes to emphasize a point or by highlighting portions of the text. Annotating a slide can help you make your points more forcefully or draw attention to issues you want your audience to consider more closely.

PowerPoint 2003 has improved annotation features that give you more options for marking on a slide. Clicking the Pointer button on the popup toolbar displays the shortcut menu shown in Figure 11-3. You can choose from the Ballpoint Pen, the Felt Tip Pen, or the Highlighter to mark on the text, with the Ballpoint Pen giving the finest line and the Highlighter the thickest. Change the ink color by clicking Ink Color and selecting a new color from the color palette.

Figure 11-3

Pointer shortcut menu

In PowerPoint 2003, annotations remain on slides even after you move to another slide. To erase annotations, you can click Eraser on the Pointer shortcut menu to change the pointer to an eraser you can use to delete selected annotations. Or, click Erase All Ink On Slide (or press E) to remove all annotations. If you don't erase annotations, you will be asked when you end the slide show if you want to keep or discard the annotations.

> **IMPORTANT**
>
> When a marking tool is active in Slide Show view, clicking the mouse does not advance the slide show to the next slide. Click Arrow on the Pointer shortcut menu to reactivate the pointer, or press Esc.

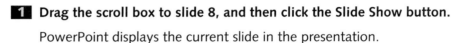

Annotate slides during a slide show

Now that you are more comfortable working in Slide Show view, you will practice marking on a slide to test the annotation tools.

1 Drag the scroll box to slide 8, and then click the Slide Show button.

PowerPoint displays the current slide in the presentation.

2 Move the mouse pointer to display the popup toolbar, and then click the Pointer button.

The Pointer shortcut menu displays PowerPoint's annotation options.

3 Click Highlighter.

The pointer changes to a thick vertical bar in the current ink color.

4 Drag the highlighter pointer over the word "Creation" in the first bullet.

The text is highlighted, just as if you were using an ink highlighter on a printed page.

5 Right-click anywhere on the slide, point to Pointer Options, point to Ink Color, and click the red color on the palette.

You have changed the ink color to red.

6 Click the Pointer button on the popup toolbar, click Felt Tip Pen, and then draw a line under the word "Implementation."

Your Slide Show window should look like the following illustration.

Figure 11-4

Annotations added to slide 8

7 **Click the Pointer button on the popup toolbar, and then click Erase All Ink On Slide.**

All annotations are erased.

ANOTHER METHOD

Press E to erase all ink on the slide.

8 **Press Esc twice.**

The slide show ends, and PowerPoint displays slide 8 in Normal view.

◆ **Keep this file open for the next exercise.**

QUICK REFERENCE ▼

Draw an annotation in slide show

1 Click the Slide Show button.

2 Click the Pointer button on the popup toolbar, or right-click anywhere on the slide and point to Pointer Options.

3 Select a marking option and, if desired, an ink color, and drag to annotate the slide.

4 To erase annotations, click the Pointer button on the popup toolbar and click Eraser to erase individual annotations or Erase All Ink On Slide to remove all annotations.

Setting Slide Transitions

Adding Transition Effects

THE BOTTOM LINE

Transitions can help to hold audience interest while one slide is replaced by another. You can apply transitions to individual slides or to all slides in the presentation and change the speed to control the transition effect.

Transition effects help your presentation make more of an impact by varying the way one slide replaces another. A slide transition is the visual effect of a slide as it moves on and off the screen during a slide show. Slide transitions include such effects as Checkerboard Across, Cover Down, Cut, and Split Vertical Out.

Use the Slide Transition task pane to apply a slide transition effect, set the transition speed and transition sound, and determine settings for advancing a slide. You can set a transition for one slide or a group of slides by first selecting the slides in Slide Sorter view or in the Slides tab in Normal view and then applying the transition. Use Apply To All Slides to apply the settings to all slides in the presentation.

Set slide transitions

In this exercise, you apply a slide transition effect to a single slide, apply a transition to multiple slides, change the transition speed, and then remove all transitions.

1 **Click the Slide Sorter View button, and then select slide 1.**

ANOTHER METHOD

On the View menu, click Slide Sorter View.

2 **On the Slide Sorter toolbar, click the Slide Transition button.**

The Slide Transition task pane appears with current slide transition options.

ANOTHER METHOD

- On the Slide Show menu, click Slide Transition.
- Right-click a blank area of a slide in Normal view, and then click Slide Transition on the shortcut menu.

3 **Under Apply To Selected Slides, scroll down, and then click Dissolve.**

PowerPoint previews the transition effect on the slide miniature for slide 1 in Slide Sorter view and places a transition symbol below the lower-left corner of the slide, as shown in the illustration below. The symbol indicates that PowerPoint has applied a slide transition effect to this slide.

Figure 11-5

Slide Transition task pane

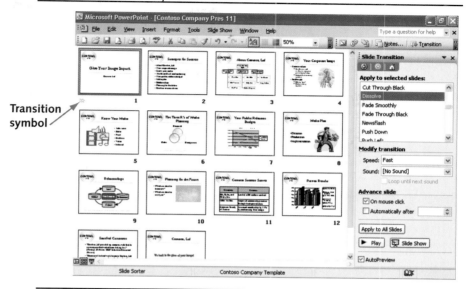

4 **Click the transition symbol below slide 1.**

PowerPoint demonstrates the Dissolve transition effect on slide 1. Now you will apply another transition effect to the other slides in the presentation.

5 **On the Edit menu, click Select All.**

All of the slides in the presentation are selected. You need to deselect slide 1 because a transition has already been applied to it.

ANOTHER METHOD

Press Ctrl + A.

6 **Hold down Ctrl, and then click slide 1 to deselect it.**

Slide 1 is deselected, but all other slides remain selected.

7 **In the Slide Transition task pane, under Apply To Selected Slides, scroll down and then click Random Bars Horizontal.**

The slide miniatures demonstrate the transition effect.

8 **Under Modify Transition, click the Speed down arrow, and then click Medium.**

PowerPoint applies the transition effect to the selected slides. Notice that all of the slides have a transition symbol below their left corners.

9 **Click the Slide Show button.**

Slide Show view displays slide 2 with the Random Bars Horizontal effect.

10 Click the mouse several times to advance through the slides and watch the transition effect, and then press Esc to end the slide show.

PowerPoint returns you to Slide Sorter view.

11 Press Ctrl+A to select all the slides.

12 In the Slide Transition task pane, under Apply To Selected Slides, scroll up and click No Transition, and then click a blank area of the presentation window.

PowerPoint removes the transition effect from all of the slides.

✕

13 In the Slide Transition task pane, click the Close button to close the task pane.

◆ Keep this file open for the next exercise.

QUICK CHECK

Q: What three speeds can you specify for a slide transition?

A: **You can specify Slow, Medium, or Fast.**

QUICK REFERENCE ▼

Apply a slide transition effect

1 Click the Slide Sorter View button or select the Slides tab in Normal view, and then select one, several, or all slides.

2 On the Slide Show menu, click Slide Transition to open the Slide Transition task pane.

3 Under Apply To Selected Slides, click a transition effect.

4 Under Modify Transition, click the Speed down arrow, and then click the desired speed.

5 Click the transition symbol below the slide to preview the effect.

Animating Slides

Animating Slides

THE BOTTOM LINE

Add animation effects to text and slide objects such as shapes and charts to create greater visual interest on a slide. Animation also allows you to control how objects come into view on the slides during the presentation.

You can make a slide show more exciting and engaging by adding animation to the text and objects on your slides. You can apply a wide variety of animation effects to almost every object on a slide, including text placeholders, pictures, tables, charts and their individual series, and shapes you have drawn on the slide. Not only are the animation effects visually interesting, they allow you to control how you want to display the objects during the presentation. For example, you can apply an effect to a title that causes it to spin around when you click the mouse button during the show, or you can control a chart's elements so that you can display the data one column at a time.

You have two options for applying animation to slide objects. You can use an Animation Scheme, or you can create custom animations for various objects on slides. Your choice depends on how much time you want to spend animating your slides.

Applying an Animation Scheme

The easiest way to apply animation effects to a slide show is to use Animation Schemes in the Slide Design task pane. The **Animation Schemes** feature gives you one-click access to professionally designed animations divided into three categories: Subtle, Moderate, and Exciting. Some of these have sound connected to them, and they are designed to animate both the title and text on a slide. You can preview each animation scheme to find the animation you want. You can apply an Animation Scheme in either Normal View or Slide Sorter view.

> **TIP**
>
> If you apply both a transition effect and an animation effect to a slide, the transition effect will occur first, followed by the animation effect.

Apply an Animation Scheme

You will start the process of animating slides by applying Animation Schemes to several slides in the presentation.

1 In Slide Sorter view, select slide 8.

2 On the Slide Show menu, click Animation Schemes.

The Slide Design task pane opens with a selection of Animation Schemes.

> **ANOTHER METHOD**
>
> Click the Slide Design button, and then click the Animation Schemes link.

3 In the Slide Design task pane, under Apply To Selected Slides, click Fade In All.

PowerPoint applies the animation effect to the slide. An animation symbol appears below the left corner of slide 8, as shown in the following illustration.

Figure 11-6

Animation symbol displays below slide

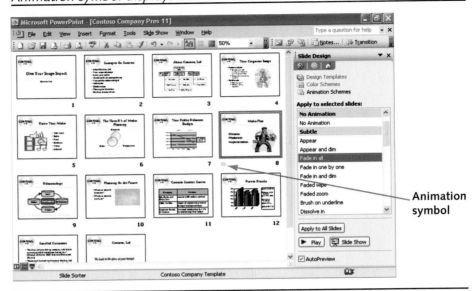

Animation
symbol

4 **Click slide 2, hold down Shift, and then click slides 3 and 4.**

Slides 2, 3, and 4 are selected.

5 **In the Slide Design task pane, under Apply To Selected Slides, click Faded Wipe.**

PowerPoint applies the animation effect to all three slides. An animation symbol appears below the left corner of each slide.

6 **With slide 2 selected, click the Slide Show button.**

As the slide show starts, the slide 2 title fades into view. On a slide that has an Animation Scheme applied, the title displays automatically, but you have to click to display the other items.

ANOTHER METHOD

Click the Slide Show button at the bottom of the Slide Design task pane.

7 **Click the mouse button to display each bullet item.**

As you click, each bullet item fades into view.

8 **Press Esc to stop the slide show.**

You return to Slide Sorter view.

◆ **Keep this file open for the next exercise.**

QUICK REFERENCE ▼

QUICK CHECK

Q: What are the three categories of Animation Schemes?

A: The three categories are Subtle, Moderate, and Exciting.

QUICK REFERENCE ▼

Apply an animation scheme

1 Click a slide in Slide Sorter or Normal view.

2 On the Slide Show menu, click Animation Schemes.

3 In the Slide Design task pane, under Apply To Selected Slides, click an animation scheme.

Applying Custom Text Animation Effects

Although Animation Schemes offer a quick and easy way to animate text on a slide, you may want to customize text animation. To apply custom animation effects to text (as well as objects), you use the Custom Animation task pane in Normal view. You must work in Normal view because you need to choose the objects on the slide that you want to animate. You can create animation effects from scratch, or you can customize effects applied by an Animation Scheme.

After you have selected the object to which you want to add an effect, click the Add Effect button in the Custom Animation task pane and choose from Entrance, Emphasis, Exit, or Motion Paths. These options describe when or how the effect will take place. Each of these categories offers a number of effects to choose among. You can then choose how to start the effect, select a direction for the effect, and adjust its speed.

After you apply an effect, you can fine-tune it by opening the effect's dialog box to choose further options. For example, you can have a title display one word or one letter at a time. You can also determine which text indent levels to animate. If a slide has multiple paragraphs and more than one level of bulleted text, for example, you can customize the animation so that the levels of text in each bulleted item animate separately.

Apply custom text animation effects

You have applied an Animation Scheme to a few slides in the presentation. In this exercise, you use the Custom Animation options to animate text on several other slides.

1 In Slide Sorter view, double-click slide 1 to switch to Normal view.

2 On the Slide Show menu, click Custom Animation.

The Custom Animation task pane opens with the text prompt *Select An Element Of The Slide, Then Click "Add Effect" To Add Animation.*

3 Click the title text "Give Your Image Impact," and then click Add Effect in the Custom Animation task pane.

The Add Effect submenu appears with four effect categories: Entrance, Emphasis, Exit, and Motion Paths.

4 Point to Entrance, and then click Fly In.

The animation effect is demonstrated on slide 1. In the Custom Animation task pane, the title text (item 1) and a description of the effect appear in the Animation Order list. A small number 1 displays to the left of the title placeholder to indicate an effect has been applied to the title.

Figure 11-7

Animating the title

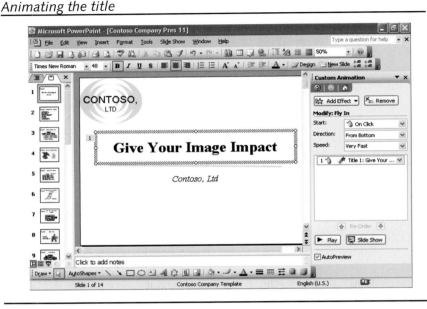

5 Click the subtitle text "Contoso, Ltd."

6 In the Custom Animation task pane, click Add Effect, point to Emphasis, and then click Spin.

The animation effect is demonstrated. In the Custom Animation task pane, the subtitle text (item 2) and a description of the effect appear in the Animation Order list. This list shows effects for the current slide only.

7 In the Custom Animation task pane, click the first animated item in the Animation Order list to select it.

A down arrow appears when the item is selected.

8 Click the down arrow, and then click Effect Options to display the Fly In dialog box.

The Fly In (the current effect) dialog box appears, showing the Effect tab.

Figure 11-8

Fly In dialog box

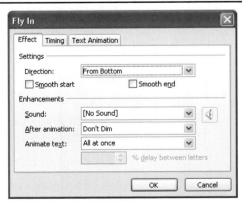

9 **Click the Animate Text down arrow, and then click By Word.**

This option animates the selected text one word at a time.

10 **Click OK.**

The dialog box closes and the revised effect previews on the slide.

11 **In the Custom Animation task pane under Modify: Fly In, click the Start down arrow, and then click With Previous.**

The animation effect is now set to play without having to click the screen during the slide show.

12 **Click the Slide Show button to start the slide show and view the new animation effects.**

The title appears one word at a time.

13 **Click the screen to spin the subtitle, and then press Esc to end the Slide Show.**

14 **Click the Next Slide button three times to advance to slide 4.**

The animation effects in the Animation Order list were supplied by the Animation Scheme you applied in the last exercise.

15 **In the Custom Animation task pane, click the second animated item in the Animation Order list, click the down arrow, and then click Effect Options.**

The Fade dialog box appears.

16 **Click the Text Animation tab, click the Group Text down arrow, and then click By 2nd Level Paragraphs.**

This option sets the text to animate the first- and second-level paragraph lines separately.

17 **Click OK.**

The Fade dialog box closes, and the effect is demonstrated. Each bullet item and subitem appears separately.

 18 **At the bottom of the Custom Animation task pane, click Slide Show.**

The title fades in.

19 **Click the screen to display each bullet item, and then press Esc to end the slide show.**

◆ **Keep this file open for the next exercise.**

QUICK REFERENCE ▼

Apply custom text animation effects

1 In Normal view, select a slide and select an object on the slide.

2 On the Slide Show menu, click Custom Animation.

3 Click Add Effect in the Custom Animation task pane.

4 Point to an effect category, and then click an effect.

5 Adjust settings for start, direction, and speed if desired.

6 In the Animation Order list, click the down arrow for an effect.

7 Click Effect Options and modify settings on the dialog box tabs as required.

8 Click OK.

QUICK CHECK

Q: What are the four categories of effects you can add to a slide object?

A: **You can choose among Entrance, Emphasis, Exit, and Motion Paths.**

Animating Slide Objects

In addition to animating text in a slide show, you can customize the animation of slide objects, such as pictures or drawn objects. As with text, to set custom animation effects, you must be in Normal view.

If an object includes text, you have an additional choice. The default is for the object and its text to be animated at the same time. If you want, however, you can animate only the text so that it flies into the stationary shape, for example.

As you add effects to a slide, you may need to adjust the order in which the effects take place. By reordering the effects in the Animation Order list, you can control when each object appears on the slide.

As you customize the animation order, you should also pay attention to the Start settings for each object. The default setting is On Click, which requires you to click the mouse to start the animation effect. Use the With Previous setting to start an animation at the same time as the object above it on the list (or when the slide displays for the first effect on the list). Use After Previous to start an effect after the previous effect has finished.

Animate slide objects

In this exercise, you animate slide objects and change the order in which objects animate.

1 In Normal view, drag the scroll box to slide 6.

2 Drag the mouse to draw a selection marquee around the three shapes and the connectors.

All five objects are selected.

3 In the Custom Animation task pane, click Add Effect, point to Entrance, click More Effects, click Peek In, and then click OK.

The three objects and two connector lines are animated with the same effect. The number 1 appears next to each of the five parts to show that they will all take place at the same time.

Slide Show

4 At the bottom of the Custom Animation task pane, click the Slide Show button, and then click the screen.

The three objects and connector lines appear all at once.

5 Press Esc to end the slide show.

Because the current animation effect isn't as exciting as it could be, you will now adjust the animation order and start settings to improve the effect.

6 In the Animation Order list, click Elbow Connector 6, click the Re-Order up arrow at the bottom of the task pane two times, click the Start down arrow, and then click After Previous.

The Elbow Connector 6 animation order changes from fourth to second, and it will now start its animation after the Research shape has finished its animation.

7 In the Animation Order list, click Elbow Connector 7, click the Re-Order up arrow once, click the Start down arrow, and then click After Previous.

The Elbow Connector 7 animation order changes from fifth to fourth. Your Animation Order list should look like the one shown in the following illustration.

Figure 11-9

Object animation order has been adjusted

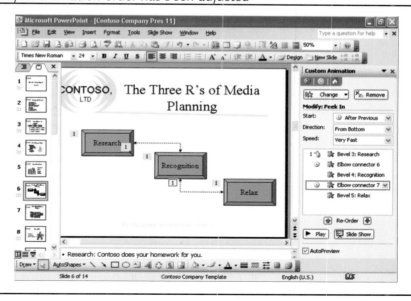

8 In the Animation Order list, click Bevel 4: Recognition, click the Start down arrow, and then click After Previous.

The Recognition shape will not animate until after the first connector has finished.

9 In the Animation Order list, click Bevel 5: Relax, click the Start down arrow, and then click After Previous.

This object will animate after the previous object has finished.

10 At the bottom of the Custom Animation task pane, click the Slide Show button, and then click the screen to view the revised animation.

[Slide Show]

The objects and connector lines appear one after another from top to bottom.

11 Press Esc to end the slide show.

◆ Keep this file open for the next exercise.

QUICK REFERENCE ▼

Animate slide objects

1 Select the object that you want to animate.

2 On the Slide Show menu, click Custom Animation to open the Custom Animation task pane.

3 In the Custom Animation task pane, click Add Effect, point to an effect category, and then click an effect.

Change animation order

1 In the Custom Animation task pane, click the item in the Animation Order list.

2 Click the Re-Order up or down arrow.

Change start option

1 In the Custom Animation task pane, click the item in the Animation Order list.

2 Click the Start down arrow, and then click On Click, With Previous, or After Previous.

Animating Chart Objects

You can also enhance a presentation by animating charts that are created with Microsoft Graph or imported from Microsoft Excel. For example, you can animate each data series in a chart to appear at a different time. This allows you to control the flow of information to the audience to add dramatic effect.

Animate chart objects

To complete your animation task, you will animate the chart to make its appearance more dramatic.

QUICK CHECK

Q: What Start option animates an object at the same time as the object above it on the Animation Order list?

A: **The With Previous setting animates an object at the same time as the previous object.**

CHECK THIS OUT ▼

Create a Motion Path Animation
The Motion Paths category in the Add Effects list lets you create a path for an object to follow on the slide. You can choose from a number of preset paths for the motion, from simple diagonals and straight lines to complex shapes such as parallelograms or arcs, or you can create your own path by drawing it. Adding motion in this way is similar to the kind of animation you can create in a program such as Macromedia Flash.

1 Scroll down to slide 12.

2 Click the chart object to select it.

3 In the Custom Animation task pane, click Add Effect, point to Entrance, and then click Blinds.

The Blinds effect is applied to the entire chart. Now you will modify settings to control the display of each data series column.

4 In the Animation Order list, select the chart effect, click the down arrow, and click Effect Options.

The Blinds dialog box opens.

5 Click the Chart Animation tab, click the Group Chart down arrow, and click By Series.

This setting displays the columns of the chart one by one as you click the mouse button.

6 Click OK.

The Custom Animation task pane looks like the following illustration. You could click the double arrow in the shaded bar below the animation effect to see the animation effect for each part of the chart.

Figure 11-10

Custom Animation task pane shows chart animation

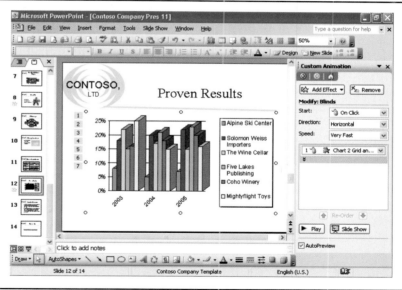

7 At the bottom of the Custom Animation task pane, click the Slide Show button, and then click the screen seven times to view the animation.

As you click, the chart framework and then each data series appears on the screen.

8 Press Esc to end the slide show.

9 In the Custom Animation task pane, click the Close button to close the task pane.

◆ Keep this file open for the next exercise.

QUICK CHECK

Q: What option do you choose in a chart effect's dialog box to have each column appear by itself?

A: **Choose By Series to animate each series separately.**

QUICK REFERENCE ▼

Animate a chart

1 Select the chart object that you want to animate.

2 On the Slide Show menu, click Custom Animation to open the Custom Animation task pane.

3 In the Custom Animation task pane, click Add Effect, point to an effect category, and click an effect.

4 In the Animation Order list, select the chart object's down arrow and click Effect Options.

5 Click the Chart Animation tab, click the Group Chart down arrow, and select an option.

6 Click OK.

Hiding a Slide

Customizing a Slide Show

THE BOTTOM LINE

Hide slides in a presentation when you don't want to display them during a slide show. This is a good way to safeguard some information or customize a show for a particular audience.

When you have a number of slides on a particular subject, you may find that you don't need to show all of them to a particular audience. If you have a presentation on the progress of putting in a new community pool, for example, you can leave out slides relating to costs when you deliver the presentation to the neighborhood children.

Rather than copy all the slides you want to use to a new presentation, you can simply hide the slides you don't want to show during a particular presentation but still want to keep in the presentation. To hide a slide, you select it in the Slides tab or in Slide Sorter view and click Hide Slide on the Slide Show menu (or click the Hide Slide button in Slide Sorter view, or right-click the slide and select Hide Slide from the shortcut menu). A hidden slide displays a special symbol below it in Slide Sorter view or the Slides tab so you know it is hidden. When you deliver the presentation, hidden slides are skipped automatically.

Even if you have hidden a slide, however, you can still display it during the slide show. Use the Navigation shortcut menu to display slide titles and then click the title of the hidden slide. Unhide a slide by using the same command or button you used to hide it.

Hide a slide

In this exercise, you hide a slide in the current slide show.

1 Click the Slide Sorter View button.

ANOTHER METHOD

On the View menu, click Slide Sorter.

2 Select slide 10.

3 On the Slide Sorter toolbar, click the Hide Slide button.

A hide symbol appears over the slide number to indicate that the slide will be hidden in a slide show, as shown in the following illustration.

Figure 11-11

Slide shows hide symbol

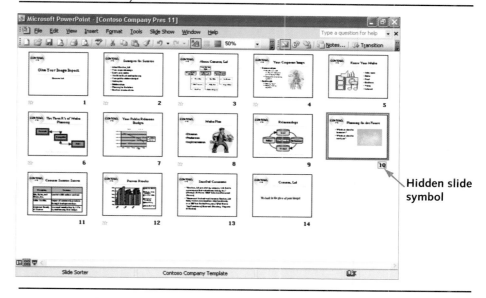

Hidden slide symbol

ANOTHER METHOD

- With the slide selected in Slides tab or Slide Sorter view, click Hide Slide on the Slide Show menu.
- Right-click the selected slide, and then click Hide Slide on the shortcut menu.

4 Select slide 9.

5 Click the Slide Show button, and then click anywhere on the screen.

The slide show hides slide 10 and displays slide 11.

6 Press P to go back to slide 9.

7 Right-click anywhere on the screen, point to Go To Slide, and then click (10) Planning for the Future, or press the H key to show the hidden slide.

Slides are designated as hidden with parentheses around their slide numbers. The hidden slide appears in Slide Show view.

8 Press Esc to end the slide show.

◆ Keep this file open for the next exercise.

QUICK REFERENCE ▼

Hide a slide

1 Select the slide that you want to hide in Slides tab or Slide Sorter view.

2 On the Slide Sorter toolbar, click the Hide Slide button, or on the Slide Show menu, click Hide Slide.

Show a hidden slide during a presentation

1 Click the Slide Show button, and then click the screen.

2 Right-click anywhere on the screen, point to Go To Slide, and then click the hidden slide in parentheses, or press H on the previous slide to show the hidden slide.

Creating and Editing a Custom Show

Customizing a Slide Show

THE BOTTOM LINE

You can use the slides in a presentation to set up custom shows of specific slides for specific audiences. This is a more efficient way to customize a presentation than hiding slides.

If you plan to present slides on a topic to more than one audience, you don't have to create separate presentations for each audience. Instead of creating multiple, nearly identical presentations for different audiences, you can create one comprehensive presentation that includes all the slides you will need and then create **custom shows** that contain selected slides for each audience. This is a much more efficient way to customize a presentation than hiding slides for each audience.

When you create a custom show, you supply a name for the show and then select slides from the presentation to add to the show. You can create as many custom shows as you need, and each show can use any of the presentation's slides. After you have created the show, you can edit it to change the order of slides or remove slides. When you deliver the presentation, you can select the custom show to present, and only the slides in the custom show appear.

Create a custom show

For your last task in preparing your presentation, you create and edit a custom show.

1 **In Slide Sorter view, on the Slide Show menu, click Custom Shows.**

The Custom Shows dialog box appears.

2 **Click New.**

The Define Custom Show dialog box appears. The default custom show name is selected in the Slide Show Name box.

3 **In the Slide Show Name box, type** Contoso Custom Show 11.

4 **In the Slides In Presentation box, click slide 1, and then click Add.**

Slide 1 appears in the Slides In Custom Show box on the right.

5 **Select and add slides 3, 4, 6, 8, 13, and 14 to the custom slide show to match the following illustration.**

You can hold down the Ctrl key to select multiple slides.

Figure 11-12

Define Custom Show dialog box

6 **Click OK.**

The Custom Shows dialog box appears, with the newly created custom show selected in the Custom Shows list.

7 **Click Show.**

Slide 1 of the custom show displays.

8 **Click through all of the slides until Slide Sorter view appears, indicating the slide show is complete.**

Slide Sorter view appears. Now you will edit the custom show to remove a slide.

9 **On the Slide Show menu, click Custom Shows.**

The Custom Shows dialog box appears.

10 **Verify that Contoso Custom Show 11 is selected, and then click Edit.**

The Define Custom Show dialog box appears.

11 In the Slides In Custom Show box, click slide 2, and then click Remove.

Slide 2 is removed from the show.

12 Click OK, and then click Close to close the Custom Shows dialog box.

◆ If you are continuing to other lessons, save the Contoso Company Pres 11 presentation with the current name and then close it. If you are not continuing to other lessons, save and close the Contoso Company Pres 11 presentation, and then click the Close button in the title bar of the PowerPoint window.

QUICK REFERENCE ▼

Create a custom show

1 On the Slide Show menu, click Custom Shows.

2 Click New.

3 In the Slide Show Name box, type the slide show name.

4 In the Slides In Presentation box, click a slide, and then click Add.

5 Select and add more slides to the custom slide show.

6 Click OK, and then click Close or Show.

QUICK CHECK

Q: What button can you use to quickly preview a custom show after you have created it?

A: **Click the Show button in the Custom Shows dialog box to preview the show.**

Key Points

✓ *You can use a variety of keystrokes or mouse actions to navigate from slide to slide in Slide Show view. Use the new popup toolbar to display a shortcut menu that gives additional options for going to the last slide viewed and specific slides.*

✓ *Use several new pointer tools to mark on slides during a presentation. You can use the Ballpoint Pen, the Felt Tip Pen, or the Highlighter to emphasize slide content for the audience.*

✓ *Apply slide transitions to slides to hold audience attention between slides with graphical effects. You can apply a transition to one, several, or all slides and modify the speed as desired.*

✓ *For additional visual interest in a presentation, animate text and objects on slides. Use Animation Schemes to apply predesigned effects to one or all slides, or create custom animations to control the effect's start options, direction and speed.*

✓ *Hide one or more slides in a presentation when you want to skip them automatically during the slide show. You can show hidden slides during the slide show using the Navigation shortcut menu.*

✓ *Create custom shows to organize slides in a presentation for different audiences. Name the show and then select the slides to include in it.*

Quick Quiz

True/False

T F   1.   To go to a specific slide during a slide show, you can use the Go To Slide command on the Navigation shortcut menu.

T F   2.   Once you have added a transition to a slide, you cannot remove it.

T F   3.   You can apply an Animation Scheme in either Normal view or Slide Sorter view.

T F   4.   You can start a slide show right from the Custom Animation task pane.

T F   5.   Hidden slides cannot be seen in any PowerPoint view.

Multiple Choice

1.   If you need to remove only one annotation on the slide, select _____ on the Pointer shortcut menu.
   a.   Erase All Ink On Slide
   b.   Remove Annotation
   c.   Remove Ink
   d.   Eraser

2.   The default start option for new custom animation effects is _____.
   a.   On Click
   b.   With Previous
   c.   After Previous
   d.   On Hover

3.   When you animate a shape that has text in it, you can choose to _____.
   a.   animate the text only
   b.   animate the text and the shape at the same time
   c.   animate either the text or the shape.
   d.   either A or B

4.   A keyboard shortcut you can use to display a hidden slide during a slide show is _____.
   a.   E
   b.   S
   c.   H
   d.   P

5.   If you need to give similar presentations to different audiences, the most efficient method to customize a presentation is to _____.
   a.   hide slides as necessary
   b.   create custom shows
   c.   create separate presentations for each audience
   d.   skip slides as you present them

Short Answer

1. How do you view the Custom Animation settings?
2. How do you eliminate a transition effect from all of the slides in a presentation?
3. How do you move forward in Slide Show view?
4. How do you animate a slide object?
5. How do you immediately end a presentation in Slide Show view?
6. How do you animate a chart?
7. How do you edit a custom show?
8. How do you change the color of the annotation marker tool?
9. How do you hide a slide during a slide show?
10. How do you create a new custom show?

On Your Own

Exercise 1

Open Contoso Company Pres 11 in the Lesson11 folder that is located in the PowerPoint Practice folder. Change the slide 1 transition to Box with a slow speed, hide slide 13, start a slide show, change the ink color to blue and select a pen tool, draw a line under the text *Contoso, Ltd* on slide 1, display each slide in the slide show, and then save and close the presentation.

Exercise 2

Open Contoso Company Pres 11 in the Lesson11 folder that is located in the PowerPoint Practice folder. Animate the clip art on slide 4 with the Fly In effect from the bottom, create and show a custom slide show named *Contoso Client* with the slides 1, 4, 6, 7, 8, 9, and 14, and then save and close the presentation.

One Step Further

Exercise 1

Open Holidays 08 from the Lesson08 folder that is located in the PowerPoint Practice folder. Save the presentation as Holidays 11 in the Lesson11 folder. Apply an animation scheme to all slides. On slide 3, animate the fireworks objects and their dotted-line paths to appear one at a time on the slide. Use the After Previous Start option for the fireworks objects so you don't have to click to display them. On slides 9 and 10, remove the animation scheme and supply custom animations for the titles and animate bulleted lists by second-level paragraphs. Save and close the presentation.

Exercise 2

Open the Holidays 11 presentation from the Lesson11 folder. Create two custom shows. In the first custom show, include all the slides relating to holidays. In the second custom show, include all the slides that relate to personal time. Supply appropriate names for the custom shows. Save and close the presentation.

Exercise 3

Open AD Sales 10 from the Lesson10 folder that is located in the PowerPoint Practice folder. Save the presentation as AD Sales 11 in the Lesson11 folder. Animate the picture on slide 1 to fly in from the bottom at medium speed. Animate all slide titles with an appropriate custom animation effect and specify the With Previous start for all titles. Animate the table, chart, and diagram as desired. Select a slide transition and apply it to all slides. Hide slide 3. Start the slide show with slide 1. On slide 2, use the Felt Tip Pen to circle the April 29 agenda topic. Use the Navigation shortcut menu to display the hidden slide. Save and close the presentation.

Creating a Multimedia Presentation

After completing this lesson, you will be able to:

✔ *Insert sounds and movies in a presentation.*
✔ *Modify sound and movie settings.*
✔ *Set slide timings.*
✔ *Set rehearsed slide timings.*
✔ *Record a narration in a slide show.*
✔ *Create a self-navigating presentation.*

KEY TERMS

- Animated pictures
- Slide timing

Insert sounds and movies in a presentation to add multimedia interest to your slides. Sounds and movies can be set to play automatically or manually. Use the custom animation options you learned about in Lesson 11 to control playback of sounds and movies during a slide show. You can transform a slide show into a self-running multimedia presentation by setting slide timings, adding narration, and setting up the show to run by itself.

As vice president of sales at Contoso, Ltd, you have been working on a company presentation. After adding transitions and animations, you decide to add sounds and movies to slides, set slide timings, rehearse the presentation, and set up the show to run by itself.

In this lesson, you will learn how to insert sounds and movies into a presentation, modify sound and movie settings, control playback of sounds and movies in a slide show, add slide timings, rehearse slide timings, record narration, and set up a self-navigating presentation.

◆ Before you can use the practice files in this lesson, you must install them from the book's companion CD to their default location. See "Using the CD-ROM" at the beginning of this book for more information. To complete the procedures in this lesson, you will need to use a file named 12 PPT Lesson in the Lesson12 folder in the PowerPoint Practice folder located on your hard disk.

Inserting Sounds and Movies in a Presentation

Inserting and Playing Sounds and Movies

THE BOTTOM LINE

Sounds and movies not only engage audience interest, they can also deliver information to the audience. Use the Clip Art task pane to locate and insert both sounds and movies, or insert files from any drive on your system.

You can add sounds and movies to a presentation to make your slide show a real multimedia experience for your audience. Besides holding audience attention, sounds and movies can deliver essential information. Adding the sound of a bamboo flute to a presentation on musical instruments, for example, helps the audience to better understand an explanation of the instrument. Inserting a movie clip that shows a potter working on a wheel gives the audience a clearer comprehension of pottery techniques.

You can insert sounds and movies from the Microsoft Clip Organizer, from a file located on your system or network, or from a CD-ROM or other disk. The process of locating a sound or movie file from the Clip Organizer is similar to locating a clip art image: you can search using keywords and then select the sound or movie file you want from the search results. Inserting a sound or movie from a file is similar to inserting a picture file: navigate to the location of the sound or movie file and then select and insert it.

In most cases, you will receive a message box when you insert a sound or movie that asks how you want the object to play in the slide show. You can choose Automatically to have the clip play as soon as the slide appears, or choose When Clicked to control the object yourself by clicking it when you're ready for it to play.

Inserting and Playing Sounds

PowerPoint offers you several ways to add sound to your slides. You can associate sound effects with slide transitions and custom animations, for example, to further spice up these effects. You can also insert sounds from the Microsoft Clip Organizer or from a file by double-clicking a media placeholder or by clicking the Movies And Sounds command on the Insert menu. The Clip Organizer contains a wide selection of sounds in the form of both sound effects and music files. You can also click the Clip Art On Office Online link to locate sounds on the Microsoft Clip Art And Media Web page.

When you insert a sound file on a slide, it appears as an icon on the slide. To play a sound manually, double-click the sound icon in the Slide pane in Normal view or click the icon during the slide show.

IMPORTANT

To play sounds, sound hardware (such as a sound card and speakers) must be installed on your computer.

Insert sounds in a presentation

You begin the process of adding multimedia interest to your presentation by adding a sound to a slide transition. You will then insert and play a sound file.

◆ Start PowerPoint, if necessary, click the Open button on the Standard toolbar, navigate to the Lesson12 folder in the PowerPoint Practice folder, and then open the 12 PPT Lesson file. Save the file as Contoso Company Pres 12 in the same folder.

1 Verify that slide 1 is visible in the Slide pane, and then on the Slide Show menu, click Slide Transition.

The Slide Transition task pane appears.

ANOTHER METHOD

Right-click a blank area of the slide, and then click Slide Transition on the shortcut menu.

2 Click the Sound down arrow, and then click Applause.

PowerPoint applies the sound to the first slide. You can click the Play button in the Slide Transition pane to hear the sound, or run the slide show to check the sound.

3 Click the Slide Show button.

The sound plays during the transition of the first slide.

ANOTHER METHOD

- Press F5.
- On the View menu, click Slide Show.

4 Press Esc to end the slide show.

5 Scroll down to slide 10.

6 On the Insert menu, point to Movies And Sounds, and then click Sound From Clip Organizer.

The Clip Art task pane appears with a selection of sounds. The Results Should Be setting has been changed to show all clips in the Sounds category.

7 In the Search For box, type explosion, and then click Go.

An explosion sound will emphasize the picture of fireworks on this slide. Several clips of explosion sound effects display. If you do not see any explosion results, search for another suitable sound.

TIP

You can preview a sound by clicking its down arrow and selecting Preview/Properties.

8 **Click one of the sound clips in the task pane.**

A message box appears, asking how you want the sound to play in the slide show.

9 **Click Automatically.**

A small sound icon appears in the middle of the slide, as shown in the margin. The sound icon is small, but you can enlarge it for easier access by dragging a resize handle.

10 **Drag the sound icon to the lower-right corner of the slide.**

Unless you hide it, the sound icon displays in the slide show just as in Normal view. Moving it to an unobtrusive location prevents it from distracting the audience.

11 **Double-click the sound icon.**

The sound plays. Your presentation window should look similar to the following illustration.

Figure 12-1

Sound icon appears on the slide

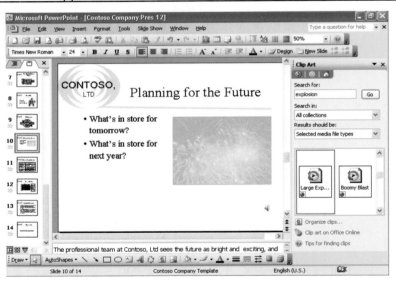

◆ **Keep this file open for the next exercise.**

QUICK CHECK

Q: What equipment do you need to play sounds on your computer?

A: **You need a sound card and speakers.**

QUICK REFERENCE ▼

Add a sound to a slide transition

1 On the Slide Show menu, click Slide Transition.

2 In the Slide Transition task pane, click the Sound down arrow, and then click a sound.

Insert a sound on a slide

1 On the Insert menu, point to Movies And Sounds, and then click Sound From Clip Organizer.

2 Click a sound, and then click Automatically or When Clicked when asked how you want the sound to play in the slide show.

Play a sound

Double-click the sound icon in Normal view, or click it in Slide Show view.

Inserting and Playing Movies

In PowerPoint, the term *movies* can mean either a digital video file produced with digital video equipment or an **animated picture**, also known as an animated GIF (Graphics Interchange Format). Most movies in the Clip Organizer are animated pictures that resemble moving cartoons. Though animated pictures look like clip art pictures, you cannot edit them in the same way as you can clip art, though you can of course resize and reposition them.

Use the Movies And Sounds command on the Insert menu to insert a movie. To locate an animated picture from the Clip Organizer, you then click Movie From Clip Organizer. To locate a movie file on your system or on a disk, click Movie From File.

You cannot play an animated picture in Normal view. To see how the animated picture looks in motion, you must switch to Slide Show view. If you have inserted a digital movie file, however, you can view it in Normal view by double-clicking it. To pause the movie, click the movie object again.

Insert a movie on a slide

You have added sound to the presentation, and you're now ready to add more visual interest. In this exercise, you'll add an animated picture and then test a movie file that has already been inserted in the presentation.

1 On the Slides tab, click slide 13.

2 On the Insert menu, point to Movies And Sounds, and then click Movie From Clip Organizer.

The Clip Art task pane displays a selection of movie clips. The Results Should Be setting has been changed to show all clips in the Movies category.

3 **In the Search For box, type** target**, and then click Go.**

The Clip Art task pane displays clips that contain or relate to targets. If you do not see target results, search for another suitable business-related movie.

4 **Click any clip that shows an arrow hitting a target.**

The animated picture appears on the slide.

5 **Drag the movie to the blank area on the right side of the slide and enlarge the clip if necessary.**

Your presentation window should look similar to the following illustration.

Figure 12-2

Position the clip as shown

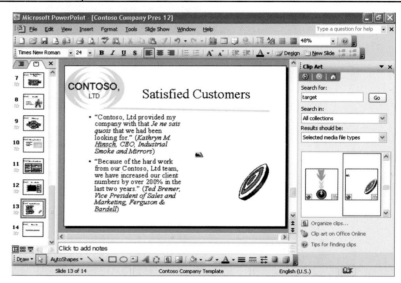

6 **In the Clip Art task pane, click the Close button to close the task pane.**

7 **Click the Slide Show button.**

You can see how the movie looks when animated in Slide Show view.

8 **Press Esc to end the slide show.**

9 **Scroll up to slide 2.**

This slide contains a movie clip that shows gears turning.

10 **Double-click the movie object.**

The movie begins to play in Normal view. You can click the movie to pause it and click again to resume playing.

◆ **Keep this file open for the next exercise.**

QUICK CHECK

Q: What is another name for the moving cartoons you insert from the Clip Organizer?

A: Another name for moving cartoons is animated GIFs or animated pictures.

QUICK REFERENCE ▼

Insert a movie

1 On the Insert menu, point to Movies And Sounds, and then click Movie From Clip Organizer or Movie From File.

2 Click a movie in the Clip Art task pane, or navigate to the location of the movie file.

3 If necessary, click Automatically or When Clicked when asked how you want the movie to play in the slide show.

Play a movie

1 Double-click the movie object.

2 Position the pointer over the movie, and then click the movie object to pause it.

3 Click the movie object again to play the rest of the movie.

Modify Sound and Movie Settings

Inserting and Playing
Sounds and Movies

> **THE BOTTOM LINE**
>
> After you have inserted sounds and movies, you can change settings that control how they play and how they perform in the slide show. Change settings to make sure all objects play correctly and in the correct order during the presentation.

After you insert a sound or movie object, you can modify object settings to change the way the object plays. PowerPoint 2003 offers improved media playback options to help you adjust sound and movie settings.

Right-click a sound object and click Edit Sound Object to open the Sound Options dialog box. In this dialog box, you can choose to loop the sound (play it over and over) until you stop it, adjust the sound's volume, or hide the sound icon on the slide during the slide show. You can also see information about the clip, such as its path and its total playing time.

Right-click a movie object and click Edit Movie Object to open the Movie Options dialog box. You can loop the movie and make sure it rewinds after it plays, adjust sound volume if the clip contains sound, hide the movie when it isn't playing, or have it zoom to full size while playing. The dialog box also tells you the path to the object and the total playing time of the movie. The Edit Movie Object command is not available for animated GIFs.

Besides adjusting settings of the sound and movie objects themselves, you can modify the way they play during a slide show and the order in which they play. To do so, you can apply custom animation effects, or you can use the Action Settings dialog box. The Action Settings dialog box lets you choose to play an object by clicking it or by moving the mouse over it.

Modify movie and sound settings

You have inserted sound and movie objects in the presentation, and now you need to adjust their playback and animation settings so they play properly during the slide show.

1 **On slide 2, right-click the movie object, and then click Edit Movie Object.**

The Movie Options dialog box appears, displaying movie play options and the total playing time of the movie.

Figure 12-3

Movie Options dialog box

2 **Select the Loop Until Stopped check box.**

Now when the movie object plays, the media clip continues to play until you stop it by clicking on the slide or pressing Esc.

3 **Click OK to close the Movie Options dialog box.**

Next you will apply and adjust animation effects to play the objects on this slide in the correct order.

4 **Right-click the movie object again, and then click Custom Animation on the shortcut menu.**

The Custom Animation task pane appears.

ANOTHER METHOD

On the Slide Show menu, click Custom Animation.

5 **In the Custom Animation task pane, click Add Effect, click Entrance, and then click Dissolve In.**

The movie object now appears in the Animation Order list with its file name, COGS.AVI.

6 Click the Start down arrow, and then click With Previous.

Changing this setting makes the movie object display along with the item above it on the list.

7 With the movie object still selected, click Add Effect, click Movie Actions, and click Play.

Note that because you are working with a movie object, a new category is available on the Add Effect menu—Movie Actions. Applying the Play effect adds a control that tells the object to play.

8 Click the Start down arrow, and then click After Previous.

You have now set the object to play after the previous effect, which is the Dissolve In entrance. The object will dissolve into view and then begin playing.

9 Click the Text 2 item in the Animation Order list and click the Re-Order up arrow at the bottom of the Custom Animation task pane one time.

The text item is now the first item in the list.

10 Click the first COGS.AVI item in the Animation Order list, and click the Re-Order up arrow one time. Then click the second COGS.AVI item, and click the Re-Order up arrow one time.

The movie objects are now below the text item, as shown in the following illustration.

Figure 12-4

Objects reordered to play correctly

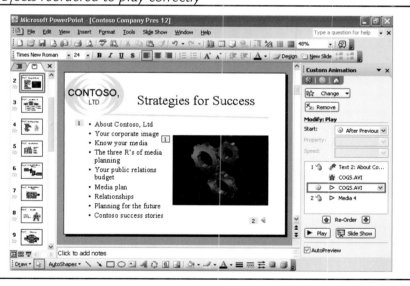

Next you will change settings for the sound icon so you can play it by moving the mouse pointer over it.

11 Click the sound icon on slide 2 to select the object.

12 On the Slide Show menu, click Action Settings.

The Action Settings dialog box appears.

Right-click the sound icon, and then click Action Settings from the shortcut menu.

13 Click the Mouse Over tab, and then click the Object Action option.

The Play option appears in the list.

14 Click OK, and then click the Slide Show button.

You can now look at your animation effects in Slide Show view to make sure they work as desired.

15 Move the pointer over the sound icon to play the sound, and then click the mouse to advance through the slide animations.

16 Press Esc to stop the movie, and then press Esc again to stop the slide show.

◆ Keep this file open for the next exercise.

QUICK REFERENCE ▼

Change movie playback options

1 Right-click the movie object, and then click Edit Movie Object.

2 Click a play option.

3 Click OK.

Change the animation settings

1 Right-click the movie object, and then click Custom Animation.

2 In the Custom Animation task pane, change the start setting or change the order to play the object.

Change action settings to play in Slide Show view

1 Click an object on a slide to select it.

2 On the Slide Show menu, click Action Settings.

3 Click the Mouse Over or Mouse Click tab.

4 Click an option.

5 Click OK.

Setting Slide Timings

Adding Slide Timings

THE BOTTOM LINE

Slide timings control the display of slides during a slide show. Setting slide timings allows you to automate a presentation so you don't have to click to advance each slide.

Slide timing refers to the length of time that a slide appears on the screen. As with transitions, you can set slide timings for one slide or a group of slides, depending on how many slides are selected when you apply the slide timing.

You advance the slide show in one of two ways: automatic advance, which you set with the timing feature, or manual advance, which you operate with the mouse. The automatic advance-timing feature moves slides through the slide show by itself, keeping each slide on the screen for the length of time that you designate beforehand. The mouse click-timing feature manually moves slides through the slide show.

You can select both advance methods if you like. With both options selected, you can click the mouse if you're done with the slide before the automatic advance timing elapses.

TIP

In Slide Show view, a mouse click always advances a slide, even if the timing that is set in the Slide Transition task pane has not elapsed. Conversely, holding down the mouse prevents a timed transition from occurring until you release the mouse, even if the set timing has elapsed.

Set slide timings

Now that you have finished working with sounds and movies, you're ready to set slide timings to control the presentation.

1 Click the Slide Sorter View button.

ANOTHER METHOD

On the View menu, click Slide Sorter.

2 On the Slide Sorter toolbar, click the Slide Transition button, or on the Slide Show menu, click Slide Transition.

The Slide Transition task pane appears.

3 In the Advance Slide area, select the Automatically After check box, and click the up arrow twice to show 00:02.

Because both check boxes in the Advance Slide section are selected, the slides advance after 2 seconds or when you click the mouse.

4 **Click Apply To All Slides.**

PowerPoint applies the current Slide Transition settings, including the new slide timing, to all of the slides and places the 00:02 timing under each slide in the Slide Sorter view.

Figure 12-5

Timings applied to all slides

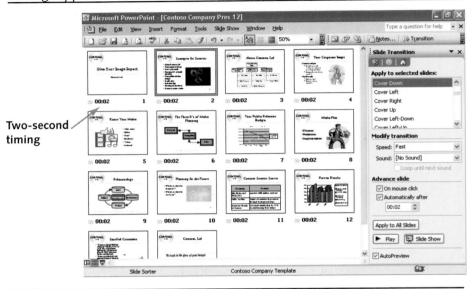

Two-second timing

TIP

It does not matter which slide is selected when you click Apply To All Slides.

5 **Scroll up (if necessary), and then click slide 1.**

6 **At the bottom of the task pane, click the Slide Show button.**

PowerPoint runs the slide show in the presentation window, using the slide timing that you set using the Slide Transition task pane.

7 **After the slide show has ended, click the Close button on the Slide Transition task pane to close the task pane.**

◆ **Keep this file open for the next exercise.**

QUICK REFERENCE ▼

Apply slide timings

1 Click the Slide Sorter View button.

2 On the Slide Sorter toolbar, click the Slide Transition button, or click Slide Transition on the Slide Show menu.

3 In the Advance Slide area, click the Automatically After check box, and then type a value.

QUICK CHECK

Q: If you have selected both manual and automatic advance options, what happens if you click the mouse button before the time has elapsed?

A: **The slide will advance even if the time has not elapsed.**

Setting Rehearsed Slide Timings

Adding Slide Timings

THE BOTTOM LINE

When you set slide timings by rehearsing the slides, you have a better idea how long each slide will take to present.

Because you might want to spend more time viewing some slides than others, setting a single timing for all slides may mean that some timings are too fast and some are too slow. Rather than guess at slide timings, you can use the Rehearse Timings feature to rehearse a slide show.

When you rehearse the show, you look at each slide in Slide Show view, allowing time for the animations and reading the text and any additional notes you may want to deliver for the slide, and then you move on to the next slide. At the end of the show, you can choose to save the new timings for each slide, and those timings are then applied to the slides for use the next time you run the slide show.

Rehearse slide timings

You have set slide timings of 2 seconds to all slides. In this exercise, you rehearse the slides to adjust those timings.

1 **In Slide Sorter view, on the Slide Sorter toolbar, click the Rehearse Timings button.**

The slide show begins. The Rehearsal dialog box is displayed in the upper-left corner of the screen, as shown in the following illustration.

Figure 12-6

Rehearsal dialog box

Next button   Repeat button

The slide time begins running as soon as the first slide appears.

2 **As soon as you feel that enough time has passed to adequately view or discuss the information on the slide, click the mouse or the Next button to select the timing for the next slide, or press O to use the original timings for the slide and move on to the next slide.**

The next slide may not appear if there are still animations that need to be applied. Continue to click the Next button or the mouse until you have advanced through all animations and proceed to the next slide.

TIP

You can click the Pause button at any time to pause the timer. Click Pause again to return to recording.

3 **If the time is inadequate, click the Repeat button and then rehearse the slide again. To stop the slide rehearsal at any time, click the Close button in the Rehearsal dialog box to return to Slide Sorter view.**

At the end of the slide rehearsal, a confirmation dialog box appears with the total time for the slide show.

4 **Click Yes to save the new slide timings.**

The slides now display the new slide time settings.

5 **At the bottom of the task pane, click the Slide Show button.**

PowerPoint runs through the slide show in the presentation window, using the slide timings that you set during the slide show rehearsal. Notice that objects you had to click to animate are now animated automatically.

◆ **Keep this file open for the next exercise.**

QUICK REFERENCE ▼

Rehearse slide timings

1 In Slide Sorter view, on the Slide Sorter toolbar, click the Rehearse Timings button.

2 As soon as you feel enough time has passed to adequately view or discuss the information on the slide, click the mouse or Next to select the timing for the next slide, or press O to use the original timings for a slide.

3 If the time is inadequate, click the Repeat button to rehearse the slide again. You can stop the slide rehearsal at any time by clicking the Close button in the Rehearsal dialog box.

4 Click Yes to save the new slide timings.

QUICK CHECK

Q: What shortcut key can you use to keep the original timing for a slide?

A: **Press O to keep the original timing for a slide.**

Recording a Narration in a Slide Show

Inserting and Playing Sounds and Movies

THE BOTTOM LINE

Use voice narration for a slide show that will run unattended. The narration can add information that you would deliver from speaker notes if giving the presentation yourself.

You can add voice narration to a slide show when creating a slide show for individuals who can't attend a presentation, or you can add it during a meeting so that presenters can review it later and hear comments made during the presentation. To record a narration, your computer needs a sound card and a microphone, as well as speakers so you can check the narration.

You can record a narration before you run a slide show, or you can record it during the presentation and include audience comments. As you record the narration, you can pause or stop the narration at any time. You can delete a voice narration icon just as you would delete any other PowerPoint object. While you are recording voice narration, you won't hear other sounds you have added to the slides.

By default, narration is stored with the presentation. But if the narration is lengthy, this can add considerably to the presentation's file size. The Rehearse Narration dialog box includes the Link Narration In option that allows you to specify a path to another location to store the narration. Just as when linking an object such as an Excel chart, linking helps to keep the presentation's file size manageable.

If you don't have hardware installed on your computer for recording or playing sounds, the Record Narration command on the Slide Show menu is grayed out. If this command is grayed out on your computer, skip this section.

Record narration in a slide show

In this exercise, you record a voice narration while running the presentation.

1 Double-click slide 1 to switch to Normal view.

2 On the Slide Show menu, click Record Narration.

The Record Narration dialog box appears, showing the amount of free disk space and the number of minutes that you can record, as shown in the following illustration.

Figure 12-7

Record Narration dialog box

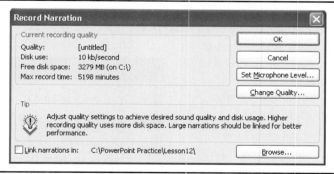

3 Click OK.

The slide show starts.

4 Use the rehearsed slide timings, or click to advance through the slide show, and add voice narration (your own explanation of the slides) as you go.

When adding narration, speak clearly and with a tone appropriate to the presentation subject.

5 Right-click anywhere on the screen, and then click Pause Narration.

The recording of voice narration pauses.

6 **Right-click anywhere on the screen, and then click Resume Narration.**

The voice narration recorder resumes, and you can step through the rest of the slide show, adding narration. At the end of the slide show, a message appears, asking if you want to save the new slide timings along with the narration.

7 **Click Save.**

A sound icon appears in the lower-right corner of each slide that has narration. You can double-click the sound icon to hear the narration for the slide.

> **TIP**
>
> To show a presentation that has narration on a computer without sound hardware installed, click Set Up Show on the Slide Show menu, and then select the Show Without Narration check box to avoid problems running the presentation.

8 **Click the Slide Show button.**

The narration plays with the slide show.

> **ANOTHER METHOD**
>
> - Press F5.
> - On the View menu, click Slide Show.

◆ **Keep this file open for the next exercise.**

QUICK REFERENCE ▼

Record a voice narration during a presentation

1 On the Slide Show menu, click Record Narration.

2 Click OK.

3 Use the rehearsed slide timings, or click to advance through the slide show, and add narration as you go.

4 Right-click anywhere on the screen, and then click Pause Narration or Resume Narration, if necessary.

5 Click Save.

QUICK CHECK

Q: What option would you select in the Record Narration dialog box if you want to store narration separate from the presentation?

A: You would click Link Narrations In and then browse to the location where the narration should be stored.

Creating a Self-Navigating Presentation

THE BOTTOM LINE

Set up a show to run by itself when you won't be present to deliver the presentation. You can select options that will allow the presentation to loop, use slide timings, or show a custom show.

Self-running slide shows are a great way to communicate information when a presenter can't be on hand to run the show. You might want to set up a presentation to run unattended in a kiosk at a trade show or place it on your company's intranet to run at the user's convenience. A self-navigating show turns off all navigation tools except action buttons and other action settings available to the user.

Use the Set Up Show dialog box to create a self-navigating presentation. In this dialog box, you can specify what slides or custom show to run, specify slide timings, and set other options such as whether to run narration or show animations.

Create a self-navigating presentation

In this exercise, you create a self-navigating presentation so that your supervisor can watch the slides without having to advance them.

1 **On the Slide Show menu, click Set Up Show.**

The Set Up Show dialog box appears.

2 **Click the Browsed At A Kiosk (Full Screen) option.**

When you click this option, the Loop Continuously Until 'Esc' check box turns on and grays out. This means that the presentation will repeat until you press the Esc key to turn it off. If you have recorded narration sound, it plays unless you choose to turn it off.

Figure 12-8

Set Up Show dialog box

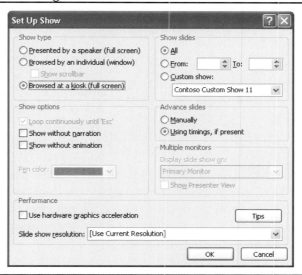

3 Click OK.

4 **In Slide Sorter view, click the slide icon for slide 13, and then click the Slide Show button.**

Slide Show runs the presentation continuously, using the slide times that you set in the previous section. The transitions that you set in the previous lesson stay the same.

ANOTHER METHOD

- Press F5.
- On the View menu, click Slide Show.

5 **Press Esc.**

The slide show stops running and Slide Sorter view reappears.

◆ If you are continuing to other lessons, save the Contoso Company Pres 12 presentation with the current name and then close it. If you are not continuing to other lessons, save and close the Contoso Company Pres 12 presentation, and then click the Close button in the title bar of the PowerPoint window.

QUICK REFERENCE ▼

Set up a self-running slide show

1 On the Slide Show menu, click Set Up Show.
2 Click the Browsed At A Kiosk (Full Screen) option and select any other relevant options.
3 Click OK.

Key Points

✓ *Add sounds and movies to a presentation to hold audience attention and deliver information. You can use the Clip Art task pane to locate and insert sounds and movies. You can also insert files from any drive on your system.*

✓ *After you insert sounds and movies, you can adjust their playback settings to make sure they are suitable for your slides. You can also add or modify animation settings and add action settings to control how objects play and the order in which they play in the presentation.*

✓ *Set slide timings to control how long slides remain in view during the slide show. You can choose to advance slides manually or automatically using the slide timings.*

✓ *If you aren't convinced your slide timings are accurate, you can rehearse the slides and then save the new timings to control the slide display the next time you run the slide show.*

✔ *Record narration for a slide show when you or another pre-senter won't be available to deliver the additional information. Narration allows you to record additional information about each slide's content that can improve comprehension.*

✔ *Create a self-running show to deliver slides when a presenter isn't available. You can choose what slides to display and turn on or off options such as narration and animation.*

Quick Quiz

True/False

T   F   1. You can play a sound in Normal view by double-clicking it.

T   F   2. You can play an animated picture in Normal view by double-clicking it.

T   F   3. You must choose either manual advance or automatic advance for slides in a slide show.

T   F   4. If you don't have enough time when rehearsing, click the Repeat button to rehearse the slide again.

T   F   5. A self-running show turns off all navigation tools except action buttons and other action settings.

Multiple Choice

1. In PowerPoint, a *movie* can mean a(n) _____.
   a. digital video file
   b. DVD
   c. animated picture
   d. either a or c

2. One adjustment you can make to a movie file's settings is to _____.
   a. change the length of the movie
   b. change the movie's sound volume
   c. browse to change the movie source
   d. change the movie's resolution

3. If you're not sure you have the right timings for your slides, use the _____ feature to refine the timings.
   a. Slide Rehearsal
   b. Rehearse Slides
   c. Rehearse Timings
   d. none of the above

4. In order to record and listen to narration for a presentation, your computer must have _____.
   a. a microphone
   b. a sound card
   c. speakers
   d. all of the above

5. What option turns on and grays out in the Set Up Show dialog box when you choose to set up a self-running show?
   a. Run Continuously
   b. Loop Twice And Stop
   c. Loop Continuously Until 'Esc'
   d. Show Until 'Esc'

Short Answer

1. How do you insert a sound from the Clip Organizer?
2. How do you insert a movie from a file?
3. How do you use slide timings and the mouse to advance a slide show?
4. How do you delete a sound object in a slide?
5. How do you record narration on a single slide?
6. How do you set up a slide show to run continuously?

On Your Own

Exercise 1

Open the Contoso Company Pres 12 file in the Lesson12 folder that is located in the PowerPoint Practice folder. Change the slide transition sound, set all the slide timings to 4 seconds, set rehearsed slide timings, play the slide show, and then save and close the presentation.

Exercise 2

Open the Contoso Company Pres 12 file in the Lesson12 folder that is located in the PowerPoint Practice folder. Delete the graphic on slide 5, insert a movie or sound from the Microsoft Clip Organizer related to the slide content, change the animation settings to play during a slide show, create a self-navigating presentation, play the slide show, and then save and close the presentation.

One Step Further

Exercise 1

Open Marx 08 from the Lesson08 folder that is stored in the PowerPoint Practice folder. Save the presentation as Marx 12 in the Lesson12 folder. If possible, record a greeting on slide 1 that welcomes Marx and Fellows employees to their five-star cafeteria and will play automatically. Display slide 6 and insert on the slide an animated picture that you locate in the Clip Organizer using the keyword *coffee*. Rehearse timings for the slides in the presentation, and then set up the show to run by itself. Save and close the presentation.

Exercise 2

Open AD Sales 11 from the Lesson11 folder that is located in the PowerPoint Practice folder. Save it as AD Sales 12 in the Lesson12 folder. Add a new slide at the end of the presentation with the title A. Datum Corporation. Add the bullet item We always hit the mark! Remove the bullet and center the text. Insert the Arrowhit.avi movie from the Lesson12 folder and center it below the text. Display slide 1. Search the Clip Organizer or your computer system for an appropriate sound file to play when the presentation starts. Display slide 4 and apply a sound effect to the display of each data series in the chart animation. (Use the Effect Options dialog box to apply the sound effects.) Save and close the presentation.

Exercise 3

Open the AD Sales 12 presentation from the Lesson12 folder. Review the custom animation for all slides and adjust the animation order as necessary to display sounds and movies in a logical way. (You may want to apply an action setting to the sound file on slide 1 to control when it plays.) Set a slide timing of 5 seconds to all slides (set the transition to No Transition). View the presentation and make any adjustments necessary to timings or animation settings. Save and close the presentation.

Creating an Internet Presentation

After completing this lesson, you will be able to:

✓ Create a summary slide.
✓ Insert a hyperlink to a slide, an Excel file, and a Web site.
✓ Create an action button.
✓ Preview a presentation as a Web page.
✓ Save and publish a presentation as a Web page.
✓ Add a digital signature.

KEY TERMS

- Action buttons
- Digital signatures
- Hyperlinks

You can use Microsoft PowerPoint to publish a presentation on the World Wide Web so that it can be viewed over the Internet. Use one of the presentation's slides as a home page for the site. You can add links and action buttons to a presentation that become active in Slide Show view or online and allow you to jump to different slides, other files, or other Web sites. After you preview a presentation as a Web page and make any final adjustments to its settings, you can publish the presentation as a Web page so that others can view it. To reassure your viewers that the Web presentation has not changed since you finished it, you can assign a digital signature to it.

As vice president of sales at Contoso, Ltd, you decide to publish a version of your current presentation on the corporate Web site and on the company intranet. After creating a basic presentation, you are ready to modify the presentation for use on the Internet.

In this lesson, you will learn how to create a summary slide; create a hyperlink to a slide, a Microsoft Excel file, and the Web; create an action button; preview a presentation as a Web page; save and publish a presentation as a Web page for the Internet; and add a digital signature.

◆ Before you can use the practice files in this lesson, you must install them from the book's companion CD to their default location. See "Using the CD-ROM" at the beginning of this book for more information. To complete the procedures in this lesson, you will need to use files named 13 PPT Lesson and 13 PR Budget in the Lesson13 folder in the PowerPoint Practice folder located on your hard disk.

Creating a Summary Slide

THE BOTTOM LINE

A summary slide shows the titles of all or selected slides in a presentation. A summary slide can be used as an agenda for the presentation or as a home page for a Web presentation.

A *summary slide* is a bulleted list of titles from selected slides in your presentation. You can create a summary slide to use as an agenda slide or as the home page for an online presentation. You can link the titles on the summary slide to their respective slides to make navigation of the presentation easy.

To create a summary slide, you select the slides that you want to include from Slide Sorter view, and then you click the Summary Slide button on the Slide Sorter toolbar. You can also select the slides in the Outline tab and click the Summary Slide button on the Outlining toolbar. A new slide appears in front of the first selected slide. This new slide, the summary slide, has a bulleted list with titles from the selected slides.

Create a summary slide

To begin preparing your presentation for publishing, you will create a summary slide to use as a home page.

◆ **Start PowerPoint, if necessary, click the Open button on the Standard toolbar, navigate to the Lesson13 folder in the PowerPoint Practice folder, and then open the 13 PPT Lesson file. Save the file as Contoso Internet Pres 13 in the same folder.**

1 Click the Slide Sorter View button.

Slide Sorter view appears with slide 1 selected.

ANOTHER METHOD

On the View menu, click Slide Sorter.

2 On the Edit menu, click Select All.

You want all slide titles to appear on the home page, so you have selected all slides in the presentation.

ANOTHER METHOD

Press Ctrl + A.

 3 On the Slide Sorter toolbar, click the Summary Slide button.

A new slide with bulleted titles from the selected slides appears in front of the first selected slide.

4 Click the Normal View button.

Slide 1, the newly created summary slide, appears in Normal view.

ANOTHER METHOD

- Double-click slide 1.
- On the View menu, click Normal.

5 Select the title text "Summary Slide."

You will change the default slide title to a more meaningful home page title.

6 Type Contoso, Ltd, and then press Enter.

7 On the Formatting toolbar, click the Font Size down arrow, and then click 28.

18 ▾

8 On the Formatting toolbar, click the Bold button, and then click the Italic button.

B

I

ANOTHER METHOD

- Press Ctrl + B.
- Press Ctrl + I.

9 Type Home Page, and then click a blank area to deselect the object.

Your slide should look like the following illustration.

Figure 13-1

Summary slide with new home page title

◆ Keep this file open for the next exercise.

QUICK REFERENCE ▼

Create a summary slide

1 Click the Slide Sorter View button, or click the Outline tab in the Outline/Slides pane.

2 Select the slides whose titles you want to include on the summary slide.

3 On the Slide Sorter or Outlining toolbar, click the Summary Slide button.

Inserting Hyperlinks

Creating Hyperlinks

Hyperlinks allow a presenter or viewer to jump from one slide to another slide, to another file, or to another Web site. Use hyperlinks to improve navigation or make it easy to access and present information from outside the presentation.

The power of an Internet presentation is its ability to link to different places: to another point in the presentation, to other slide shows or files on your computer or your company's intranet, or to Web site addresses (called Uniform Resource Locators, or URLs). You can use the Action Settings command or the Insert Hyperlink dialog box to create **hyperlinks** that link to another slide, a different presentation or another file, or a Web site.

You can add a hyperlink to any text or object, such as a shape, table, graph, or picture, to directly link it to another location when you click the object or hold the mouse over it to start its action. If you have text within a shape, you can establish separate hyperlinks for both the shape and the text. You can edit or change the object without losing the hyperlink, but if you delete all of the text or the entire object, you will lose the link.

Create a Hyperlink to a Slide

Create a hyperlink from one slide in a presentation to another to speed navigation and control the flow of information in the presentation. For example, on a slide that summarizes causes of disappointing sales for a quarter, you may want to include a hyperlink to a slide with a chart that shows the sales figures graphically.

You can use the Action Settings dialog box to set up a hyperlink from one slide to another. Click the Hyperlink To option and then select one of the slides listed, such as First Slide or Next Slide, or click Slide to see a list of slide titles from which you can choose.

Create a hyperlink to a slide

In this exercise, you create a hyperlink to a slide using the text in a shape.

1 In the Slides tab, click slide 3.

2 Select the text "Relax" in the bottom text box.

Drag the pointer over the text to select only the text, not the AutoShape.

3 On the Slide Show menu, click Action Settings.

The Action Settings dialog box appears with the Mouse Click tab on top.

ANOTHER METHOD

Right-click the selected text, and then click Action Settings on the shortcut menu.

4 Click the Hyperlink To option.

The Hyperlink To down list becomes available.

5 Click the Hyperlink To down arrow.

The Action Settings dialog box should look like the following illustration.

Figure 13-2

Action Settings dialog box

6 Scroll down the list of objects and click Slide.

The Hyperlink To Slide dialog box appears, showing a list of the presentation's slide titles.

7 In the Slide Title list, click Media Plan.

The Hyperlink To Slide dialog box displays a preview of the selected slide, as shown in the following illustration, so you can be sure you're linking to the correct slide.

Figure 13-3

Hyperlink To Slide dialog box

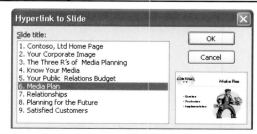

8 **Click OK.**

You return to the Action Settings dialog box. The title of the slide that you selected appears in the text box below the Hyperlink To option.

9 **Click OK, and then click a blank area of the slide.**

The hyperlink text is underlined and in light blue, which is the accent and hyperlink color in the slide color scheme.

> **TIP**
>
> You can change the color of hyperlinks by editing the current color scheme.

 10 **Click the Slide Show button.**

The slide displays in Slide Show view.

 11 **Move the mouse to display the pointer, and then position the pointer (which changes to the hand pointer) over the text "Relax."**

12 **Click the underlined text.**

The slide show links to slide 6, Media Plan.

13 **Press Esc to end the slide show.**

◆ **Keep this file open for the next exercise.**

QUICK REFERENCE ▼

Create a hyperlink to a slide

1 Select the text or object you want as a hyperlink.

2 On the Slide Show menu, click Action Settings.

3 Click the Hyperlink To option, click the down arrow, and then click Slide.

4 In the Slide Title list, click a slide to which to link.

5 Click OK, and then click OK again.

QUICK CHECK

Q: What dialog box lets you select the title of the slide to which you want to link?

A: The Hyperlink To Slide dialog box lets you select the correct slide title.

Creating a Hyperlink to an Excel File

You can create a hyperlink to another PowerPoint presentation or to a file from another program. For example, you can set up a link to jump to a Microsoft Excel worksheet that displays additional detail on a topic, such as a chart. When you create a link to a file from another program, that program opens after you click the link, so you have access to its tools and features.

Create a hyperlink to an Excel file

You have created a link from one slide to another. Now you create a link from the presentation to an Excel file that contains charts you want viewers to see during the presentation. You will use the chart itself as the hyperlink on this slide. When a viewer clicks the chart, Excel will open to show additional chart information.

1 On the Slides tab, click slide 5, and then click the chart object.

Selection handles display around the chart.

2 On the Slide Show menu, click Action Settings.

The Action Settings dialog box appears.

ANOTHER METHOD

Right-click the selected object, and then click Action Settings on the shortcut menu.

3 Click the Hyperlink To option, click the Hyperlink To down arrow, scroll down the list, and then click Other File.

The Hyperlink To Other File dialog box appears, allowing you to locate the file to which you want to link.

4 In the Look In box, navigate to the Lesson13 folder in the PowerPoint Practice folder.

5 In the list of file and folder names, click 13 PR Budget, and then click OK.

The Action Settings dialog box appears. The file name that you selected and its location appear in the text box below the Hyperlink To option.

6 Click OK, and then click the Slide Show button.

7 Move the mouse to display the pointer, position the pointer (which changes to the hand pointer) over the chart object, and then click the chart object.

Excel opens and displays two pie charts showing past and projected PR budgets.

8 In Excel, on the File menu, click Exit, and then click No, if necessary.

Excel quits and returns you to the slide show.

9 Press Esc to end the slide show.

◆ **Keep this file open for the next exercise.**

QUICK REFERENCE ▼

Create a hyperlink to an Excel file

1 Select the text or object that will become the link.

2 On the Slide Show menu, click Action Settings.

3 Click the Hyperlink To option, click the down arrow, and then click Other File.

4 In the Look In box, navigate to the location of the Excel file.

5 Click the file to which you want to create a hyperlink.

6 Click OK, and then click OK again.

Creating a Hyperlink to a Web Site

Create a hyperlink to a Web site to take viewers to another Internet site that has information related to your presentation's subject. You may, for example, want to include a link to your school's Web site in a presentation for prospective students. You can jump to that site to show more information about the school.

To set up a link to a Web site, use the Insert Hyperlink dialog box. You can type the Web address right in the Address box, or use the Browse The Web button to go to the Web site to which you want to link. When you return to the Insert Hyperlink dialog box from the Web site, the Web site address appears in the Address box. A Web site address consists of three parts: the prefix *http://*, which indicates an address on the Internet; a network identification, such as *www* for World Wide Web; and a Web site name or domain name, such as *microsoft.com*.

> **TIP**
>
> You can also use the Insert Hyperlink dialog box to set up links to other slides in the presentation, to external files such as Excel documents, or to e-mail addresses. Click Place In This Document in the Link To area to see a list of slide titles and standard linking options such as First Slide, Last Slide, and so on.

Create a hyperlink to a Web site

You complete your linking tasks in this exercise by setting up a link to Contoso's Web site that will appear on all slides in the presentation.

1 **On the View menu, point to Master, and then click Slide Master.**

The Slide Master appears. You are going to set up the hyperlink on the Slide Master so that it will appear automatically on all slides that use the master.

2 Select the text "www.contoso.com" at the bottom right of the slide by dragging over the text.

A slanted-line selection box appears around the highlighted text.

3 On the Standard toolbar, click the Insert Hyperlink button.

The Insert Hyperlink dialog box appears, with the insertion point blinking in the Address box.

CHECK THIS OUT ▼

Link to New Presentation
The Insert Hyperlink dialog box includes an option that lets you link to and create a new presentation in one easy step. Click the Create New Document option in the Link To area, supply a name for the new presentation, and choose to edit it now or later. The new presentation is automatically linked to the text or object you selected before you opened the Insert Hyperlink dialog box.

ANOTHER METHOD

On the Insert menu, click Hyperlink.

4 Type http://www.contoso.com.

As you type, the top URL in the Address list box appears. This list box stores recently used addresses to make it easy to use them again. Ignore any URL that appears in the box; the new text that you type replaces it. Your Insert Hyperlink dialog box should be similar to the following illustration.

Figure 13-4

Insert Hyperlink dialog box with new Web address

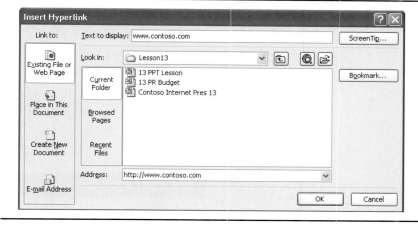

5 Click OK, and then on the Slide Master View toolbar, click Close Master View.

Slide 5 appears in Normal view, and the Web site address is underlined. You will not test this hyperlink in Slide Show view because it is not a real Web site address.

QUICK CHECK

Q: In the Web address http://www.contoso.com, what part of the address is the domain name?

A: The domain name is contoso.com.

TIP

If the hyperlink is marked with a wavy red underline like a spelling error, right-click on the hyperlink in the Slide Master and click Ignore All.

◆ Keep this file open for the next exercise.

Creating an Action Button

Creating Hyperlinks

THE BOTTOM LINE

Action buttons let you put navigation aids anywhere on a slide. Use specific action buttons for specific actions, or use the Custom button to create your own actions.

Action buttons are a set of predefined buttons that perform a specific action. The Home button, for example, is programmed to return the presentation to its first slide. Buttons such as Information and Help can be used to link to pages that provide additional information for the viewer, or you can use the Custom button to perform any action. Action buttons have a graphic appearance that tells you their function. The Home button has a house on it, for instance.

You create an action button by selecting a button from the Action Buttons submenu on the Slide Show menu (or from the AutoShapes popup menu) and then dragging the pointer on the slide to draw the button to the desired size. As soon as you finish drawing, the Action Settings dialog box opens to allow you to modify the link settings if necessary.

Create an action button

In this exercise, you create a home page action button that viewers can use to jump quickly back to the home page from any slide.

1 **On the View menu, point to Master, and then click Slide Master.**

The Slide Master appears. You will add the action button to the Slide Master to make it available on all slides that use the master.

2 **On the Slide Show menu, point to Action Buttons.**

The Action Buttons submenu appears, as shown in the margin.

ANOTHER METHOD

On the Drawing toolbar, click AutoShapes, and then point to Action Buttons.

3 **Click the Home button in the top row, second column.**

The pointer changes to the cross-hair pointer.

+ **4** **Position the cross-hair pointer in the lower-right corner of the slide, next to the Contoso Web site link, and drag to draw the Home button.**

The button fills with the default fill color and displays the default Home symbol. Your Home button should be similar in size and position to the button shown in the following illustration.

Figure 13-5

Home action button

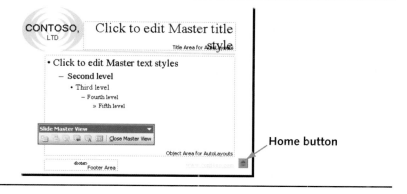

When you release the mouse, the Action Settings dialog box opens with the Hyperlink To option already set to First Slide.

5 **In the Action Settings dialog box, select the Play Sound check box.**

The Play Sound option activates the down menu.

6 **Click the Play Sound down arrow, scroll down, click Camera, and then click OK.**

 7 **With the Home button still selected, click the Fill Color button down arrow on the Drawing toolbar. Click the light gray color that has been added to the color menu.**

The Home button's fill changes from green to a more subtle gray.

8 **On the Slide Master View toolbar, click Close Master View.**

The Home button now appears on all slides in the presentation.

9 **Click the Slide Show button.**

The slide titled "Your Public Relations Budget" appears.

10 **Click the Home button.**

The slide show returns to the first slide or home page, and the camera sound plays.

11 **Press Esc to end the slide show.**

◆ **Keep this file open for the next exercise.**

QUICK REFERENCE ▼

Create an action button

1 On the Slide Show menu, point to Action Buttons.

2 Click the desired action button.

3 Drag the pointer to draw the button.

4 In the Action Settings dialog box, modify the link option and add a sound if desired.

5 Click OK.

Previewing a Presentation as a Web Page

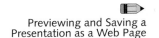

Previewing and Saving a Presentation as a Web Page

THE BOTTOM LINE

Use Web Page Preview to check how a presentation will look when published as a Web page. After you have previewed the presentation, you can adjust Web options as necessary to improve the look or performance of the presentation.

Before you save your presentation as a Web page, you can preview it to see what it will look like as a Web page using the Web Page Preview command on the File menu. The presentation opens in the default browser with the page divided into frames. The slides themselves appear in the largest frame in the window. Slide titles appear in a navigation frame at the left side of the window. Another set of navigation controls usually appears in a frame at the bottom of the window. Navigate through the presentation using any of these navigation controls or using links or buttons on the slides.

After you preview the presentation, you can adjust Web settings in the Options dialog box. Clicking Web Options on the General tab takes you to the Web Options dialog box, where you can adjust screen colors and navigation controls. You can also choose to save the graphics in a presentation in PNG (Portable Network Graphics) format. PNG graphic files are smaller, so they download from the Web more rapidly.

TIP

If you do not have Microsoft Internet Explorer as your Web browser, click the necessary prompts to proceed in Netscape Navigator or another browser.

Preview a presentation as a Web page

You are now ready to preview your presentation as a Web page. You will also make sure that your graphics can be saved in PNG format.

1 **On the File menu, click Web Page Preview.**

The message *Preparing For Web Page Preview*, along with a status indicator, appears in the status bar, and then your browser opens, displaying your presentation as a Web page. PowerPoint lists all of the slide titles in a frame on the left side of the window.

2 **Click Satisfied Customers in the list of slide titles. The frame on the right jumps to that slide in the presentation, as shown in the following illustration.**

Figure 13-6

Preview of Web presentation

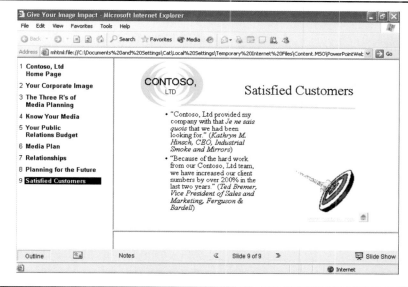

TROUBLESHOOTING

Your screen colors may not match those shown in the illustration as a result of different Web settings. You have the option to select new colors when you publish the presentation in the next section.

3 **Click the Home button to jump to the first slide.**

The action button works just as it does in Slide Show view.

4 **On your browser's File menu, click Close.**

The browser closes, and you return to the presentation in Normal view.

5 **On the Tools menu, click Options.**

The Options dialog box opens.

6 **Click the General tab, if necessary, and then click Web Options.**

The Web Options dialog box appears.

7 Click the Browsers tab.

This tab allows you to choose browser versions and set other browser options.

8 Make sure the Allow PNG As A Graphics Format check box is selected, and then click OK.

The Web Options dialog box closes.

IMPORTANT

Not all browsers support PNG format, which is recommended for Microsoft Internet Explorer 5.0 or later.

9 Click OK in the Options dialog box.

The Options dialog box closes.

QUICK CHECK

Q: When you preview a presentation in the browser, where do the slides display?

A: The slides display in the largest frame at the right of the window.

◆ Keep this file open for the next exercise.

QUICK REFERENCE ▼

Preview a presentation as a Web page

1 On the File menu, click Web Page Preview.

2 Click a title in the slide title list to jump to that slide, or use navigation controls on the slides.

3 On your browser's File menu, click Close

Save graphics in PNG format

1 On the Tools menu, click Options.

2 Click the General tab, and then click Web Options.

3 Click the Browsers tab.

4 Select the Allow PNG As A Graphics Format check box.

5 Click OK.

6 Click OK in the Options dialog box.

Saving and Publishing a Presentation as a Web Page

THE BOTTOM LINE

Save or publish a presentation to make it available on the Internet or a corporate or school intranet. Use publishing options to have more control over the appearance and functionality of the Web presentation.

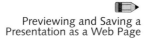
Previewing and Saving a
Presentation as a Web Page

You can easily save a presentation as a Web page in HTML (Hypertext Markup Language) format with the extension .htm. HTML is a markup language of tags that determine how text and graphics are displayed in a browser. The Save As Web Page command on the File menu creates a Web page from a presentation.

When saving, you have two options for creating a Web presentation. Use the Save As Web Page command, give the presentation a new name if desired, and click the Save button to create a Web presentation using the default Web settings. Or, if you want more control over the process of creating the Web presentation, click Publish instead of Save in the Save As dialog box. Clicking the Publish button opens the Publish As Web Page dialog box, where you can specify what slides to include, choose whether to display speaker notes, and select browser versions. You can also click the Web Options button to open the same Web Options dialog box you reviewed in the last exercise to fine-tune the Web settings.

When you save a presentation as a Web page, PowerPoint creates a folder with the same name as the Web page presentation. In this folder is a set of files that are used to display the presentation as a Web page. If you move the Web page presentation to another location, you need to move this folder as well.

After you create a Web presentation, you can open it in PowerPoint for further editing, or you can open it from PowerPoint to display it in the browser for review.

Publish a presentation as a Web page

You are ready to create a Web presentation. In this exercise, you publish the Contoso presentation as a Web page and then open the presentation in your browser.

1 **On the File menu, click Save As Web Page.**

The Save As dialog box appears. Notice that the Save As Type list box at the bottom of the dialog box displays Single File Web Page.

2 **Click the mouse in the File Name text box so that the insertion point follows the existing file name, press the spacebar, and then type Web Page.**

PowerPoint will save the presentation as Contoso Internet Pres 13 Web Page.

3 **In the Save In box, navigate to the Lesson13 folder in the PowerPoint Practice folder.**

4 **Click Publish.**

The Publish As Web Page dialog box appears, as shown in the following illustration.

Figure 13-7

Publish As Web Page dialog box

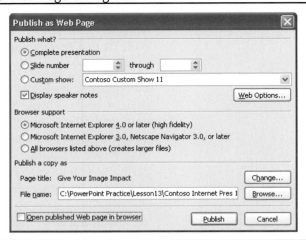

5   Click the Complete Presentation option, if necessary, and then click the All Browsers Listed Above (Creates Larger Files) option.

6   Click Web Options.

The Web Options dialog box appears.

7   Click the General tab, select the Add Slide Navigation Controls check box, if necessary, click the Colors down arrow, and then select a color scheme.

You want to make sure the forward and back navigation controls are included in the presentation. Use this opportunity as well to change the colors of the navigation controls.

8   Select the Show Slide Animation While Browsing check box.

9   Click OK.

TROUBLESHOOTING

Before you click the Publish button in the next step, check the path in the File Name box to make sure the presentation name is correct.

10   Clear the Open Published Web Page In Browser check box, if necessary, and then click Publish.

The presentation is published and stored in the Lesson13 folder, and you see the original presentation in Normal view.

11   On the Standard toolbar, click the Open button.

The Open dialog box appears.

12   In the Look In box, navigate to the Lesson13 folder in the PowerPoint Practice folder.

Notice that there is a new folder at the top of the file list with the same name as the Web page file that you just saved.

13 In the list, click Contoso Internet Pres 13 Web Page.htm.

TROUBLESHOOTING

Depending on the computer's current Windows settings, the .htm extension might not appear in the file list.

---

14 Click the Open button down arrow, and then click Open In Browser.

You may see a message warning you that hyperlinks can be harmful. Click yes to continue loading the presentation in your browser.

15 On your browser's File menu, click Close.

Your browser closes and returns you to PowerPoint.

◆ Keep this file open for the next exercise.

QUICK CHECK

Q: What language determines how a presentation's text and graphics display in a browser?

A: **HTML is the markup language that determines how text and graphics display in a browser.**

QUICK REFERENCE ▼

Publish a presentation as a Web page

1 On the File menu, click Save As Web Page.
2 In the File Name text box, type the Web page name.
3 In the Save In box, navigate to the location where you want to publish the presentation.
4 Click Publish.
5 In the Publish As Web Page dialog box, select options as desired.
6 Click Publish.

Open a presentation in the browser

1 On the Standard toolbar, click the Open button.
2 In the Look In box, navigate to the location of the presentation that you want to open in a browser.
3 In the list, click the presentation .htm file that you want to open.
4 Click the Open button down arrow, and then click Open In Browser.

Adding a Digital Signature

THE BOTTOM LINE

Add a digital signature to a presentation to let viewers know it has not been changed since you completed your work on it. Digital signatures help to maintain security.

Once you've finalized your Web document, you might consider adding a **digital signature**, an electronic, secure stamp of authentication on a document. When you apply your digital signature to a document, you verify the contents of the file and confirm that the file has not changed since you attached the signature. If someone modifies the file, the digital signature is removed.

You can create your own digital signature using an application available with Microsoft Office, or you can acquire a digital signature from a company such as VeriSign that is in the business of providing security applications.

When you add a digital signature to your file, you can sign either a file or a macro project. Sign a file when you are working with an unconverted PowerPoint presentation; sign a macro project when you are working with a presentation that has been converted to a Web page. To sign a file, you click the Security tab in the Options dialog box, click Digital Signatures, click Add, click a certificate, and then click OK three times.

To sign a macro project, you open the Microsoft Visual Basic Editor using the Macro submenu on the Tools menu. The Visual Basic Editor window is probably unfamiliar to you. This window shows the programming needed to create a Web document. If you were a software developer, you would need to know the programming in detail. However, to apply a digital signature, you need only to confirm that you see the name of your file in the left pane of the window.

Add a digital signature

In this exercise, you open your Web page in PowerPoint and then assign a digital signature to your Web page using the macro project.

◆ **Before you can start this exercise, you must install and run the Selfcert.exe file from the Microsoft Office CD. Install the file by using Add Or Remove Features in the Office Setup screen, then display Office Shared Features, click Digital Signature For VBA Projects, and click Run From My Computer. To run the Selfcert.exe file, start Windows Explorer using the Start button on the taskbar and then locate and double-click the Selfcert.exe file. The program is typically located in the Program Files\Microsoft Office\Office11 folder. In the Create Digital Certificate dialog box, type a name for the certificate as instructed, and then click OK.**

1 **On the Standard toolbar, click the Open button.**

The Open dialog box appears.

2 **In the Look In box, navigate to the Lesson13 folder in the PowerPoint Practice folder.**

3 **In the list, click Contoso Internet Pres 13 Web Page.htm, then click the Open button.**

The Web presentation opens in PowerPoint.

4 **On the Tools menu, point to Macro, and then click Visual Basic Editor.**

The Microsoft Visual Basic window opens.

ANOTHER METHOD

Press Alt + F11.

5 Verify that the Contoso Internet Pres 13 Web Page file name is at the top of the Project – VBAProject pane, at the upper-left of the window.

You can enlarge the Project – VBAProject pane to verify the file name by dragging its right border.

6 On the Tools menu in the Microsoft Visual Basic window, click Digital Signature.

The Digital Signature dialog box appears, indicating that no certificate is assigned to the document.

7 Click Choose.

The Select Certificate dialog box appears with currently available certificates, as shown in the following illustration. If you followed the instructions to create your own signature, you should see the name you typed in this dialog box.

Figure 13-8

Select Certificate dialog box

8 Select a certificate from the list, and then click View Certificate.

The Certificate dialog box appears. If you created your own certificate, a message will tell you the certificate is not trusted. The certificate is adequate, however, for this exercise.

9 Click OK to close the Certificate dialog box.

The Select Certificate dialog box reappears.

10 Click OK to close the Select Certificate dialog box, and then click OK to close the Digital Signature dialog box.

11 Click the Close button in the Microsoft Visual Basic window.

12 Click the Close Window button in the Contoso Internet Pres 13 Web Page presentation, and click Yes to save changes.

The Web presentation closes, leaving Contoso Internet Pres 13 still open.

◆ If you are continuing to other lessons, save the Contoso Internet Pres 13 presentation with the current name and then close it. If you are not continuing to other lessons, save and close the Contoso Internet Pres 13 presentation, and then click the Close button in the title bar of the PowerPoint window.

QUICK REFERENCE ▼

Add a digital signature to a published presentation

1 On the Tools menu, point to Macro, and then click Visual Basic Editor.

2 Verify that the published presentation name appears at the top of the Project – VBAProject pane.

3 On the Tools menu in the Visual Basic window, click Digital Signature.

4 Click Choose, and then select a certificate from the list.

5 Click View Certificate.

6 Click OK to close the Certificate dialog box, then click OK to close the Select Certificate dialog box.

7 Click OK to close the Digital Signature dialog box.

8 Click the Close button in the Visual Basic window.

QUICK CHECK

Q: What menu do you use to open Microsoft Visual Basic Editor?

A: You use the Macro submenu on the Tools menu.

Key Points

✔ *Create a summary slide that shows titles of selected (or all) slides in a presentation to use as an agenda slide or as a home page for a Web presentation.*

✔ *To improve navigation or access information outside the presentation, create hyperlinks. You can link to another slide in the presentation, to a file in another program, or to another Web site.*

✔ *Add an action button to one or more slides to perform a specific task, such as display the first slide of a presentation or go to the next slide. Draw an action button to the desired size and change its settings, if necessary, in the Action Settings dialog box.*

✔ *Before you publish a presentation as a Web page, preview it in the browser to see how it will look. You can then make any needed changes in the Web Options dialog box.*

✔ *Save or publish a presentation as a Web page to make it available on the Web or on a company or school intranet. Publish the presentation to have more control over the final form of the Web presentation.*

✔ *Add a digital signature to a file or project to let reviewers know that no changes have been made to the presentation since you finished it. Digital signatures provide a form of security for the presentation.*

Quick Quiz

True/False

T F   1. When you create a summary slide, it appears after the last selected slide.

T F   2. You can add a hyperlink to any text or object on a slide.

T F   3. When you link to another program, that program will open to display its file when you click the link in Slide Show view.

T F   4. An action button that has a left-pointing arrow on it will most likely take you to the previous slide when clicked.

T F   5. Web presentations are saved in the XML markup language.

Multiple Choice

1. Web site addresses are called _____.
   a. WSAs
   b. WWWs
   c. URLs
   d. either a or c

2. When you place the pointer over a hyperlink in Slide Show view, it takes the shape of a(n) _____.
   a. hand with a pointing finger
   b. cross-hair
   c. arrow
   d. fist with a thumb extending upward.

3. In a Web site address, the prefix http:// indicates a(n) _____.
   a. network identification
   b. domain name
   c. address on the Internet
   d. file name

4. A reason for saving graphics in PNG format is that PNG files are _____.
   a. more colorful
   b. smaller
   c. more widely used on the Web
   d. higher quality than other graphic formats

5. If someone modifies a file that has a digital signature applied, the digital signature is _____.
   a. updated to reflect modifications
   b. unchanged
   c. regenerated
   d. removed

Short Answer

1. How do you create a home page slide?
2. How do you create a hyperlink to a slide?
3. Name three objects to which you can add a hyperlink.

4. How do you preview a presentation as a Web page?

5. How do you add an action button to a slide?

6. How do you add a digital signature to a presentation before saving it as a Web page?

On Your Own

Exercise 1

Open Contoso Internet Pres 13 in the Lesson13 folder that is located in the PowerPoint Practice folder. On slide 1, create a hyperlink from the text *Satisfied Customers* to slide 9, create a sound action button with the Applause sound on slide 9, and then save and close the presentation.

Exercise 2

Open Contoso Internet Pres 13 in the Lesson13 folder that is located in the PowerPoint Practice folder. Preview the presentation slides in a Web browser, save the presentation as a Web page named **Contoso Web Pres 13** in the Lesson13 folder, and then close the presentation.

One Step Further

Exercise 1

Open Holidays 11 from the Lesson11 folder that is located in the PowerPoint Practice folder. Save the presentation as Holidays 13 in the Lesson13 folder. On slide 2, create links from Holidays and Personal Time to the slides that introduce these sections of the presentation. On slide 10, type a new subordinate bullet item under Disability: Disability information. Link this text to the Americans with Disabilities Act home page at http://www.usdoj.gov/crt/ada/adahom1.htm. Run the slide show and test all links. Save and close the presentation.

Exercise 2

Open Marx 12 from the Lesson12 folder that is located in the PowerPoint Practice folder. Save the presentation as Marx 13 in the Lesson13 folder. Display the Slide Master and delete the Footer area on the Slide Master. Insert a Back or Previous action button and a Forward or Next action button at the bottom of the slide where the Footer area was. (Make sure you copy the buttons and paste them on all masters that control slides in the presentation.) Preview the presentation as a Web page and then publish it with the name Marx Online 13. Choose not to display speaker notes and have the presentation open in the browser after publishing. Use the action buttons in the browser. Close the browser. Save and close the presentation.

Exercise 3

In Microsoft Excel, create a new workbook and save it as AD Data 13 in the Lesson13 folder. On the first worksheet, type A. Datum Corporation in cell A1 and type Client Data in cell A2. (You intend to insert client sales data in this worksheet before the sales conference.) Save changes and close the workbook. Open AD Sales 12 from the Lesson12 folder that is located in the PowerPoint Practice folder. Save the presentation as AD Sales 13 in the Lesson13 folder. Create a summary slide immediately after the first slide in the presentation that includes all slides but the first and last slide. Change the summary slide's default title to something more appropriate, such as Conference Information. Link each item on the agenda slide to the appropriate slide in the presentation. Unhide slide 4. On slide 5, insert an action button (you may want to use the Custom button and add text inside it) that links to the AD Data 13 workbook you created in this exercise. Add a sound effect to the action button. Run the presentation and test the links and the button. Save and close the presentation. Close the Excel workbook.

LESSON

14

Reviewing and Sharing a Presentation

After completing this lesson, you will be able to:

✔ *Add comments to a presentation.*
✔ *Add password protection to a presentation.*
✔ *Send a presentation via e-mail.*
✔ *Handle reviewer changes.*
✔ *Broadcast a presentation online.*
✔ *Use Package For CD and the PowerPoint Viewer.*

KEY TERMS

■ PowerPoint Viewer

After you create a draft of a presentation, you might want to distribute it to your coworkers for feedback. Collaborating with others can help you produce accurate and thorough presentations.

You can send a Microsoft PowerPoint presentation to reviewers electronically so that they can read, revise, and comment on the presentation without having to print it. When reviewers return the edited presentations to you, you can merge the reviewed presentations into the original presentation and then accept or reject the changes your reviewers suggest. To safeguard a presentation during the reviewing process, you can apply a password that restricts modifying or opening the presentation.

You can use Microsoft Producer to create an online broadcast of your presentation. Broadcasting a presentation allows you to present it to a group of people who might not all work at the same physical location. If you prefer to take the presentation to another location to present it, PowerPoint includes features to help you pack a presentation to deliver it at another location and show it if PowerPoint isn't available.

As vice president of sales at Contoso, Ltd, you have been working on a company presentation. After completing it, you are ready to send the presentation out for review. In particular, you are going to review the slide show over the company network with CEO Wendy Beth Kahn before you take the presentation to the next monthly staff meeting.

In this lesson, you will learn how to use comments in a presentation, add password protection to the presentation, send a presentation for review via e-mail, merge and handle changes in a presentation, broadcast a presentation online, and use the Package For CD feature and the PowerPoint Viewer.

◆ **Before you can use the practice files in this lesson, you must install them from the book's companion CD to their default location. See "Using the CD-ROM" at the beginning of this book for more information. To complete the procedures in this lesson, you will need to use files named 14 PPT Lesson and 14 PPT Edit in the Lesson14 folder in the PowerPoint Practice folder located on your hard disk.**

Adding Comments to a Presentation

Adding Comments

THE BOTTOM LINE

Add comments to a presentation as reminders of tasks that need to be done or suggestions for improvements to the slides. The Reviewing toolbar makes it easy to work with comments and review changes.

Asking others to review and comment on your presentation can assist you in improving the presentation before it is final. You or your reviewers can insert comments, which are notes about text or other parts of the presentation. Once comments are added to a presentation, you can edit or delete them, and you can choose to show or hide them.

You add a comment by clicking Comment on the Insert menu. To edit or delete a comment, you right-click the commented text and then click Edit Comment or Delete Comment. To hide or show a comment, you need to open the Reviewing toolbar and click the Show/Hide Markup button, which toggles comments on and off. You can also use the functions on the Reviewing toolbar to insert, delete, or edit comments.

Once you begin working with comments, you can open the Revisions task pane to view comments made for each slide. Open the Revisions task pane by first right-clicking on any toolbar and then selecting Revisions from the menu.

Add comments to a presentation

In this exercise, you review the slides in the presentation and add comments that you will then send with the presentation to Wendy Beth Kahn.

◆ **Start PowerPoint, if necessary, click the Open button on the Standard toolbar, navigate to the Lesson14 folder in the PowerPoint Practice folder, and then open the 14 PPT Lesson file. Save the file as Contoso Company Pres 14 in the same folder.**

1 **In the Slides tab, click slide 2.**

2 **On the Insert menu, click Comment.**

A comment box opens with your name, today's date, and a blinking cursor where you can begin typing your comment. The Reviewing toolbar also displays.

3 **In the comment box, type** Any ideas for improving this slide?

Your slide should look like the following illustration (the name and date on the slide will differ).

Figure 14-1

Comment appears on slide

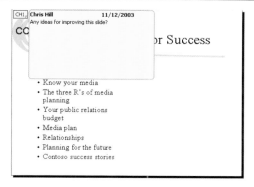

4 **Click anywhere outside of the comment box.**

The comment box closes, and a small box with your initials and a number appears in the upper-left corner of the slide.

5 **Point to the small box to display the comment, and then double-click the small box.**

The comment box reopens, allowing you to edit your comment.

6 **Click after the word "slide" to place the insertion point, press the Spacebar, type** visually, **and then click outside of the comment box.**

The edit is made, and the comment box closes.

 7 **On the Reviewing toolbar, click the Show/Hide Markup button.**

The small comment box on slide 2 disappears.

 8 **On the Reviewing toolbar, click the Show/Hide Markup button again.**

The Show/Hide Markup button toggles on, and the comment box reappears.

9 Drag the scroll box to slide 3, and then on the Reviewing toolbar, click the Insert Comment button.

A comment box appears on the slide.

10 In the comment box, type Ask Sandra to update this chart as necessary.

11 Click anywhere outside of the comment box to close it.

12 Drag the scroll box to slide 11, and then on the Reviewing toolbar, click the Insert Comment button.

13 In the comment box, type Can we update these success stories?

14 Right-click on any toolbar, and then click Revisions.

The Revisions task pane opens, showing comment 3 in the Slide Changes box, as shown in the following illustration.

Figure 14-2

Comment in Revisions task pane

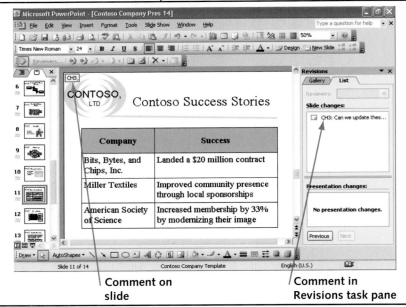

Comment on slide — Comment in Revisions task pane

TIP

To change the size of the Revisions task pane, position the pointer (which changes to the two-headed arrow pointer) on the left edge of the task pane, and then drag the edge.

15 Right-click anywhere on the comment box, and then click Delete Comment.

The comment is deleted from the slide and also from the Revisions task pane.

16 In the Revisions task pane, click Previous at the bottom of the pane.

Slide 3 appears with comment 2 in the Revisions task pane.

17 In the Revisions task pane, click Previous at the bottom of the pane.

Slide 2 appears with comment 1 in the Revisions task pane.

×

18 In the Revisions task pane, click the Close button to close the pane.

◆ Keep this file open for the next exercise.

QUICK REFERENCE ▼

Add comments to a presentation

1 On the Insert menu, click Comment, or click the Insert Comment button on the Reviewing toolbar.

2 In the comment box, type the comment.

3 Click anywhere outside of the comment box.

Edit a Presentation by Hand

If you are using a Tablet PC that allows you to capture handwritten ink, you can edit a presentation by marking directly onto slides in Normal view. Turn markup on and off using the Show/Hide Comments and Changes button on the Ink Annotations toolbar. This toolbar (and the Ink Annotations option) is available only if you have a system that will accept handwritten input.

You can use the pen styles and colors you learned about in Lesson 11 for your annotations. If you later open the edited presentation on a desktop or laptop computer that doesn't support inking, your handwritten notes appear as objects on the slides that you can move, resize, or delete.

To add ink annotations while editing a presentation on a Tablet PC:

1 Display the presentation in Normal view.

2 On the Insert menu, click Ink Annotations to display the Ink Annotations toolbar.

3 Display the slide you want to edit and mark your edits directly on the PC screen.

4 When finished, click Stop Inking on the Ink Annotations toolbar.

Adding Password Protection to a Presentation

THE BOTTOM LINE

Add a password to limit access to a presentation. You can allow users to open a read-only copy for review, or you can prevent anyone from opening a presentation without the correct password.

You can use a password to protect the integrity of your presentation as it moves from person to person. A password can prevent unwanted editing or safeguard the presentation from prying eyes.

The Security tab in the Options dialog box gives you two options for applying a password. Type a password in the Password To Modify box if you want to prevent a reviewer from modifying the presentation. This is useful when you want a presentation, such as a company-wide bulletin, to be distributed and read, but not changed. For greater protection, type a password in the Password To Open dialog box. This prevents anyone from opening the presentation in any form unless they know the correct password.

Figure 14-3

Options dialog box

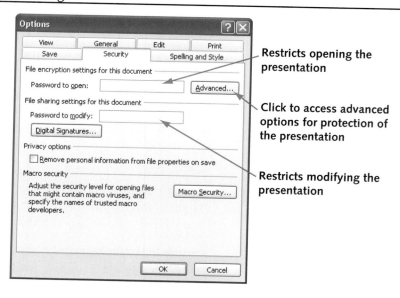

Restricts opening the presentation

Click to access advanced options for protection of the presentation

Restricts modifying the presentation

If you set a password in the Password To Modify box, when you open the presentation you have the option to type the correct password to open the presentation or click Read Only to open a read-only version of the presentation. With the read-only version, you can view the slides, but you can't make any changes to them.

When you set a password, take a moment to write it down. PowerPoint doesn't keep a list of passwords. If you lose or forget a password for a protected presentation, you will not be able to open it. To open a protected presentation, you need to enter the password in the exact same way that it was set, which includes spaces, symbols, and uppercase and lowercase characters.

Add password protection to a presentation

In this exercise, you will set a password for the presentation, close and open the presentation to test the password, and then remove the password.

1 On the Tools menu, click Options.

The Options dialog box appears.

2 Click the Security tab to display security options.

3 **In the Password To Modify box, type** contoso.

You have entered the password. Bullets appear in place of the characters you typed.

4 **Click OK to close the Options dialog box.**

The Confirm Password dialog box appears and asks you to reenter the password to confirm the way you entered it in the Options dialog box.

5 **In the Reenter Password To Modify box, type** contoso, **and then click OK.**

The password is set. You will close the presentation and open it again to test the password protection.

6 **On the Standard toolbar, click the Save button to save the presentation.**

7 **Click the Close Window button to close the presentation window.**

Using the Close Window button closes the presentation without closing PowerPoint, so you will be able to easily open the presentation from the File menu.

8 **On the File menu, click Contoso Company Pres 14.**

The Password dialog box appears. You will type the wrong password to see what happens.

9 **In the Password box, type** company, **and then click OK.**

As you type the password, bullets appear to keep your password confidential. An alert message appears, indicating an incorrect password.

TIP

To protect your presentations from being opened by unauthorized people, you should never use common words or phrases as passwords. The same password should never be used for multiple presentations.

---

10 **Click OK, and then click Read Only.**

A read-only version of the presentation opens, displaying slide 1 in Normal view. Notice that you cannot change anything on the slide.

11 **Click the Close Window button to close the presentation window.**

Now, you'll open the presentation and use the correct password.

12 **On the File menu, click Contoso Company Pres 14.**

The Password dialog box appears.

13 **In the Password box, type** contoso, **and then click OK.**

The presentation opens, displaying slide 1 in Normal view.

14 **On the Tools menu, click Options, and then click the Security tab, if necessary.**

15 **Select the contents in the Password To Modify box, and then press the Delete key to remove the password protection.**

You have now removed password protection so you can open the presentation freely.

16 Click OK to close the Options dialog box.

◆ Keep this file open for the next exercise.

QUICK REFERENCE ▼

Add password protection to a presentation

1 On the Tools menu, click Options, and then click the Security tab.

2 In the Password To Modify box or the Password To Open box, type a password.

3 Click OK.

4 Type the password again to confirm.

5 Click OK.

Remove password protection

1 On the Tools menu, click Options, and then click the Security tab.

2 In the Password To Modify box or the Password To Open box, clear all text.

3 Click OK.

Information Rights Management

PowerPoint 2003 allows you to restrict access to presentations using the new Information Rights Management feature of Microsoft Office 2003. Using Information Rights Management, you can assign permissions to users or workgroups to control who can change, print, or copy a presentation. Permissions can be set to expire after a certain time period for further security.

To implement Information Rights Management, you must download Windows Rights Management software to your computer. Once you have the software installed, you can set permissions for an open presentation as follows:

1 Click the Permission button on the Standard toolbar.

The Permission dialog box opens.

2 Click the Restrict Permission To This Presentation check box to activate other features in the dialog box.

3 For read-only permission, enter a user's e-mail address in the Read box. To allow a user to read, edit, and save changes (but not print), enter the user's e-mail address in the Change box.

4 To grant additional permissions, click More Options, set permissions, and click OK.

Sending a Presentation for Review Using E-Mail

THE BOTTOM LINE

Using e-mail is a quick and easy way to distribute a presentation to reviewers. PowerPoint's Mail Recipient (For Review) option saves time by attaching the presentation, inserting a subject line, and adding a message line to the e-mail.

PowerPoint allows you to send presentations out for review using e-mail. You can send the presentation from within the application so that you do not have to manually open your e-mail program. To share your presentation with others, click the File menu and then point to Send To.

The Send To menu includes the Mail Recipient (For Review) and Mail Recipient (As Attachment) commands. Click one of these commands to open an e-mail window in which the presentation is already listed as an attachment. If you use the Mail Recipient (for Review) command, the message also includes the text *Please review the attached document*. To send the presentation, enter the destination e-mail address and the Cc e-mail address for anyone who should receive a copy of the message and its attachments. The subject line of the e-mail will already contain the file name of the presentation you are sending.

If your team uses Windows SharePoint Services, you can create a Document Workspace that allows you to work on a document with other team members. To create a Document Workspace, you send a document as a shared attachment, or you can create a new Document Workspace using the Shared Workspace task pane in PowerPoint 2003. All the recipients of the document become members of the Document Workspace and can work on the presentation in the Document Workspace.

To send a document as a shared attachment, click the Attachment Options button in the e-mail message window to open the Attachment Options task pane. Scroll down and click the Shared Attachments option.

IMPORTANT

To complete this exercise, you need to have an e-mail program installed on your computer and an e-mail account set up.

Sending a presentation for review via e-mail

You are now ready to send your presentation out for review. You will use your default e-mail program to send the presentation.

1 **On the File menu, point to Send To, and then click Mail Recipient (For Review).**

Your default e-mail program window opens, ready for you to type in the recipient's address.

Figure 14-4

E-mail window with message inserted

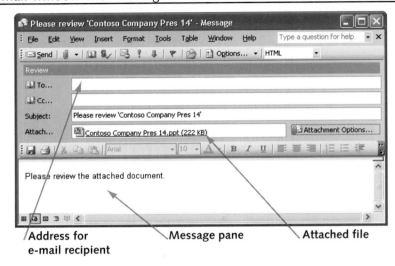

Address for   Message pane   Attached file
e-mail recipient

TIP

To send a copy of the current presentation as an attachment in an e-mail message, click the E-Mail (As Attachment) button on the Standard toolbar.

2 **Click in the To box, if necessary, and type** someone@example.com.

This e-mail address is an account at Microsoft that will automatically send a response for the message.

3 **On the Message toolbar, click the Send button.**

The e-mail with the attached presentation is sent out for review, and you return to your PowerPoint presentation.

◆ **Keep this file open for the next exercise.**

QUICK REFERENCE ▼

Send a presentation via e-mail

1 On the File menu, point to Send To, and then click Mail Recipient (For Review).

2 Click To.

3 Type the e-mail address.

4 If desired, click Cc and type an address.

5 On the toolbar, click Send.

Handling Reviewer Changes

Merging Versions of a Presentation

> **THE BOTTOM LINE**
>
> Compare and merge presentations so you can see in one presentation all the edits that have been made by all reviewers. The Reviewing toolbar provides tools to help you handle the changes suggested by other reviewers.

As part of the process of finalizing a presentation, you may have to deal with changes from reviewers as well as your own edits of a presentation. PowerPoint's reviewing features can help you to compare versions of a presentation as well as accept and reject corrections from all reviewers.

It is a common practice for several members of a team to review a presentation, inserting comments and making changes to text and objects. Handling a number of corrections from several reviewers would be a challenge if not for PowerPoint's compare and merge feature. This feature allows you to compare the various versions of the presentation and merge all of the revisions and comments into the original presentation. You can merge more than one presentation into the original presentation, so you can see all comments and changes from all reviewers at one time.

Merge an edited presentation into the original presentation

You will begin the process of tracking changes by comparing and merging an edited version of the current presentation with the original version now open in PowerPoint.

1 If the Reviewing toolbar isn't displayed, on the View menu, point to Toolbars, and then click Reviewing.

2 On the Tools menu, click Compare And Merge Presentations.

The Choose Files To Merge With Current Presentation dialog box appears.

3 Navigate to the Lesson14 folder that is located in the PowerPoint Practice folder, click 14 PPT Edit, and then click Merge.

A message box appears, indicating that the presentation you selected was not sent for review by pointing to Send To on the File menu and then clicking Mail Recipient (For Review).

4 Click Continue.

The comments and changes from both presentations appear on the screen in the current presentation.

Figure 14-5

Reviewer comments appear on the slide

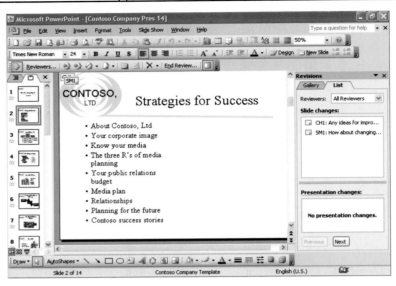

◆ **Keep this file open for the next exercise.**

QUICK CHECK

Q: What message might you receive as you compare and merge presentations?

A: You might receive a message saying the presentation has not been sent for review.

QUICK REFERENCE ▼

Compare and merge presentations

1 On the Tools menu, click Compare And Merge Presentations.

2 Navigate to the location of the presentation that you want to compare and merge it with the currently opened presentation.

3 Click a presentation file, click Merge, and then click Continue.

The merged presentation shows all comments and changes from all reviewers. Comments from other reviewers look just like the comments you inserted earlier in this lesson. Changes to text or objects are denoted by small *change markers*. These markers show changes in detail without obscuring the presentation or affecting its layout. They also give you a more visible and comprehensive view of the changes that have been made. You can click on a marker to display a box that shows what has been inserted and/or deleted. PowerPoint uses a different color marker for each reviewer and adds the reviewer's name or initials so you can easily identify who has made changes.

You can use the Reviewing toolbar to track, accept, and reject revisions. The Reviewing toolbar gives you a variety of views and options when reviewing presentations. As you review the comments and changes, you can accept or reject them one at a time or all at once. When you accept a change, PowerPoint deletes the text or inserts it into the presentation, as appropriate. When you reject a change, PowerPoint restores the original text.

When you are handling changes, you can also open the Revisions task pane to easily identify the changes a reviewer has made to a presentation. You can see a list of the changes made by a given reviewer or get a graphical representation of the changes in the Gallery tab. A drop-down menu makes it simple to apply or unapply changes that the reviewer has made.

Handle changes in a merged presentation

The edited presentation you merged in the last exercise contained changes made by Sandra Martinez, who received a copy for review. In this exercise, you will handle her corrections as well as the comments you added earlier.

1 **On the Reviewing toolbar, click the Show/Hide Markup button, if necessary, to display all comments and changes.**

2 **Display slide 2, if necessary.**

You have asked for input on changing the visual impact of the slide, and Sandra has a comment on the slide.

3 **In the Revisions task pane, click SM1 to see Sandra's suggestion.**

Sandra suggests changing the slide to a two-column layout.

4 **Change the slide layout to Title and 2-Column Text, move the last four items of the list to the new second column, and adjust the text size in the first column to match the size of the text in the right-hand column.**

You have handled this suggestion by improving the slide layout.

5 **On the Reviewing toolbar, click the Delete Comment down arrow, and then click Delete All Markup On The Current Slide.**

Both comment markers are removed from the slide.

6 **On the Reviewing toolbar, click the Next Item button to display changes on slide 3.**

You asked Sandra to update the organization chart as necessary. She has edited the chart, and a change marker appears on the slide to let you know she has made a change to the chart.

7 **Click the Gallery tab in the Revisions task pane to see the changed organization chart.**

The Gallery tab shows the slide with Sandra's changes to the organization chart.

8 **On the Reviewing toolbar, click the Apply button down arrow, and then click Apply All Changes To The Current Slide, or click the slide in the Gallery tab.**

The organization chart is updated to show a new name for one employee and a new employee in Sandra Martinez's area. The change marker on the slide shows a check mark to indicate the change has been made.

9 **Delete all markup on the current slide, and then click the Next Item button.**

Slide 4 appears, showing a changes box listing changes Sandra Martinez has made to the text, as shown in the following illustration.

Figure 14-6

Sandra's changes to text

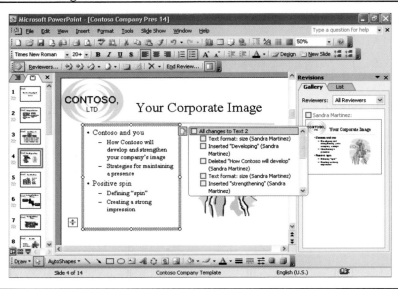

10 **In the changes box on the slide, select the second check box, Inserted "Developing" (Sandra Martinez).**

You click the second check box to see how Sandra has changed the text. (The first check box changes text size of the first-level bullet item.) Sandra's text change appears in the bulleted text box.

11 **Click in a blank area of the slide to close the changes box, and click the Apply button on the Reviewing toolbar.**

All of the changes proposed by Sandra Martinez are applied to the slide and the change marker shows a check mark.

12 **On the Reviewing toolbar, click the Delete Marker button.**

The change marker is deleted from the slide.

13 **On the Revisions task pane, click the List tab, and then click the Next button at the bottom of the List tab.**

PowerPoint takes you to slide 13, where Sandra has added a revision.

14 **Click the change marker to see the revision.**

Sandra has inserted *Hirsch* and deleted the word *Hinsch*. This change is not correct, however, so you will reject her suggestion by deleting the comment.

15 **Click on the slide to close the change box, and then delete the marker on the slide.**

16 **On the File menu, click Save As, click at the end of the current file name in the File Name box, press the Spacebar, and type Edited.**

You are saving a new version of the presentation that includes all edits.

17 **Click Save.**

The presentation is saved and the Reviewing toolbar and Revisions pane close.

◆ **Keep this file open for the next exercise.**

QUICK REFERENCE ▼

Handle changes from reviewers

1 On the Reviewing toolbar, click the Show/Hide Markup button, if necessary, to display comments and changes.

2 Use the Reviewing toolbar or Revisions task pane to move to each correction.

3 Use the Reviewing toolbar or Revisions task pane to accept or reject changes.

4 Click the Close button in the Revisions task pane.

Broadcasting a Presentation Online

THE BOTTOM LINE

Use an online broadcast to reach an audience that may not all be at the same physical location. Broadcasting online can save time and money by allowing all participants to view a presentation from their own computers.

When you need to reach an audience that is not gathered in one physical location, you can use online broadcasting to present a slide show in real time over a computer network or on the Internet. Online broadcasting can save a great deal of time and money because viewers can run the presentation and view it from their own computers, rather than travel to a distant location to view the presentation.

You can use Microsoft Producer to prepare a presentation for online broadcast. This program is not installed by default with Microsoft Office 2003 but can be downloaded for free from Microsoft. Using Microsoft Producer, you can import a presentation, add the slides to a Timeline, create an introduction page, and publish the presentation for playback. You then have the option of previewing the broadcast so you can determine if you need to make any further changes to the presentation.

Prepare a presentation for online broadcast

You are ready to publish your edited presentation for online broadcast. In this exercise, you will use Microsoft Producer to set up an online broadcast on your computer to test the presentation before publishing it to the company network.

◆ **Before you begin this exercise, you must download and install Microsoft Producer. Connect to the Internet, if necessary, and then on PowerPoint's Help menu, click Microsoft Office Online. Click Downloads in the left pane of the Office Online home page. On the**

Downloads page, click in the Search box and type **Producer** and click the **Click To Search** button. In the list of search results, locate PowerPoint 2003 Add-in: Microsoft Producer, click the link, and follow instructions to download and install the program.

1 Click the Start button, point to All Programs, point to Microsoft Office, and then click Microsoft Producer for PowerPoint 2003.

You may receive a message as the program starts that your screen resolution could be changed for better display. Click OK to continue loading the program. A dialog box displays to ask how you want to create your presentation.

2 Click Cancel to close the dialog box.

Rather than use one of the default options, you will import a presentation.

3 On the File menu, click Import.

The Import File dialog box opens.

4 Navigate to the Lesson14 folder that is located in the PowerPoint Practice folder, click Contoso Company Pres 14 Edited, and click Open.

Producer imports the file, showing you the progress of the import. When the process is complete, you should see your presentation on the Media tab in the Producer window, as shown in the following illustration.

Figure 14-7

The presentation displays in Microsoft Producer

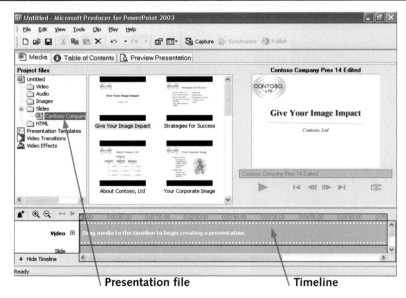

Presentation file   Timeline

5 In the Project Files pane, click the Contoso Company Pres 14 Edited presentation, drag it to Timeline at the bottom of the screen, and drop it in the Slide track.

The slides display in the Slide track as individual units, as shown in the illustration below. Slides that have animation effects display the blue animation symbol.

Figure 14-8

The slides have been added to the Timeline

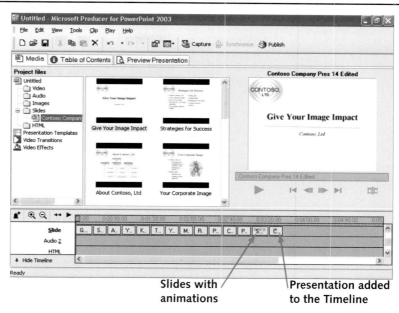

Slides with animations

Presentation added to the Timeline

6 **Click the Table Of Contents tab.**

You can add information for an introduction page on this tab. You will insert a title for the broadcast and your name.

7 **In the Title box, type** Contoso Company Presentation.

8 **In the Presenter (Optional) box, type your name.**

Your window should look similar to the following illustration. You can also insert an image to use on the introduction page as well as a description of the presentation. Notice the table of contents information at the left side of the window, which shows all slide titles, the time in the presentation that each slide appears, and the duration of each slide.

Figure 14-9

Introduction information on the Table Of Contents tab

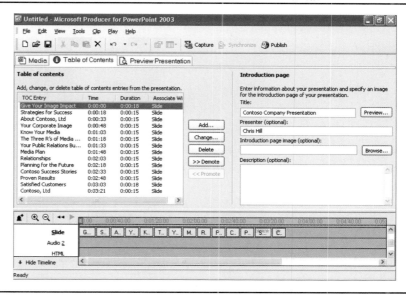

You are now ready to publish the production.

9 **On the toolbar, click the Publish button.**

The Publish Wizard starts and displays its first screen to ask you to select a playback site. You will accept the default option of My Computer, but you could also choose to publish to a network location or Web server to create an online broadcast.

10 **Click Next to move to the Publishing Destination window.**

You are prompted to enter a file name for the production and a location to publish the files. You will accept the default file location but change the default file name.

11 **In the File Name box, type** Contoso Online, **and then click Next.**

The Presentation Information window appears. This window gives you another opportunity to set up the opening page of the broadcast, but since you already entered the necessary information, you can move on.

12 **Click Next to open the Publish Setting window.**

You will accept the default settings in this window.

13 **Click Next to open the Publish Your Presentation window, and then click Next again.**

The publishing process begins. You can monitor the process of publishing in the Publishing Presentation bar. When the process completes, the Presentation Preview window appears to give you the option of previewing the broadcast.

14 **In the Presentation Preview window, click the Internet Explorer 5.0 Or Later For Windows link.**

The introduction page displays in Internet Explorer, as shown in the following illustration.

Figure 14-10

Introduction page in the browser

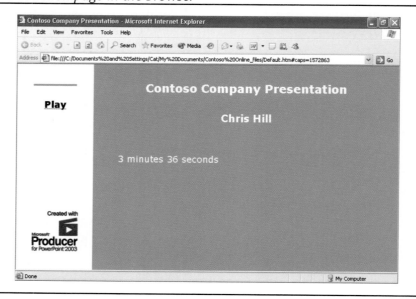

15 **Click the Play link to start the presentation.**

The broadcast uses the slide timings to advance and plays available animations. You can use the control bar at the left side of the screen to display the next or previous slide or any slide in the list of titles.

TROUBLESHOOTING

You may notice that animations don't play correctly on slide 1 in the preview.

---

16 **When the presentation ends, scroll up and click the first slide to retest the animations.**

The animations should display correctly this time.

 17 **Click the browser's Close button to return to Producer.**

18 **Click the Finish button in the last Publish Wizard window.**

At this point, you could save the broadcast for future use, but you will not save the current project.

 19 **Click Microsoft Producer's Close button, and then click No to close without saving.**

Producer closes and you return to PowerPoint.

◆ **Keep this file open for the next exercise.**

QUICK REFERENCE ▼

Prepare an online broadcast using Microsoft Producer

1 Start Microsoft Producer.

2 On the File menu, click Import.

3 Navigate to the location of the presentation you want to import, select the file, and click Open.

4 Drag the presentation to the Timeline and make any necessary adjustments to the slide timings.

5 Click the Table Of Contents tab and enter a title and presenter name for the production.

6 Click Publish to start the Publish Wizard.

7 Proceed with the Wizard to select a playback site, enter a file name and publish location, set presentation information, modify publish settings, and then publish the presentation.

8 Click the Internet Explorer 5.0 Or Later For Windows link to preview, then close the browser.

9 Click Finish, and then save the production if desired.

QUICK CHECK

Q: Where in Producer can you enter a description of the presentation?

A: You can enter a description in the Description box on the Table Of Contents tab or in the Presentation Information window of the Publish Wizard.

Packaging a Presentation for Delivery

Taking a Slide Show on the Road

THE BOTTOM LINE

To take a slide show with you to present at a remote location, you can use the Package For CD feature to gather and store all files required to deliver the presentation. You can present the slides on a computer that doesn't have PowerPoint by using the PowerPoint Viewer.

If you need to transport your presentation to another computer, you can use the Package For CD feature to compress and save the presentation to a CD or to a drive or other removable media. Package For CD includes linked files such as images by default so they are available with the slides on which they appear.

You also have the option of embedding TrueType fonts on the slides. When you select the Embed TrueType Fonts option, TrueType fonts are stored in the presentation. It is especially important to select this option if you are using fonts in a presentation that are not typically installed by Windows. Then when you open or show a presentation on another computer that doesn't have these TrueType fonts, the presentation looks the same as it did on your computer. Be aware that including embedded fonts in a presentation increases its file size.

TIP

You can also embed fonts when you save a presentation. In the Save As dialog box, click Tools, click Save Options, select the Embed TrueType Fonts check box, and then click Embed Characters In Use Only (Best For Reducing File Size) option to embed only those characters used in the presentation or click Embed All Characters (Best For Editing By Others) option to embed all the characters in the font set.

PowerPoint offers a special program called the **PowerPoint Viewer** that allows you to show a slide show on a computer that does not have PowerPoint installed. Package For CD automatically includes the PowerPoint Viewer, but you can deselect this option if you know you will have access to PowerPoint on the computer you will use for the presentation. The PowerPoint Viewer has been improved in PowerPoint 2003 with better support for graphics, animations, and media playback.

When you complete the packaging process, PowerPoint stores the presentation file in the folder you designate. If you add the PowerPoint Viewer, several additional files are stored in the folder, including the Viewer program. When you are ready to show the presentation, you can open the folder, right-click the presentation stored there, and choose to show the presentation or open it with the PowerPoint viewer.

Package a presentation for delivery elsewhere

You have completed your work on the Contoso company presentation and are now ready to pack it up to deliver it at the next staff meeting. In this exercise, you will package the presentation and then view it using the PowerPoint Viewer.

1 **On the File menu, click Package For CD.**

The Package For CD dialog box opens, as shown in the following illustration.

Figure 14-11

Package For CD dialog box

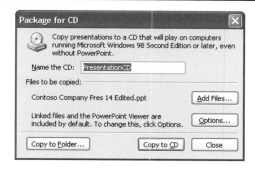

TROUBLESHOOTING

You may see a message box prompting you to install this feature if it is not already installed.

2 **In the Name The CD box, type** Contoso Show**.**

You are supplying the name for the folder that will contain the presentation materials.

3 **Click Options to open the Options dialog box, and then click Embedded TrueType Fonts.**

Embedding the TrueType fonts ensures they will be available wherever you show the presentation.

4 **Click OK, and then click Copy To Folder.**

The Copy To Folder dialog box opens to allow you to select a location to store the folder.

5 **Click Browse, and then navigate to the Lesson14 folder in the PowerPoint Practice folder and click Select.**

6 **Click OK.**

The files are packaged in the folder and stored in the location you specified.

7 **In the Package For CD dialog box, click Close.**

The dialog box closes. You are now ready to take your presentation on the road.

8 On the File menu, click Exit.

If a dialog box appears asking whether you want to save the changes to your presentation, click Yes.

9 On the taskbar, click the Start button, and then click My Computer.

The My Computer window opens.

10 Navigate to the Lesson14 folder in the PowerPoint Practice folder.

11 In the list of files and folders, double-click the Contoso Show folder to open it.

The contents of the folder should look similar to the following illustration. Your screen may vary, depending on the current Windows display settings.

Figure 14-12

Contents of packaged folder

12 Right-click the Contoso Company Pres 14 Edited file, point to Open With, and click Microsoft PowerPoint Viewer.

The PowerPoint Viewer shows Contoso Company Pres 14 Edited as a slide show.

13 Click the mouse to advance to the next slide, and then press Esc.

The slide show ends and you're returned to the Contoso Show folder.

14 Click the Close button to close the Contoso Show folder.

QUICK REFERENCE ▼

Use Package For CD

1 On the File menu, click Package For CD.

2 In the Name The CD box, type a name for the folder that will store the files.

3 Click Options and select the Embed TrueType Fonts check box.

4 Click OK, and then click Copy To CD or Copy To Folder.

5 Specify a location to store the folder, and click OK.

6 Click Close.

Show a presentation with the PowerPoint Viewer

1 On the Windows taskbar, click Start, and then click My Computer.

2 In the Look In box, navigate to the location of the packaged folder, and double-click the folder to open it.

3 Right-click the presentation name, point to Open With, and click Microsoft PowerPoint Viewer.

4 Click the mouse to advance through the presentation slides.

QUICK CHECK

Q: What button do you click in the Package For CD dialog box to select the Embed TrueType Fonts check box?

A: Click the Options button to open the Options dialog box.

Key Points

✔ *Add comments to a presentation as reminders of tasks to complete or suggestions for improvements. You can edit and delete comments as needed.*

✔ *To safeguard a presentation during the editing process, you can apply a password. The password can prevent a reviewer from changing the presentation or prevent anyone from opening the presentation without the correct password.*

✔ *Sending a presentation for review using e-mail is a quick way to distribute it to all members of a team.*

✔ *Use PowerPoint's compare and merge feature to combine all reviewer versions with the original version so all changes can be addressed in one presentation. Use the Reviewing toolbar and the Revisions task pane to view, accept, and reject changes.*

✔ *Use Microsoft Producer to set up an online broadcast of a presentation that viewers can access on their computers.*

✔ *To show a presentation on another computer, pack it up using the Package For CD feature. You can link and embed files and include the PowerPoint Viewer, which enables you to show the presentation on a computer that doesn't have PowerPoint installed.*

Quick Quiz

True/False

T F 1. To remove comment boxes from sight, you use the Show/Hide Comments button on the Reviewing toolbar.

T F 2. If you have forgotten your password, PowerPoint will supply it if you answer a specified question.

T F 3. You can merge more than one presentation into the original presentation to see changes from all reviewers in one presentation.

T F 4. You can install Microsoft Producer from the Microsoft Office 2003 CD.

T F 5. By default, Package For CD links related presentation files.

Multiple Choice

1. You can edit a presentation by drawing right on the screen if you have a(n) _____.
   a. Desktop PC
   b. Laptop PC
   c. Tablet PC
   d. Annotating PC

2. As you type a password, _____ characters take the place of the letters and numbers you typed.
   a. asterisk
   b. bullet
   c. zero
   d. dash

3. To see a graphical representation of changes to a slide, click the _____ tab in the Revisions task pane.
   a. Gallery
   b. Images
   c. Album
   d. Review

4. To move to the next change in a presentation, you can click _____.
   a. Go To on the Reviewing toolbar
   b. Next Item on the Reviewing toolbar
   c. Next button on the Revisions task pane
   d. either b or c

5. When you choose to preview an online broadcast, the presentation displays in _____.
   a. Producer
   b. PowerPoint
   c. Internet Explorer
   d. Windows Explorer

Short Answer

1. How do you add comments to a presentation?
2. How do you protect a presentation with a password?
3. How do you send a presentation using e-mail?
4. How do you accept all changes on a slide at once?
5. How do you set up a presentation broadcast using Microsoft Producer?
6. How do you embed TrueType fonts when packaging the presentation?
7. How do you run a slide show using the PowerPoint Viewer?
8. How do you merge changes from several edited presentations into one for editing?

On Your Own

Exercise 1

Open Contoso Company Pres 14 in the Lesson14 folder that is located in the PowerPoint Practice folder. On slide 3, add a comment that reads Move Kevin M. Homer to the Production group and add Rebecca Laszlo to the Technology group. Send the presentation as an attachment in an e-mail. Save and close the presentation.

Exercise 2

Open Contoso Company Pres 14 in the Lesson14 folder that is located in the PowerPoint Practice folder. Use Package For CD to save the presentation in a folder on your hard drive, close the presentation, and then play the presentation slide show using the PowerPoint Viewer.

One Step Further

Exercise 1

Open Holidays 13 from the Lesson13 folder that is located in the PowerPoint Practice folder. Save the presentation as Holidays 14 in the Lesson14 folder. Add a comment to slide 1 asking for general review comments. Use the Send To command to e-mail the presentation to a classmate and ask the classmate to review and comment on the presentation. When you receive the reviewed presentation back, merge it with your original version and make any necessary corrections. Save and close the presentation.

Exercise 2

Open AD Sales 13 from the Lesson13 folder that is located in the PowerPoint Practice folder. Save the presentation as AD Sales 14 in the

Lesson14 folder. Apply a password to the presentation to safeguard its contents. Use the Package For CD feature to copy the presentation to a CD if your computer has a CD recorder, or copy files to another removable medium such as floppy or zip disk. Take the disk to a computer that doesn't have PowerPoint installed and run the presentation using the PowerPoint Viewer.

Exercise 3

Open AD Sales 14 from the Lesson 14 folder. Set up the presentation for an online broadcast using Microsoft Producer. Create an introduction page that uses your name and gives a description of the presentation. Preview the presentation and then save it if desired. Save and close the AD Sales 14 presentation.

Customizing PowerPoint

Microsoft PowerPoint has many optional settings that can affect either the screen display or the operation of certain functions. You can change PowerPoint's optional settings to customize the way you work and perform tasks. For example, you can change toolbars so that the tools you use most often are easy to find. Or, you can change the initial font type and style of text that appear in text boxes. If you frequently perform a repetitive task in PowerPoint, you can also record the sequence of steps as a macro to automate the task and save you time.

In this appendix, you will learn how to customize the PowerPoint screen display to meet your needs. You will learn how to change your toolbars so that the tools you use most often are easy to find. In addition, you will find out how to customize your default font and drawing attributes. Finally, you will create macros to help you automate a repetitive task and learn about PowerPoint add-ins.

Customizing PowerPoint Toolbars

PowerPoint comes with several preset toolbars with buttons that can save you time and effort. The toolbars that appear depend on which view is active. In Normal view, for example, you see three default toolbars: Standard, Formatting, and Drawing. You have already used these toolbars, as well as the Outlining and Reviewing toolbars, in earlier lessons.

By default, the Standard and the Formatting toolbars are on the same row below the menu bar. If you like, you can customize this option so that each of these toolbars is displayed on its own row. If you leave the Standard and Formatting toolbars on one row, they self-adjust. That is, commands you use more often stay on the toolbars, and commands that you use less often are replaced with more frequently used commands. Toolbars are also movable. You can drag entire toolbars to new locations on the screen.

Customize PowerPoint toolbars

In this exercise, you reposition the Formatting toolbar, put the Standard and Formatting toolbars on the same row, and reset toolbar buttons to display the default setting.

 1 **Position the pointer over the dotted vertical bar at the left edge of the Formatting toolbar.**

The pointer changes to the four-headed arrow.

Figure A-1

Formatting toolbar

2 **Drag the toolbar to the middle of the screen.**

The floating toolbar now has a title bar, a Toolbar Options down arrow, and a Close box.

Figure A-2

Toolbar is now floating

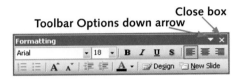

3 **On the Tools menu, click Customize.**

The Customize dialog box appears.

4 **Click the Options tab.**

Figure A-3

Options tab of the Customize dialog box

5 **Clear the Show Standard And Formatting Toolbars On Two Rows check box to display the toolbars on one row.**

6 **Click Reset Menu And Toolbar Usage Data, and then click Yes in the alert box.**

7 **Click Close.**

The toolbars appear on one row.

Adding or Removing Toolbar Buttons

Both the Standard and Formatting toolbars have additional buttons that you can add to the toolbar itself or to the Add Or Remove Buttons list under Toolbar Options.

Add and remove toolbar buttons

In this exercise, you add and remove a toolbar button.

1 On the Formatting toolbar, click the Toolbar Options down arrow.

2 Click Add Or Remove Buttons, and then click Formatting.

A submenu displays a list of buttons that you can add to or delete from the Formatting toolbar.

3 Point to the down arrow at the bottom of the list, if necessary.

The list scrolls to the end. The buttons with check marks next to them already appear on the Formatting toolbar or on the Toolbar Options list.

4 Click the Layout button in the list.

A check mark appears next to it, and the button appears on the Formatting toolbar just to the left of the Toolbar Options down arrow.

5 Click the Layout button again.

The button is removed from the toolbar.

6 Click anywhere in the presentation window to close the list.

Creating a Toolbar and Adding Buttons

You can also create new toolbars that contain only the buttons that you need or use most frequently. You can customize the arrangement of buttons on a new or existing toolbar, or you can move buttons from one toolbar to another.

Create a toolbar and add buttons

In this exercise, you create a toolbar and add and arrange buttons.

1 On the Tools menu, click Customize.

The Customize dialog box appears.

2 Click the Toolbars tab.

Figure A-4

Toolbars tab of the Customize dialog box

3 **Click New.**

The New Toolbar dialog box appears.

4 **In the Toolbar Name text box, type Special, and then click OK.**

Special is added to the toolbar list with a check mark next to it, and a small, empty toolbar appears in the presentation window, as shown in the left margin. You might need to drag the dialog box out of the way to see the new toolbar.

5 **Click the Commands tab.**

6 **In the Categories list box, click Slide Show.**

7 **Drag the Action Settings button to the Special toolbar you created.**

A black insertion bar appears as you drag the button onto the Special toolbar to indicate the new location of the button. An icon for Action Settings appears in the Special toolbar.

8 **In the Commands list, scroll to the bottom of the list, and then drag the Custom Shows button to the Special toolbar.**

The Custom Shows button appears on the Special toolbar. You can move a toolbar button to another location on a different toolbar by dragging the button.

9 **Drag the Custom Shows button to the other side of the Action Settings button.**

The Custom Shows button now appears to the left of the Action Settings button. If you add the wrong button, you can remove it by dragging the button off the toolbar to a blank area of the window.

10 **Drag the Custom Shows button off the toolbar.**

The button is removed. If you decide you don't want the new toolbar, you can delete it.

11 **In the Customize dialog box, click the Toolbars tab.**

12 In the Toolbars list, click Special, click Delete, and then in the alert box, click OK.

The toolbar is deleted.

13 In the Customize dialog box, click Close.

Changing Font Defaults

Default settings are the initial attributes that PowerPoint applies when you create an object. Some examples of PowerPoint font default settings include font style, size, and formatting, such as bold, italic, and underline. To find out the current font default settings for your presentation, you can create a text object and check the object's attributes.

Change font defaults

In this exercise, you change font defaults.

1 Open any presentation and switch to Normal view.

2 On the Drawing toolbar, click the Text Box button.

3 Click a blank area of the Slide pane to create a text box.

4 On the Format menu, click Font.

The Font dialog box appears with the current default font and size.

5 In the Font list, click Book Antiqua.

6 In the Size list, click 18.

7 Select the Default For New Objects check box.

8 Click OK.

The text styles are applied to the text defaults.

9 In the text object, type Book Antiqua, size 18, is now the default font.

10 Select the text object, then press Delete.

Changing Object Attribute Defaults

You can also change the default settings for a drawn object. Some examples of PowerPoint object default settings include fill color, shadow, and line style. To find out the current default settings for your presentation, you can draw an object or create a text object and check the object's attributes.

Change object attribute defaults

In this exercise, you change object attribute defaults.

1 On the Drawing toolbar, click the Oval button.

2 Drag in the Slide pane to draw an oval.

Notice the current default fill color and line style settings.

3 On the Format menu, click AutoShape.

The Format AutoShape dialog box appears.

4 Click the Color down arrow in the Fill section, and then change the fill color.

Make any additional formatting changes you want to the object.

5 Select the Default For New Objects check box.

6 Click OK.

7 On the Drawing toolbar, click the Oval button.

8 Drag in the Slide pane to draw an oval.

Both oval objects have the new attributes you just selected.

9 Press Shift, click the original oval object, and then press Delete.

TIP

To distinguish between the headings and responses, use the Formatting toolbar to change the appearance of the headings. In this example, the headings are bold.

Simplifying Tasks with Macros

If you perform a task repeatedly, you can record a macro that automates the task. A macro is a series of commands and functions—stored in a Visual Basic module—that you can run with one step whenever you need to perform a task. You can record a macro in PowerPoint to combine multiple commands into one, speed up routine editing and formatting tasks, or make a dialog box option more accessible.

Before you record or write a macro, you need to plan the steps and commands you want the macro to perform. If you make a mistake while recording, you can record a correction instead of rerecording.

With the Macro dialog box, you can run a macro completely or step through it one command at a time. You can also create, edit, or delete a macro.

Record and run a macro

In this exercise, you record and run a macro to insert a Title Only slide.

1 **On the Tools menu, point to Macro, and then click Record New Macro.**

The Record Macro dialog box appears. The default macro name is selected in the Macro Name box.

Figure A-5

Record Macro dialog box

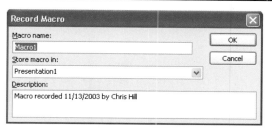

2 **Type InsertTitleOnlySlide (macro names cannot contain spaces).**

3 **Click OK.**

The Stop Recording toolbar appears, as shown in the margin, with a Stop Recording button.

4 **On the Formatting toolbar, click the New Slide button.**

The Slide Layout task pane appears.

5 **In the Slide Layout task pane under Text Layouts, click the Title Only layout to change the layout of the new slide.**

6 **On the Stop Recording toolbar, click the Stop Recording button.**

The macro is recorded, and the Stop Recording toolbar closes.

7 **On the Tools menu, point to Macro, and then click Macros.**

The Macro dialog box appears.

Figure A-6

Macro dialog box

8 In the Macro Name area, click InsertTitleOnlySlide, if necessary, to select the macro.

9 Click Run.

The Macro dialog box closes and executes the macro.

TIP

You can create more advanced macros by entering Visual Basic commands in the Visual Basic Editor. To open the Visual Basic Editor, point to Macro on the Tools menu, and then click Visual Basic Editor. You can click the Help button to learn how to use the program.

Expanding PowerPoint Functionality with Add-Ins

Add-ins are supplemental programs that extend the capabilities of PowerPoint by adding custom commands and specialized features. You obtain add-ins from independent software vendors, or you can write your own using the PowerPoint Visual Basic Editor. You can also find PowerPoint add-ins on the Microsoft Office Online Web site. To use an add-in, you must first install it on your computer and then load it into PowerPoint. PowerPoint add-ins have the filename extension .ppa.

Load and unload an add-in

In this exercise, you load and unload an add-in program.

1 On the Tools menu, click Add-Ins.

The Add-Ins dialog box appears.

2 Click Add New.

The Add New PowerPoint Add-In dialog box appears.

3 In the Look In down arrow, click the folder where you stored your PowerPoint add-in programs.

4 In the list of file and folder names, click a PowerPoint add-in program.

5 Click OK.

The add-in program is loaded.

6 In the Available Add-Ins list, click the add-in that you want to load, and then click Load.

The add-in program is registered and appears in the list of available add-ins.

7 Click Close.

The Add-Ins dialog box closes, and the add-in program is available for use in PowerPoint. To conserve memory and maintain PowerPoint's running speed, it's a good idea to unload add-in programs you don't use often. When you unload an add-in, its features and commands are removed from PowerPoint. However, the program itself remains on your computer for easy reloading.

8 **On the Tools menu, click Add-Ins.**

The Add-Ins dialog box appears.

9 **Click the add-in that you want to unload.**

10 **Click Unload to remove the add-in from memory but keep its name in the list, or click Remove to remove the add-in from the list and from the registry file.**

11 **Click Close.**

Glossary

Action buttons Predefined buttons, such as Home, Help, Information, Back, Next, Beginning, End, and Return, that perform a specific action.

Adjustable objects Objects that have an adjustment handle (which looks like a small yellow diamond) positioned on one side of the object next to a resize handle. This handle allows you to alter the appearance of the object without changing its size.

Animated pictures GIF (Graphics Interchange Format) files that you can insert into a slide presentation as a movie.

Animation Schemes A set of professionally designed animations divided into three categories: Subtle, Moderate, and Exciting.

Background The underlying colors, shading, texture, and shading style of the color scheme.

Bullet text A list of items in which each item is preceded by a symbol.

Cell The intersection of a row and a column.

Clip art Professionally drawn images that can be used to illustrate a slide.

Color menu The color palette associated with Drawing toolbar buttons, such as Fill Color, Line Color, or Font Color.

Color scheme The basic set of eight colors provided for any slide. The color scheme consists of a background color, a color for lines and text, and six additional colors balanced to provide a professional look to a presentation.

Connection sites Small blue handles on each side of an object that allow you add a connection line between two objects.

Custom show A named group of slides from a presentation that can be run separately from the entire presentation.

Design template A presentation with a professionally designed format and color scheme.

Digital signature An electronic, secure stamp of authentication on a document.

Dotted selection box The border of a selected object that indicates that you can manipulate the entire object.

Embedded object An object that is created with another program but is stored in PowerPoint. You can update an embedded object in PowerPoint.

Export The process of converting and saving a file format to be used in another program.

Grayscale A black and white image that displays shades of gray.

Hanging indent Paragraph formatting adjusted by small triangles on the ruler where the second and subsequent lines of text are indented more than the first.

Hyperlinks "Hot spots" or "jumps" to a location in the same file, another file, or an HTML page that are represented by colored and underlined text or by a graphic.

Import To convert a file format that was created in another program.

Indent markers Markers on the ruler that control the indent levels of the master text object.

Landscape Horizontal orientation of an image on the output media.

Linked object An object that is created in another program that maintains a connection to its source. A linked object, unlike an embedded object, is stored in its source document, where it was created. You update a linked object within its source program.

Margin markers Small squares on the ruler that move both the upper and lower indent markers.

Masters Special slides that control the properties of slides in a presentation.

Menu A list of commands or options available in a program.

Normal view View that contains three panes: Outline/Slides, Slide, and Notes.

Notes Page view View where you can add speaker notes and related graphics.

Notes pane Area in Normal view where you can add speaker notes.

Object Any entity in PowerPoint that you can manipulate.

Office Clipboard Storage of multiple pieces of information from several different sources in one storage area shared by all Office programs.

Offset The direction in which a shadow falls from the object.

Outline/Slides pane Area in Normal view where you can organize and develop presentation content in text form as well as display thumbnails of all slides in a presentation.

Paragraph Text that begins when you press Enter and ends when you press Enter again.

Portrait Vertical orientation of an image on the output media.

PowerPoint Viewer A program that allows you to run a slide show on a computer that does not have PowerPoint installed.

Presentation window The electronic canvas on which you type text, draw shapes, create graphs, add color, and insert objects.

Print Preview View that allows you to see how slides, notes pages, handouts, and the outline will look if printed.

Pure black and white A black and white image that displays only black and white without any shades of gray.

Resize handles White circles that you use to adjust the size of an object. The circles appear in the corners and around the perimeter of a selection box.

Rich Text Format (RTF) A common text format that many programs can open.

Scaling Resizing an entire object by a set percentage.

ScreenTip A yellow box that tells you the name of or more information about a button, icon, or other item on the screen when you place the pointer over the item.

Selection box The gray slanted line or dotted outline around an object that indicates it is selected.

Slanted-line selection box The border of a selected object that indicates you can edit the object's content.

Slide Master A master slide that controls the characteristics (background color, text color, font, and font size) of a presentation.

Slide pane Area in Normal view where you can view a slide and add text, graphics, and other items to the slide.

Slide Show view View where you can preview slides as an electronic presentation.

Slide Sorter view View where you can see all the slides in a presentation in miniature.

Slide timing The length of time that a slide appears on the screen.

Source document The original document that is created in the source program.

Source program The program that created a document that is a linked object in PowerPoint.

Status bar The bar at the bottom of the presentation window that displays messages about the current state of PowerPoint.

Task pane A pane that allows you to quickly access commands related to a specific task without having to use menus and toolbars.

Template A presentation whose format and color scheme you apply to another presentation.

Text box A box that contains text in a slide.

Text label A text object used primarily for short phrases or notes.

Text object An object containing slide text.

Text placeholder A box with dotted outlines that you can click to add text.

Title Master A master slide that contains placeholders that are similar to those of the Slide Master but that affect the title slide only.

Title slide The first slide in the presentation.

Title text Text that identifies the name or purpose of a slide.

Toolbar A graphical bar in the presentation window with buttons that perform some of the common commands in PowerPoint.

Window An area of the screen that is used to display a PowerPoint program or presentation window.

Word processing box A text object used primarily for longer text.

Word wrap A feature that automatically moves the insertion point to the next line within an object as you type.

Index

System Requirements

Your computer system must meet the following minimum requirements for you to install the practice files from the CD-ROM included with this book and to run Microsoft PowerPoint 2003.

- A personal computer running Microsoft PowerPoint 2003 on a Pentium 233-megahertz (MHz) or higher processor.
- Microsoft Windows® 2000 with Service Pack 3 (SP3), Windows XP, or later.
- 128 MB of RAM or greater.
- At least 2 MB of available disk space (after installing PowerPoint 2003 or Microsoft Office).
- A CD-ROM or DVD drive.
- A monitor with Super VGA (800 X 600) or higher resolution with 256 colors.
- A Microsoft mouse, a Microsoft IntelliMouse, or other compatible pointing device.